Love and authority in
the work of Paula Rego

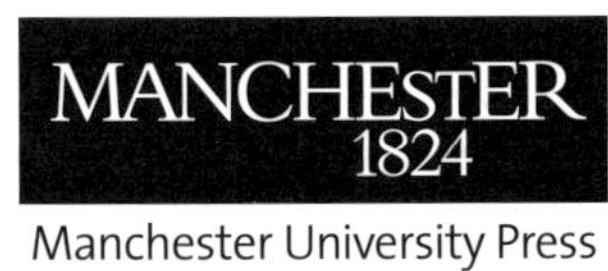

Manchester University Press

In loving memory of Ian Garton

Love and authority in the work of Paula Rego

Narrating the family romance

Ruth Rosengarten

Manchester University Press

Manchester and New York

distributed in the United States exclusively by Palgrave Macmillan

Published by Manchester University Press
Oxford Road, Manchester M13 9NR, UK
and Room 400, 175 Fifth Avenue, New York, NY 10010, USA
www.manchesteruniversitypress.co.uk

Distributed in the United States exclusively by
Palgrave Macmillan, 175 Fifth Avenue, New York,
NY 10010, USA

Distributed in Canada exclusively by
UBC Press, University of British Columbia, 2029 West Mall,
Vancouver, BC, Canada V6T 1Z2

British Library Cataloguing-in-Publication Data
A catalogue record for this book is available from the British Library

Library of Congress Cataloging-in-Publication Data applied for

ISBN   978 0 7190 8070 8 hardback

First published 2011

The publisher has no responsibility for the persistence or accuracy of URLs for any external or third-party internet websites referred to in this book, and does not guarantee that any content on such websites is, or will remain, accurate or appropriate.

Typeset
by Servis Filmsetting Ltd, Stockport, Cheshire
Printed in Great Britain
by TJ International Ltd, Padstow

Contents

List of illustrations

Plates

Colour plates appear between pages 118 and 119

Figures

Acknowledgements

I first came to know Paula Rego's work in London, at the time of her first solo exhibition there. Later, when I moved to Portugal, my interest in her gained substance as I came into contact with the cultural foundations of her artistic imagination. My thanks to her for facilitating my work over the years, for opening her studio doors to me so generously, and for permission to publish the images of her work. I would like to express my gratitude to Memory Holloway, Jessica Dubow and João de Pina Cabral for much encouragement and stimulating discussion along the way. My thanks to the staff at Marlborough Fine Art in London for their assistance. I am indebted to the Museu Nacional de Belas Artes in Rio de Janeiro and the Biblioteca Nacional in Lisbon for providing me with the two indispensible historical images that are reproduced here. Above all, for the scepticism that keeps a check on my flights of fancy, for his good sense and humour, my profound thanks go to my husband Ian Garton, to whose memory I dedicate this book.

Introduction

For many viewers, to think of the artist Paula Rego's work is to conjure an inevitable pair of words: narrative, and Portugal. 'To paint,' begins John McEwen's monograph, 'Paula Rego must have a story; and her favourite way of telling a story is to paint' (McEwen, 2006: 16). 'The older Rego gets, the more stridently and obviously Portuguese her art becomes' writes Waldemar Januszczak (Januszczak, 2001: 6), without properly explaining what a 'Portuguese art' might be. The ends to which painting may use storytelling, and the sustained significance of being a native of Portugal are, indeed, two issues that any serious study of Rego's work has to tackle. It is Rego herself who reinforced this portrayal of her art, not only because her work embodies both a narrative impulse and a sense of ownership of Portuguese iconography, but also because she variously rehearses and reiterates these concerns in the way she verbally reconstructs her working process: on the one hand 'I can only work things out through stories' (Rego, in conversation), and on the other 'everything I paint comes from Portugal' (Pinharanda and Melo, 1987: 14).

While the conflation of Portugueseness and narrative has at times contributed to their mutual mythification and served to obscure the more challenging ambiguities in Rego's work, it also, like all clichés, harbours a truth. Yet the most enlightening comments on Rego's work – sometimes, though not always, her own – underline the self-subversive aspects of storytelling,[1] or the entirely subjective contours of 'Portugal': when asked what it was like to return to Portugal from London in the 1950s, she quipped: 'Portugal was my house in the country' (Melo, 1988: 70).

Born in Portugal in 1935 to anglophile parents, Paula Rego

studied fine arts at the Slade School of Art in London between 1952 and 1956. Here she met the man she was to marry: the artist Victor Willing. For the following two decades, together with Willing and their children, Rego divided her time between England and Portugal. Living and working in London definitively since 1976, and steeped in the traditions of Western art, Rego continues to feel most at home when making images that in one way or another hark back to her childhood in Portugal. That 'Portugal' of her youth is filtered through memory, fabulation and political concerns, where the artist's own narrations of self play a significant role: narrations that underline the fetishistic dimensions of autobiography, its valuation of the minute and the graspable.[2] Explicitly mimetic since the 1980s, Rego's work links subjectivity itself to a vivid and almost ethnographically specific Portuguese iconography, probing the visual culture that informed her childhood, asking how a turn of phrase in the Portuguese language might be performed as image, and exploring how the articulation of 'Portugueseness' and 'Englishness' might be constituted visually.

But it is above all in its many allusions to the *Estado Novo* – the authoritarian New State that, under António de Oliveira Salazar, held Portugal in its grip between 1933 and 1974[3] – that Rego most consistently evokes 'Portugueseness': evokes it as both pastness and as trace; an indexical, physical vestige. But the past, in Rego's work, is not only a burden borne in the present: arguably, its very existence is elicited by, and projected from, present perception, as if to say: 'I remember it when I see it', or 'I recognise it as I make it'.

Crucially, too, where iteration brings into focus something hidden but not entirely forgotten, Rego invokes not only the convoluted routes of historiography, but also the circuitous chronologies that inform the encounter between analyst and analysand in the scene of psychoanalysis. Such an encounter between past and present goes by the name of transference, a projection of affect from patient to analyst that brings to light an inchoate past. In their unfolding, the narratives brought into the analytic arena animate an anteriority immersed in immediacy, where current action stands in the place of a muffled memory. Rego's use of memory might gladly suffer the transferential analogy: for her, the remembrance of political oppression is not only stirred by her probing of current formations of authority structuring private life and organising the home. It is also realised by a concrete and material exploration of homely motifs in the present tense; from the standpoint, in other words, of the contemporary. The revived – because pictorially performed – recollection of a political past becomes, in her hands, a vehicle for the exploration of the dynamics of authority framed by the home. And, contrariwise, despotic power, while scaled down and mocked as that of the domestic tyrant or play-yard bully, nevertheless remains politicised.

The home in this context is not a prosthesis of the enveloping maternal body. It is, rather, the dwelling place of strategy and intrigue: an arena in which boundaries are delineated, negotiated, re-drawn, policed. If, for Freud, the uncanny – the *unheimlich* – is the name for everything that is unremembered but not forgotten, that ought to have remained secret and hidden but that has, instead, come to light, then unnervingly, its opposite, the *heimlich* or homely is the condition in which all that is secret and hidden must persist so. The homely is the breeding place of secrets. And with secrets come alliances, collusions. Prototype to all subsequent triangles, the parents–child threesome, in other words, is nothing short of politics. Concealment and disclosure, sanction and reward, coercion and betrayal: these are plotted in the home, and their intertwinement and articulation map the subject's relation to its primary caretakers, and, via them, more broadly and abstractly to both love and authority. Crucially, since the object of love gains empowerment through the possibility for withdrawal (and this is how the object of love holds the subject to ransom), love and authority are ineluctably intertwined, rendering the loving subject always enthralled, by definition subjected (Figure 1). (Throughout this book, I use the term 'object' in the psychoanalytic sense, as the person or thing through which an instinct aims to be satisfied, as the recipient of the subject's fantasies, actions or desires.)

Constituting the backbone of this book, the relationship between love and authority links the public arena of history and politics to the private realm of domesticity. It is a relationship that, in Rego's work, plays itself out upon the body. The body not only mediates inside and outside, subject and world, but is also the site of their mutual impact. Concomitantly, in the home, Rego's figures also perform a political drama. Here, we see the staging of the relationship of subordinates to superiors, a relationship that, in Rego's work, paradoxically both endorses and reverses traditional gender roles. Conversely, the political finds its most apposite setting in the intimate relationship between two or three people. So in the reprises – always idiosyncratically transformed – of stories from

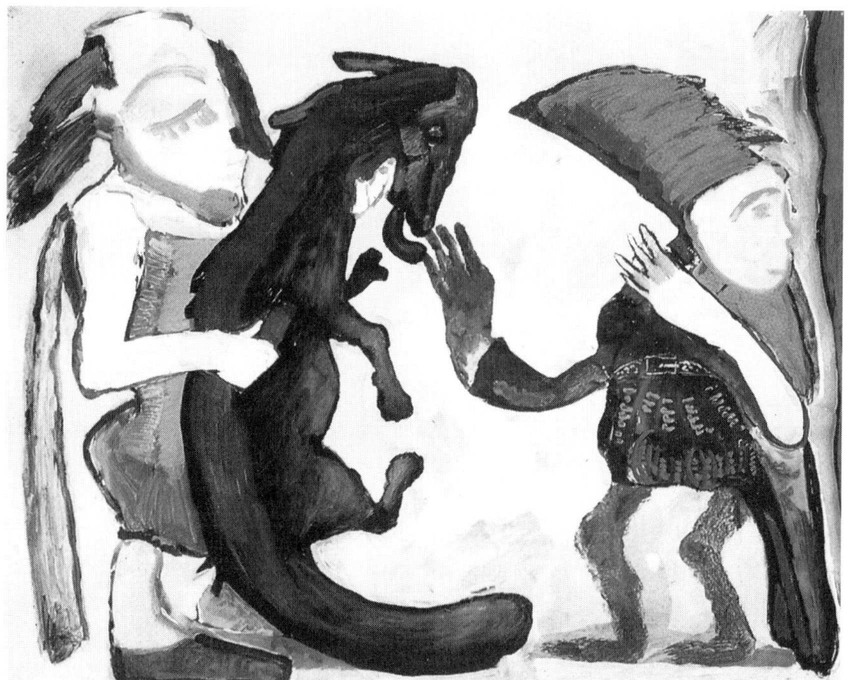

Figure 1   Paula Rego, *Lovers*, 1982

Portuguese history, from folklore, or literature, Rego's art constantly rephrases a private question: what does it mean to love? And how does this adherence to an-Other form and affect the subject? What is it to be submissive or subversive, obedient or rebellious: as a citizen, as a mother or daughter, a wife or lover – and also as an artist? The question is an important one, yet the way it is phrased is, perhaps, specious. For to separate these roles is merely to schematise the overlapping and imbricated positions and forms of agency that any subject assumes, and it is their mutuality, the complex negotiations between them, that Rego's work powerfully embodies.

And so it is that while many of Rego's works are staged in a domestic interior, the studio itself, more or less disguised, sets the scene for a considerable number of images, particularly from the mid-1990s on, when drawing directly from the model became crucial to the artist. Importantly, several paintings thematise the making of art, the labour in the studio, as a viable alternative to the family romance. From *Time – Past and Present* (1990–91) and *Joseph's Dream* (1990; see Figure 17), through *The Artist in her Studio* (1993), to *Martha,*

Mary and Mary Magdalene (1998) and *Border Patrol: Self Portrait with Lila, Reflection and Ana* (2004), they posit production in the studio through the agency of a robust, generative female body. Such characterisation sets itself up in opposition to the male gendering of the painter's body in the canon of Western painting, signalling the equivalence between Culture and masculinity. But it also pits itself against twin ideals of the female body within that same canonicity: either as the fetishistic redress of a lack (she must appease even as she threatens), or as a vehicle of genealogical reproduction, borne out especially in the traditional iconography of the Madonna and Child. Both ideals had for centuries informed traditional representations of women, pandering to male anxieties of loss of mastery: the first by disavowing loss, the second by guaranteeing continuity.

As an imperative of patriarchal succession, the conflation of femininity with reproduction has proved useful to authoritarian regimes. The ideology of Nazism lent support to the formal, institutional and military power of men, while women were idealised as the bearers of more men. In the droll words of Claudia Koonz, 'the ideal Nazi man was a fighter; the ideal Nazi woman, his mother' (Koonz, 1988: 447). In Fascist ideology too, the cult of virile masculinity laid emphasis on the symbolic primacy of maternity as the vehicle of its own perpetuation. Maternity, then, was not only naturalised as the sine qua non of womanhood, but also served as the incubator of ideology itself, spawning an 'epidemic of familiarism', where the proverbial Angel in the House served as a 'link between patriarchy and fascist tyranny' (Macciocchi, 1979: 73). If one of the responsibilities of the state was to safeguard the family as a source of racial and social conservation, the family in turn served as a blueprint for the nation itself. As in Fascism, for the *Estado Novo*, the family, hierarchically structured around the moral authority of the father, operated as the seat of transmission and cohesion of the larger social unit. While it was within the bounds of the family that the symbolic and institutional power of paternity was privately embodied, it was also through the support of wide-ranging social institutions (legal, educational, medical, religious, technological and so forth) that the actual father came to approximate the symbolic father and that paternal and political power became mutually representative. It is just such authority that Rego satirises and avenges in her political works of the late 1950s and 1960s, or in the tableaux of domestic revenge of the 1980s (see Figure 6, *Nursery Violence*).

While this relation of the female subject to male/paternal

authority suggests that Rego might idealise maternity, even the most casual perusal of her work reveals ambivalence towards motherhood, figured not as the 'connivance' between a girl and her mother,[4] but as the power to destroy. Indeed, the annihilating effectiveness of maternal power is more prevalent in Rego's work than any bond of feminine complicity. Whether across the generations or within them, women are as often as not competitors: the *Dancing Ostriches from Disney's 'Fantasia'* (1995) are preening and prancing, vying for the attention of men, while *Snow White and her Stepmother* (1995) are more explicitly sexual adversaries. In the vindictiveness with which girls treat their canine custody in works of the mid-1980s, Rego not only exposes the imprinting of the maternal bond as the prototype for other attachments, but also explores the possibilities of aggression underpinning acts of nurturing. In the six works constituting the *Girl and Dog* series of 1984, the dog is an infantilised invalid. His ductile, passive body is cradled and supported; he is spoon-fed, exercised, shaved; medicine is administered. The vitality of the nursing figure is clearly empowering. The girl – in effect a little woman – is practical and kind, but she also delights in the delicious, collapsing weight of the dog/man/child. Disgust and anger lurk behind her manifest disposition of patience and compassion. The dog extending his neck to the shaving blade is exposed and vulnerable, at the mercy of his carer's clemency (Figure 2). For her part, she is the scarcely disguised bearer of an aggression whose *modus operandi*, as Maria Manuel Lisboa observes, 'is the simulacrum of a variety of stereotypical female nurturing roles', transforming the acts of nursing, feeding and shaving into 'preludes to murder' (Lisboa, 2003: 38).

The murder underlying family plots and the love stories that succeed them is clearly and famously articulated in Freud's formulation of the Oedipus complex. And it is Oedipus that structures Rego's explorations of the mutual imbrication of love and authority. Considering the series of four paintings constituting the *Snow White* series (1995), Fiona Bradley observes:

> Rego's re-telling of the story is a variant on the story of Oedipus as enshrined in Sigmund Freud's identification of the Oedipus complex as a significant stage in the psycho-sexual development of an individual. . . . Rego investigates a female variant of Freud's hypothesis, the series examining, as do many of her earlier family narrative paintings, the struggle between the women of a family for the sexual attention of the male. A chain of women striving for

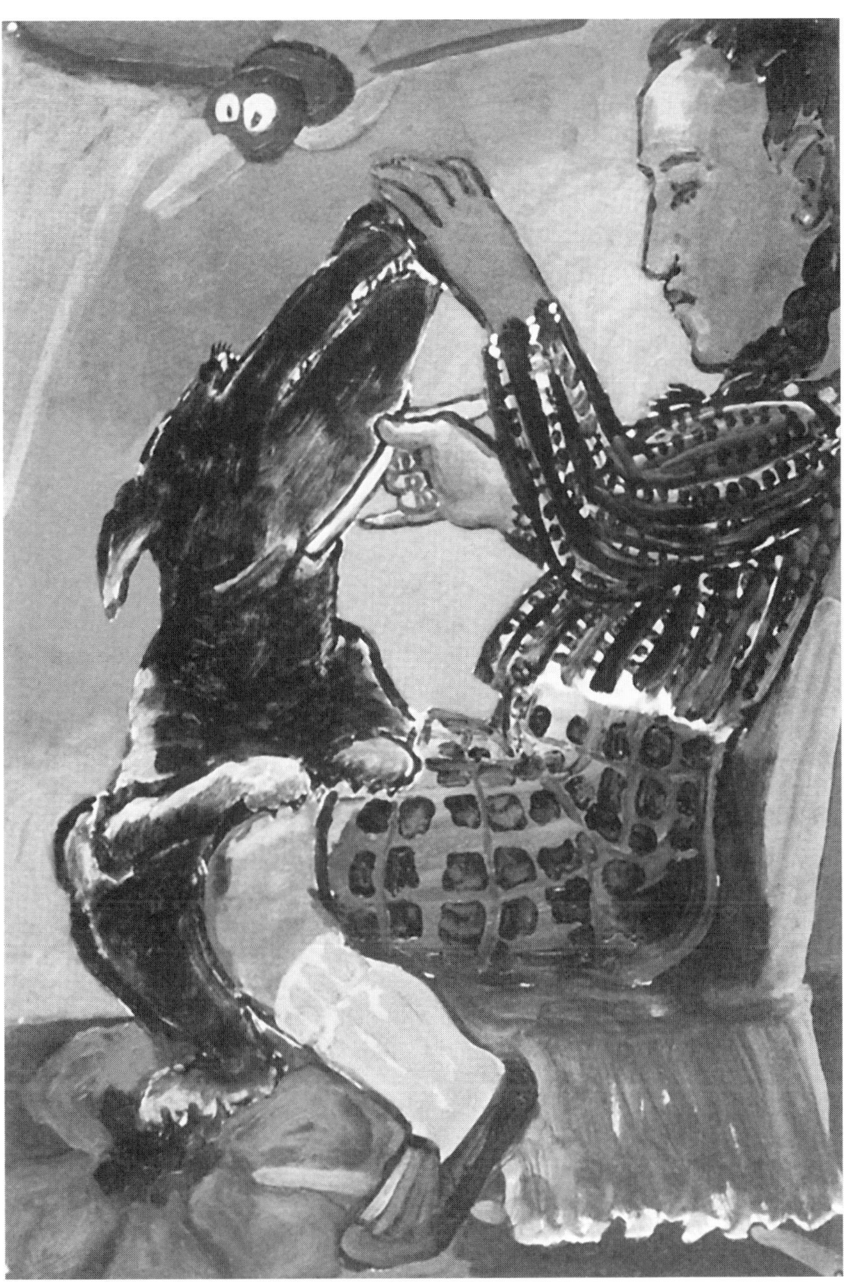

Paula Rego, *Girl Shaving a Dog*, from *Girl and Dog* series, 1986　　Figure 2

> recognition and attention from their father/husband links together much of Rego's work. (Bradley, 2002: 79)

The Oedipus narrative is, as I shall attempt to show, profoundly embedded in the narrative structuring of Rego's work. Sophocles' drama served Freud and his followers not only as a paradigm for familial relations, but also as a prototype of how the subject's desire is engendered. For many feminists, however, adhering to the concept of Oedipalisation is an ideological position that would imply an acceptance of the patriarchal family: an acceptance through which the female might find herself crippled by a sense of inadequacy unless she adhered to the procreative model and aligned herself with 'the qualities of passivity, exhibitionism, and masochism which make her the perfect "match" for the properly Oedipalized male subject' (Silverman, 1983: 143). In line with such feminist readings of Oedipus – and it is important to note here at the outset that in fact it is perfectly possible to be a feminist *and* to acknowledge the process of Oedipalisation – Rego's numerous exegetes[5] have repeatedly stressed that underpinning her work is an intention 'not so much to reform as to wreak havoc' at the very 'heart of the established order' (Lisboa, 2003: 92), undermining its patriarchal tenets, thereby disqualifying the Oedipal model that structures relations of kinship and affinity.

In the following chapters, I shall argue that, rather than unalloyed subversion, Rego's work evinces an ambiguity with regard to the implications of patriarchy and the position of the female subject within it. My use of the term 'patriarchy' refers to the hierarchic system that structures, and indeed defines, the Symbolic Order as we know it. As a pay-off for anatomical difference, patriarchy safeguards the father's purchase on his offspring by consigning to it a symbolic value. But, more concretely, it is the system of transmission of name and property – and with them, of symbolic capital – along the male line.

Here, I am using Lacan's now widely accepted concept of the Symbolic Order, one of the three orders of the psychoanalytic field, the other two being the Imaginary and the Real. The Symbolic Order is the register of culture and language, of the exchanges and contracts underpinning the social sphere. It incorporates all the discursive activities characterised by systems of symbolic substitution. In the Lacanian scheme, the Symbolic Order intrudes upon, and takes shape within, the life of individual subjects through the intervention of a third term, for which the father is traditionally a placeholder, disrupting the dyadic relationship between a child and its mother. As in Freud's concept of Oedipalisation, such an intervention introduces triangulation as a structuring principle: the pair becomes a trio, and the child gains consciousness not only of a 'me' (child) and a 'you' (mother), but also of a third party ('him'/'her', other). Contrariwise, the Imaginary Order is characterised by the unstable flow of attachments preceding the acquisition of language. The Imaginary Order, in other words, is marked by homology, identification and duality: a relationship with a counterpart, someone in whom the subject identifies a likeness with him or herself, 'another who is me' (Laplanche and Pontalis, 1973: 210). Although, in the life of the infant, the Imaginary precedes the Symbolic, the latter does not supplant the former and the two continue to co-exist in the psychic life of the subject.

In their amalgamation of compliance and rebellion, the female subjects of Rego's works from the mid-1980s to the present expose the origin of their desire as existing in a symbolic field invested with paternal authority. Logically, the inevitable outcome of such investment is a sense of inadequacy: for the mother, because of a tautologically defined sense of lack; for the daughter because, ostensibly, she cannot identify with the position of power except through masculinisation. Rego's work, I shall argue, shows the female subject to be obliged to negotiate with the Symbolic Order if she is to occupy this position of power, if she is to have any voice at all. It acknowledges, in other words, that entry into the Symbolic entails entertaining a network of privileged cultural signifiers – such as power, knowledge, the law, authority – with which the father's name traditionally enjoys proximity. (It should already be clear that such an analysis entails an attempt to define the artist's position with regard to feminism, and this endeavour underpins the present book.)

Such submission to the Symbolic became explicit in Rego's practice at a significant moment: in 1990, during her year as Associate Artist at the National Gallery in London. In interviews of the prior two decades, Rego had always insisted that she looked for inspiration to popular sources, to the marginal and the outcast, and never to the canonical, never to the Old Masters (see Melo, 1988: 67–71). However, in the rendezvous with the Old Masters at the National Gallery, her work began consciously to contend with, rather than contest, a version of the Western art-historical canon, with its conflation of patrimony and artistic paternity.

In effect, there had been precursors to this change, in the series of paintings of 'heroic handmaidens' (Kent, 1989: 158) of the late 1980s: the daughters and sisters of the intrepid men traditionally represented in history painting. Rego has often made clear her aversion to the authorised version, the traditional view of history as a tale told by victors. Instead, she proclaims an allegiance with a narrative told from the sidelines; with historians of everyday life. Talking to Susie Mackenzie in 1991, she quipped: 'Were I to paint the Burning of Rome, it would still be the cook in the kitchen plucking feathers' (Mackenzie, 1991: 15) The women in the background – those who stay at home and sew and weep while their men pledge war in Jacques-Louis David's *Oath of the Horatii* (1784) – are brought to the foreground in Rego's work, amplified and animated as protagonists in their own right. Behind the scenes, her work tells us, History is made possible by the invisible humdrum work – the histories – of ordinary human beings. As Bertolt Brecht rhetorically asks: 'Young Alexander Conquered India. He alone? Caesar beat the Gauls. Was there not even a cook in his army?' (Brecht, 1972: 30). If Rego enters the Great Tradition of mimetic figurative painting, she does so with the cook, so to speak: through the kitchen door.

It is an art-historical commonplace that, since the Renaissance, one of the precepts of such naturalistic painting – at least in the Italianate tradition[6] – is that that which came, through the procedures of perspectival construction, to be called a 'picture' is both generated by, and addressed to, a single viewer: a measurable world addressed to a centralised and sovereign subject. This defines the classical model of vision. Perspective not only masters vision, separating objects in space, but also inaugurates a regime of 'truth in painting' that hides the tenets of its own ideologically based axioms. The perspectival picture opens out onto an 'as if' world, reassuringly presenting the illusion, later inherited by photography, of an all-present and neutral instantaneity. It gives us an image of potentially infinite phenomenological plenitude, geometrically ordered by the gaze of the spectator; a world that presents itself as both punctual and incontrovertible. Since the early 1970s, numerous critics have recognised that the logic of such an address – the logic of the gaze as construed by perspectival spatial construction – takes for granted a male producer, and a male spectator later occupying his position.[7]

In light of this, Rego's works of the early 1980s – for instance the *Operas* (1983) or the *Vivian Girls* (1984; Figure 3) – may be seen as

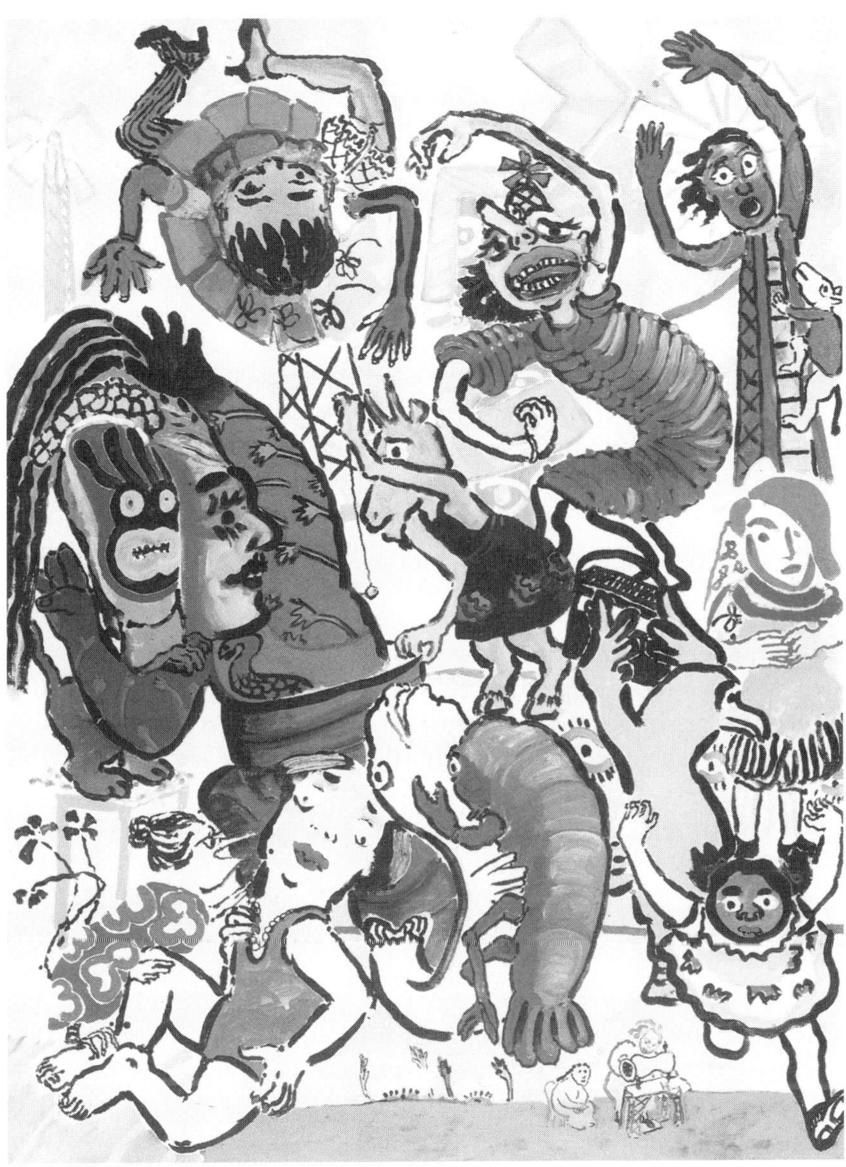

Paula Rego, *The Vivian Girls as Windmills*, 1984

Figure 3

countering the connotative burden of such pictorial construction. In a world of un-mastered fluidity, girls, animals and vegetables cavort with malicious pleasure, intermingle and are mutually transformed into polymorphous hybrids with a lightness and joy unparalleled even in Rego's own work. A buoyant and often hilarious figuration is rendered with luminous, breathy candour. Though images are foreshortened, there is no clearly marked distinction between foreground and background, no orthogonals and no depth. Rather, the space is organised as a network of surface events. With the greatest speed of execution, yet with the fine precision in mimetic capture of a cartoonist, the picture seems to have unfurled straight from the artist's imagination, pictorial incident piling upon pictorial incident. This is the kind of imaging one might compare to spirited babble or free association. In this respect – in the way these works seem to spill directly from an uncensored imagination – their precedents reside not in the works that precede them, but in Rego's work of the early 1960s. Though the works separated by over a decade differ in both form and spirit, they share the fact of an immense assurance and an extraordinarily idiosyncratic vision.

Arguably, Rego's paintings and collages from the first half of the 1960s are the most unambiguously insubordinate she has produced. Many are satirical and political in their manifest content – *Salazar Vomiting the Homeland* (1960) is the most famous example, but there are numerous others, such as the smaller works on paper *Order Has Been Established* or *Always at Your Excellency's Service* (both of 1961), or *When We Had a House in the Country* (1962; Plate 6). But in their mockery of tyranny, they also hit out against the self-importance of the domestic despot (usually, though not exclusively, the father). These works, whether painted or including collaged bits of newspaper or found materials, are voluptuously tactile and bodily, exuding unfeigned energy and pleasure in the visceral carnality so fluently translated into image.

While today we are accustomed to such confidence and boldness in art made by women, in the mid-1960s feminism as a social and artistic movement had only just begun to emerge in the UK and America. Marco Livingstone gives us an idea of how confounding such works were when they were made. He notes that while such 'robust libidinousness' was, at the time, 'accepted in the work of a hard-drinking, boorish male artist such as the recently deceased American Jackson Pollock', it was perhaps unseemly 'for a nice mother in her mid-twenties to paint such pictures' and 'the English galleries and critics who saw them considered them unexhibitable' (Livingstone, 2007: 44).

In eschewing a homogeneous mode of production, while at the same time materially exposing the procedures of pictorial construction, the dense, elaborately made, yet visceral figurations of the first half of the 1960s challenge both coherence and authoritative mastery. They draw sustenance not only from the physical action of drawing, painting and collage, but also from multiple narrative and visual sources: daily experience, events reported in the newspaper, stories recollected from childhood, comic strips and popular arte-facts. Alhough she now confesses never to have seen the Dubuffet exhibition at the ICA in London in 1959 that so strongly marked her work at the time,[8] the effect of Rego's admiration of Dubuffet and, a little later, of Arshile Gorky is manifest in the licence she grants the energetically drawn, or cut and pasted, biomorphic forms of her works in the late 1950s and early 1960s. Heir to Surrealist automatism, the narrative in Rego's work at this time is constructed and transformed during the making of the work: a fierce libidinal energy invested in process.

In the evisceration, decomposition, the stretching and shatter-ing of forms in these works, there occurs that de-structuring – or declassification – that Yve-Alain Bois and Rosalind Krauss, following Georges Bataille, identified as the *informe*, the formless (Bois and Krauss, 1997). Such unravelling of a coherent and cohesive picto-rial gestalt, such breaking down of classificatory boundaries and flattening of hierarchies, performs an operation that Bataille called *declassification*, foreshadowing Julia Kristeva's notion of the abject (Kristeva, 1982). This describes the blurred boundaries – the per-meable borders – between the inside and the outside of the personal body, announcing instability in the social body at large. The abject is a quality that hovers between subject and object, and, as such, one of its more apposite representations is the liminal maternal body. As the expression of a smudging of distinctions, a leak between boundaries, the abject heralds a collapse of hierarchy and meaning. Pictorially, it erupts less in the representation of such leakage than in its *performance* through the dissolution of identifiable objects and of the geometrical sureties provided by perspectival construction. In their spillings and splittings, their evasions of bodily integrity and of univocal signification, Rego's works of the first half of the 1960s embody such a relation to the abject.

By the middle of the 1960s, in works such as *Centaur and Harpy*, *Stray Dogs* and *Regicide* (Figure 4) (all of 1965), Rego's paintings had begun to include cut or torn sections of her own drawings and paintings. Unlike the earlier incorporation of found materials, the plasticity of these fragments is now shaped and contained by strong outlines, so that, in the works, a visceral quality is counterbalanced

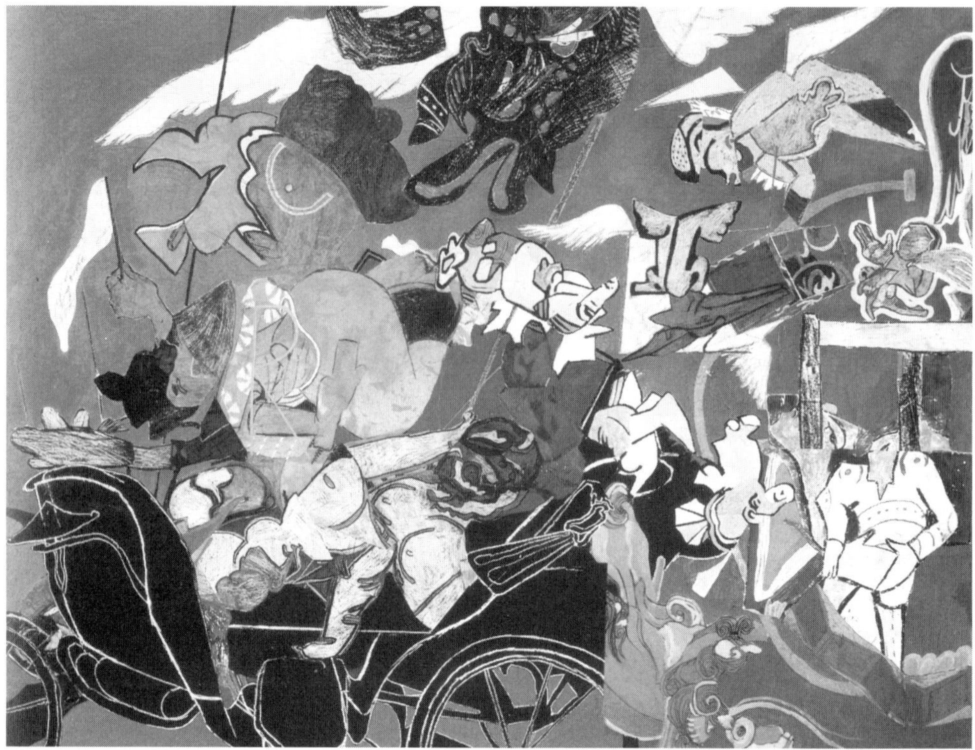

Figure 4   Paula Rego, *Regicide*, 1965

by a strong sense of graphic design. While in Rego's works of the late 1960s this graphic sense approached the more contrived idiom of Pop Art, it was, as we have seen, in the first half of the 1980s that it erupted again in a more assuredly personal way. That this sense of design owed a great debt to the narrative, linear traditions of comic strips is manifestly clear in such works as the *Operas* (1983) or *The Proles' Wall* (1984).

In 1981, Rego abandoned these complex procedures of collage and over-painting. Her works from the early 1980s seem to breathe more freely, shedding the belaboured quality of pictorial production, and gaining a fresh material homogeneity. If such homogeneity undermines the work's power to disrupt,[9] nevertheless its refusal to address a stationary and sovereign viewer keeps alive a rebellious streak in the very design of Rego's pictures. If a new range of more skittish, playful images tumbles into view, images that are less overtly political, these nevertheless always prod the relationship between the powerful and the impotent, and such exploration is expressed in the sense of reckless abandon, the refutation of overt compositional discipline.

But the 'heroic handmaidens' of the late 1980s and, after them, the four easel paintings produced at the National Gallery and the large panels of *Crivelli's Garden* (1990–91) painted for the restaurant of the Sainsbury Wing at the same venue, put a clamp on such spontaneity. There are certainly many reasons for this shift of emphasis in Rego's working procedure and, indeed, in her pictorial concerns. But, as Dalila Rodrigues has pointed out in an essay dealing with Rego and the Old Masters, they all relate directly to the artist's continued search for the appropriate idiom in which to tell her own story (Rodrigues, 2009). Rego engages, in other words, in a kind of self-telling in which other images – whether those of comic strips or canonical paintings – serve as a kind of mirror, or, in the Lacanian sense, counterpart: a relationship with a someone in whom the subject identifies a likeness with him or herself, 'another who is me' (Laplanche and Pontalis, 1973: 210).

Immersed for a year in an institutional space that allowed her privileged access to works that define the canon of Western art, she came to recognise how richly these could serve her. In particular, their narrative strategies provided her with a copious stock of pictorial devices. Rather than seeing in them the epitome of a great patriarchal plot, Rego began to regard the Old Masters as an endless resource. Instead of spurning the 'fathers' of the Great Tradition, Rego now negotiates with them for a legitimate position within the lineage. Such an engagement with the canon was reinforced when Rego once again worked with the National Gallery collection in the year 2000, for the exhibition *Encounters: New Art from Old*, when she chose Hogarth's series *Marriage à la Mode* as the point of departure for her eponymous triptych (1999).

Since Linda Nochlin first unsettled female viewers in 1971 by suggesting that setting the record straight by disinterring some of art's 'old mistresses' neither addresses the question of canonicity nor explores the gendered social conditions enabling artistic production, feminists have made divergent claims for what being a woman artist might entail. For Rego, the turn towards the canon – a turn that, she understood, did not involve moving away from other, more popular spheres of influence – clearly meant engaging in some form of negotiation with issues of gender. 'You're a man when you're painting', she startlingly observed in 1999. 'Part of me that's male comes to the fore' (Gee, 1999: 19). Arguably, a dialogue with the discipline of the paternal now also emerges in the very structure of Rego's work, its obedience to an overriding design. In place of amniotic fluidity and a non-hierarchical pictorial organisation, we see compositions mastered by a unitary gaze and grounded by a horizon line that divides fore- from background. Such simple pictorial division serves as a prelude to her later essays in perspective.

By the early 1990s, Rego was working increasingly – and later, exclusively – from the model. The narratives of these works were elaborated partially in advance, partially during the process of the work's production as new meanings unfolded in the artist's contact with the model's bodily performance. The freshness of *alla prima* painting and the luminosity of rapidly executed washes cedes again to a laboured surface, now cobbled together from slow looking, a surface that bears the evidence of the work required to manufacture this 'hard-won image',[10] first in acrylic paint, and, from the series *Dog Women* (1994) onwards, in pastel.

The change to pastel was a momentous one. In this medium, Rego found great freedom, afforded by its unique capacity to combine techniques from both drawing and painting. Pastel suited better her particular practice of mimetic representation than the slow drying – and, to her, often fiddly – medium of oil paint, or the rather too quick drying leatheriness of acrylic. In defining painting as 'a category of bounded surface having descriptive or expressive or representational properties that are the result of some means of coloring or marking or otherwise modifying their appearances', Charles Harrison recognises that the category of painting may include works in pastel that might also otherwise be conceived 'as heavily worked drawings' (Harrison, 2005: 10). Rego's definition of the more densely elaborated works in pastel as paintings seems, therefore, perfectly acceptable.

The heavy working and reworking and close attention to perception that Rego's work continues to manifest places the artist at odds with the predominant model of wan, purposefully de-skilled painting of contemporary artists such as Luc Tuymans, Elizabeth Peyton, Chantal Joffe, Karen Kilimnick or even Peter Doig. Drawing, painting, over-painting, drawing and finding the outline again: these procedures are meshed together in the service of what Rego frequently speaks of as 'getting it right', a doing that eventually embodies an emotion that would otherwise have remained inchoate.

Yet against the controls exerted by the demands of mimetic figuration, rebellion now erupts more surreptitiously in the facture itself, in the insistent presence of the artist's hand, the intransigent physicality of the medium: whether the scratchy intensity of the pen, the gouging and scoring of the etching tool, or the friction of pastel on paper. The resulting surfaces often have about them an impacted sense of emotion angrily contained, intensity violently restrained. Conflict and rage erupt in a certain harshness – an obduracy – of surface. For, arguably, if a beautiful, smooth surface acts as a fetish (a sign that disavows loss), then a belaboured or ugly one bars such imaginative completion by exposing the traces of a founding loss. The spurning of apparently effortless facture, I am urging, operates as a form of internal revolt against the phallic authority of the paintbrush and its capacity for skilful aestheticisation. Likewise, while adhering to an overall perspectival design, she nevertheless disrupts the incremental and logical diminution of figures in relation to the viewing position, occasionally introducing spatial pockets where scale is ruled by an emotional and symbolic logic rather than strictly by the impersonal rationale of perspectival geometry, similarly allowing misrule to clamour against the laws of perspective.

Nevertheless, it must be conceded that, unlike the early work, the figuration of these more recent works strives towards some kind of closure – there is no more spilling from broken forms – and, in so doing, insistently and perhaps nostalgically evokes a past where such a call to order had distinctly political overtones. The problems inherent in such a revival of mimetic representation have been nowhere more starkly and critically outlined than by Benjamin Buchloh in his important essay 'Figures of Authority Ciphers of Regression', presciently written in 1980. Examining the return to traditional modes of figuration in the late 1970s in terms of an ideological backlash, Buchloh pits this revival against earlier 'chains of restorative phenomena' (Buchloh, 1984: 107) occurring after the conceptual and material paradigm shifts effected by Duchamp and Malevich. Buchloh is here convinced that, under the aspect of liberal humanism, the return to forms of figuration that idealise 'the perennial monuments of art history and its masters' (Buchloh, 1984: 111) scarcely disguises an academicism or a degraded classicism directly reflecting the political realities of the day. 'Is there a simple causal connection', he asks at the outset of the essay, 'a mechanical reaction, by which growing political oppression necessarily and irreversibly generates traditional representation?' Furiously, he queries to what extent

> the rediscovery and recapitulation of these modes of figurative representation . . . reflect[s] and dismantle[s] the ideological impact of growing authoritarianism; or to what extent they simply indulge and reap the benefits of the increasingly apparent political practice; or, worse yet, to what extent they cynically generate a cultural climate of authoritarianism to familiarize us with the political realities to come. (Buchloh, 1984: 107–108)

An adulation of the canon as embodied by past masters invokes, for Buchloh, an analogy with kowtowing to 'the paternal principle of the master' and, with grave aesthetic and ideological implications, 'serves as a screen upon which the configurations of a failed historical presence can be projected' (Buchloh, 1984: 111). With his theoretical roots in the Frankfurt School, Buchloh regards as insurmountable the conflict between autonomy and social determinism: for him, an aesthetic vanguard would by definition be politically radical. Put another way, for Buchloh aesthetic value is inextricably intertwined with social value.

But Rego's work from around 1988 onwards uses the type of pictorial idiom Buchloh deplores precisely *because* it is cathected to historical meaning, and for the complex array of both orthodox and subversive impulses it rehearses. It does, furthermore, at the level of the surface what the bodies within it do at the level of narrative, and that is perform historical revision, not as the affirmation of a concluded meaning, but as epistemological pursuit. In this, Rego's work invites a serious reading in relation to the historical referents that have served it. But in its invocation of delayed and revised temporalities, it also – as I have already hinted – begs for analysis deploying the terms brought into being by psychoanalysis, terms that pertain not only to mnemonic construction, but also to subject formation. The first task of psychoanalysis is to bring what is unconscious into consciousness, and in this sense, deferring to psychoanalytic models, I will be prying into the unconscious of Rego's work: not, of course, her personal unconscious, but the historical and ideological forces working behind the scenes.

Although Freud paid much attention to literary works by a wide range of writers – Sophocles, Shakespeare, Dostoyevsky, Goethe and Schiller, among others – his only extensive analysis of works of art were those he dedicated to Michelangelo's *Moses*, his speculative psychoanalytic biography of Leonardo da Vinci, and a discussion of a fictional work of art in Jensen's *Gradiva*. Reading Rego's work together with Freud's in particular, as I propose to do in this book, does not entail aligning it with Freud's style of image analysis. Neither does it entail equating it with a kind of dreaming. But it does involve tapping into the psychoanalytic model of temporalisation. Freud's model of psychic life, and his proposition of a process through which it might come to be signified, not only grafts the past onto the present, the old onto the new; it also tells us that, in effect, there is little that is new. As Peter Brooks observes, Freud summons us to 'engage the dynamic of memory and desire that can reconnect, however provisionally and tenuously, time lost and time continuing' (Brooks, 1984: 284).

But if Rego's works – and, particularly, her single-figure works – offer, at the level of the body, a narrativisation of the very condition of being a subject, they also, in their evocations of realism of the 1930s and 1940s, perform the psychoanalytic desideratum of unleashing memory of the past through present utterance. They are, in other words, memory embodied.

In setting out the initial parameters for this book, I was prompted by my own interests in the possible relationship of psychoanalysis and history,[11] in how feminism thinks the law, and in the signifying procedures and mutual interdependence of visual and verbal narrative. As Rego's is an oeuvre that invites a productive engagement in these concerns, I was eager to find their points of intersection or mutual evasion. Using as my springboard the psychoanalytic conception of the family as a vital relay between subjectivity and the broader cultural field, I begin by thinking through the Freudian concept of the family romance as the theoretical frame for an exploration of Rego's work. Immersed, at first, in the critical discourse in which Rego situates her own work – carnivalesque inversions of the weak and the strong, erosions of the desiderata of patriarchy – I set off to explore the insubordinate daughter and subversive mother, only time and again to confront the father. This perhaps should not have surprised me, yet it is unexpectedly that the paternal has, from early on, haunted my writing of this book. At the same time, Rego's work seemed undeniably feminist in its desire, where feminism may be defined, in Griselda Pollock's formulation, not as 'an alibi for female expressivity', but as a means of 'seeking to secure women's equal right to the "body of the painter"' (Pollock, 2001: 80). What is the relationship between such a desire for a female occupation of the body of the painter, and paternal law?

In tracking female subject formation in Rego's work – and, more specifically, in asking how that subject either slots into, or sabotages, the patriarchal family romance – I examine not the contexts of this work's reception, but the forces that have shaped its production of meaning and that have informed its symbolic resources. In this sense, my enquiry follows a historicist model, as did Maria Manuel Lisboa in her monograph on Rego (Lisboa, 2003). But unlike Lisboa, my findings point not to radical subversion, but to a greater ambivalence in Rego's work.

Looking at Rego's work together with the historical resources that have served it suggests that my approach has been iconographic, and this is of course true: Rego's work is irresistible to iconographers. In the strictest sense, as the traditional relationship of a sign to pre-existing knowledge, iconography sounds its own limitations when pressed at the service of works that do not themselves deploy such standardised imagery. Yet many of Rego's images *are* drawn from a common cultural reservoir. The importance of existing narratives – stories, opera plots, poems, fairy-tales, novels – standing in a relation of pre-text to her works, reveals the extent to which her paintings, drawings and graphic work relate to a textual order. This anterior textuality manifests itself variously: through titling; in the frequent use of literary texts as points of departure; in the discursive web the artist weaves about her work in interviews; and, in the early work, in the inclusion of words scribbled on the surface of the works themselves.

But the longer one looks at Rego's work, the more clear it becomes that her relationship to existing texts – and indeed, to existing images – is an expedient one. 'Could it serve me?' is the question that underlies all her pictorial encounters with both art and literature. Put otherwise, it is not so much that Rego's work pays homage to her predecessors, but rather that the artist actively intervenes in the material that she mines. Such intervention – such invention – is governed by an intuition that is often formal, pictorial. The improvisatory nature of pictorial construction; the combination of intention and contingency, purpose and unconscious association; the uses to which textual sources are put and the extreme transformations they undergo; the dynamic relation with the model; and the performative extemporisation in the studio all serve to tilt an iconographic approach to Rego's work in the direction of both psychoanalysis and semiotics.[12]

If iconography teases out the specific, culturally honed meanings of signs from a given repertoire by superimposing a conventional meaning on a purported natural meaning, semiotics is, by its very nature, anti-positivist, focusing more broadly on the socially constructed nature of signs. Here, a key role is played by intertextuality: the idea that every present utterance incorporates past 'texts'. As Mieke Bal and Norman Bryson have argued (Bal and Bryson, 1991) – and as Svetlana Alpers (1983) and Michael Baxandall (1985) have importantly revealed in their close scrutiny of individual works – intertextuality differs from iconography in disallowing source to stand as origin,[13] emphasising the extent to which verbal or visual texts are cross-fertilised by other textual material, both at the point of production and at the point of reception. To view an image intertextually is to undo authorial omnipotence and contextualise, historicise or deconstruct antecedence itself. It is to disallow the present from enshrining the past as complete, ready-made and already given.

How the past resides in the present; how significations shaped by culture are taken in by the subject: these count, of course, among the concerns of psychoanalysis. So it is no surprise that in their call for a 'semiotic turn for art history' Bal and Bryson link semiotics to psychoanalysis. But they also link it to feminism, for psychoanalysis and feminism share an attention to difference and gender construction. Noting that '[p]sychoanalysis connects semiotics with an awareness of gender differentiation as pervasively relevant, indeed as a crucial basis for the heterogeneous and polysemous nature of looking', they also invoke a 'feminist turn' in semiotics (Bal and Bryson, 1991: 176). The intersection of psychoanalysis and feminism – uncomfortable bedfellows – in readings of the family romance by numerous critics, mostly feminist, informs the theoretical considerations I undertake in Chapter 1.

Thinking psychoanalysis together with art history poses its own problems, for the relationship between psychoanalytic models and works of art cannot be contained by direct 'applicability',[14] by one being used diagnostically on the other. As Jacqueline Rose has pertinently asked, what application could there be of psychoanalysis to the work of art 'which does not reduce one field to the other or inhibit by interpretation the potential meaning of both?' (Rose, 1986: 231). Freud's own interpretations of works of art may be considered in terms of such reductionism or determinism, treating visual art as he would a dream or a symptom. This leads him ultimately to use the work of art as a tautological source of bio-graphical intelligibility, pushing the material to fit in with his own interpretative desire. For Richard Wollheim, the shortcomings of Freud's aesthetics reflect contradictions in his conception of unconscious processes. Wollheim concludes that by the time Freud found himself theoretically in a position to deal with those contradictions in relation to aesthetic concerns, 'the necessary resources of leisure and energy were, we must believe, no longer available to him' (Wollheim, 1973: 266).

If Wollheim's subtle reading of Freud takes into account his use of the work of art as evidential proof of a complex or syndrome or anxiety, Meyer Schapiro offers the most explicit dismantling of Freud's foray into the interpretation of art (Schapiro, 1956). He exposes the extent to which a psychoanalytic approach to works of art cannot be symptomal – a hermeneutics constructed, moreover, on a misguided and indeed erroneous selection and interpretation of material – and makes a convincing case for the necessity of overlaying psychoanalytic models with a consideration of historical, social and linguistic contexts. Schapiro's model is one that certainly underpins my present endeavour.

Since the early 1980s, many nuanced voices have been added to the debate. In her interpretation of Freud's aesthetics, Sarah Kofman recognises that 'for Freud, works of art are like all other psychic productions insofar as they are compromises and constitute "riddles" to be solved' (Kofman, 1988: 4). Yet, for Kofman, Freud's methods cannot be described as 'applications': Freud 'does not apply to art, from the outside, a method belonging to a supposedly alien sphere. If the method is coherent, it is because each of its objects of study is but a different repetition of the same' (Kofman, 1988: 4). In her elaboration on the narcissistic investment that constitutes the connoisseurship underpinning the very idea of a canon, and in reading the 'cult of the artist' as an adulation of both the father and the hero, Kofman – much as Freud had done – considers the appositeness of a psychoanalytic model for the analysis of art as one of demystification.

Clearly, however, while attuned to the possibility of reconstructing the artist's psychic biography through his works, Freud was not alive to the formal and material concerns of the visual arts. Donald Kuspit points out that Freud 'makes scant mention of the Herculean body of Michelangelo's Moses, or of the figura serpentina that is the artist's great accomplishment', focusing instead on the secondary matter of the tablets of the law (Kuspit, 1993: 307), a matter of obvious interest to Freud himself. Furthermore, in making meaning a matter of private association, Freud's view of aesthetics does not take the social – or, indeed, the ideological – into account, except inasmuch as the ideological is present in any superego.

Kofman's study of the scope and implication of Freud's aesthetics (Kofman, 1988) is an exemplary performance of psychoanalytic exegesis, as indeed is Malcolm Bowie's exploration of how Michelangeo's *Moses* mediates thought and action (Bowie, 1993: 58), while Leo Bersani offers, as an antidote to applied psychoanalysis, the notion of 'moments of textual embarrassment' in Freud that make it impossible to read him literally (Bersani, 1986: 2). But I have found the most valuable model aligning psychoanalysis and art in Mieke Bal and Norman Bryson's suggestion that the work of art cannot illustrate the psychoanalytic concept, but stands, rather, as a 'representation of a unique instance of it' (Bal and Bryson, 1991: 197). They offer a systematised classification of the possible uses to which art history might put psychoanalysis, from the simpler models of 'application' (the analogical model), through 'interpretation' (the hermeneutic model) to a more elaborate procedure that they call the 'specification' model, a 'searchlight theory allowing specific features to be illuminated, sometimes explained but primarily read, by means of psychoanalytic concepts' (Bal and Bryson, 1991: 197).

Following the specification model, Bal and Bryson suggest, 'it remains possible to use Lacan's terms (the Symbolic, the Imaginary, the Real, the gaze)' – or indeed, of course, Freud's own (Oedipus, castration, sublimation, disavowal, narcissism, fetish) – 'to make explicit those features in a given work that these terms, and perhaps only these terms, describe' (Bal and Bryson, 1991: 201). This is the principal way in which I shall mobilise psychoanalytic theory in this book. Importantly, the authors observe that some of the more interesting and illuminating instances of this model in recent art history have utilised it self-subversively, 'to provide principles of resistance and counter-example' (Bal and Bryson, 1991: 201) to psychoanalytic theory itself: the theories of Freud or Lacan themselves then undergo revision in the light of particular works.

Because of the primacy it grants narrative, Rego's work invites psychoanalytic readings. For narrative lies at the heart of the psychoanalytic procedure: it is the backbone of that form of didactic biography and that style of exemplarity that is the psychoanalytic case study. Indeed, in Freud's case studies we find an instantiation of the procedures, conundrums and limitations of storytelling that underline the subject's imperative that life be narratable. If the structure of deferral and retroaction, intrinsic to Freud's style of writing, renders the plots of these case studies self-subversive, nevertheless, 'telling the self's story remains our indispensable thread in the labyrinth of temporality' (Brooks, 1984: 284). In the mutual configuration of past and present, telling the self is what Rego's work does.

Such narrativity leads us straight into the mined terrain of literalism, intentionality and biographism, the fallacy of confusing art with life, or searching in art for too close parallels with the lived life of the type parodied by Waldemar Januszczak when, identifying the little girls in Rego's composite narrative scenes of 2000–01 as self-portraits, he warns against a critique of the 'the little girl being sick whom the maid is helping is surely young Paula having her first illicit drink' variety (Januszczak, 2001: 6).

However, rather than sustaining biographism and intentionalism, a psychoanalytically inflected reading goes against the grain of both, for it points precisely to that which slips the net of conscious objectives. A psychoanalytic turn in art history would then be less concerned with the idiosyncrasies of individual biography than with the meanings introjected from the cultural arena at large, exposing the extent to which, in Freud's famous formulation, 'the ego is not master in its own house' (Freud, 1917a: 143).[15] In such a reading, causal inference – the forward thrust of the term 'intention' – has, as Michael Baxandall wonderfully illustrates, more to do with what pictures themselves do than with the painters who make them (Baxandall, 1985: 42).

It therefore goes without saying that my use of psychoanalytic theory in no way concerns itself with Rego personally. Rather, it is a particular account of how the subject identifies with others, of the construction of sexual difference in its relation to subject formation that psychoanalysis contributes to a reading of her work. Any allusions I make to the artist's life are not aimed at supporting the slipperiness of testimonial claims of the work. Instead, if the dynamics of memory are mobilised in Rego's work in a bid to 'give fear a face' (Lacerda, 1965: n.p.), my approach to that fear – or anxiety, or ambivalence – is never conflated with the artist's person, but, rather, is examined in relation to the constellation of elements (and their cultural resonance) in which it finds itself in the pictorial event. In such an operation, it is my hope that psychoanalytic theory will come to illuminate the work, but also that the visual may be a prism through which to re-engage with that theory.

Freud's talking cure, and the primacy it grants language, presents us with the subject as a signifying complex. But in the acting-out that goes by the name of a symptom, it also sponsors a semiotisation of the body that is readily visualised. In the first instance, it is the body as symptomatic in Rego's work that I propose to study here: as both a generator of meanings and a site where meaning is performed. While Rego's dense, multi-figured compositions explore the interplay of the psychic and the social, it is in the single-figure works that the body itself narrativises the webs of psychic, sexual, linguistic and ideological signification in which the subject is ensnared. In these works, the tension between the social and the psychic is palpable, each vying for agency in a teleology of self, yet each unable to account in full for subjectivity. Rego prods, in other words, the points where the enticements and constraints of the cultural meet with the aberrant psychic material that must be relinquished in order that the law take hold. Arguably, her work also explores the efficacy and limitations of resistance to that law.

In what follows, I focus on this labour of socialisation and resistance in terms of the ambiguities that Rego's work evinces in relation to the Freudian model of the family romance. At the same time, I explore some of the vexations in Freud's own writings, its dissonances, gaps and thwarted coherence. I have selected as the nuclei – the focal points out of which my analysis grows – three paintings dated between 1987 and 2000: *The Policeman's Daughter* (1987, Plate 1), *The Interrogator's Garden* (2000, Plate 2), and *The First Mass in Brazil* (1993, Plate 3). The analysis of these single-figure works (the background figure in *The Interrogator's Garden* is not, I argue, personalised as a protagonist) structures each of my three principal chapters, and, cutting across linear chronologies, each exploration prompts discussions of other works by the artist, without deliberating on any notion of stylistic progress, which has been discussed by many writers on Rego. My text therefore weaves back and forth in time, implying that the work has a certain underlying coherence, now functioning as an 'oeuvre'. Such coherence is perhaps tautological and is certainly retrospective, and is produced by the accrued, collective meanings generated by the works as they communicate with one another across time. Although allowing analysis to grow out of a limited number of individual works has meant paying honed and concentrated attention to those particular works, contrary to my expectations, my analysis has not followed the model of 'reading in detail' so wonderfully exemplified in the writing of critics like Naomi Schor, whose excellent book *Reading in Detail: Aesthetics and the Feminine* (Schor, 1987) might be dubbed a handbook of feminist aesthetics.[16]

The detail is the hiding place of the significant, a *punctum* that unleashes the repressed meaning of the work. Reading through the detail provides, for Schor, a path out of the totalising histories associated with a male-centred epistemological model. For, as she observes, in taking its place in the 'vast field of insignificance which Freud undertook to reclaim', the detail holds a 'privileged and problematic status' in psychoanalysis (Schor, 1987: 68). This is everywhere implicit in Freud's work, and is literally spelled out in his essay on Michelangelo's *Moses*, where he speaks of trifling and apparently irrelevant details as the 'despised or unnoticed features, from the rubbish-heap, as it were, of our observations' (Freud, 1914b: 222). It is not by chance that, in this essay, Freud expresses particular interest in the writing of Giovanni Morelli, who, writing in the 1870s and 1880s under a Russian pseudonym, constructed a method of connoisseurship – of distinguishing original works of art from copies – by a minute examination of apparently insignificant and unconscious detail (such as the depiction of earlobes or fingertips in paintings).[17] The methods of both Morelli and Freud have been compared to the work of detectives and to the genre of detective stories. Such analogies are not capricious: any purview of Freud's case studies reveals his process of sleuthing through apparently insignificant details, and of course *The Interpretation of Dreams* is a thesaurus of them.

The art historical method to which Schor's theorisation points is most explicitly found in the writing of Mieke Bal, who employs semiotic and narratological tools more frequently used in studies of literature, to prod the repressed or disavowed meanings of a picture that are unleashed by the infinitesimal and subordinate. A similar approach is taken to Rego's work in Maria Manuel Lisboa's study, where 'the interpretative practice ... [seeks] to emulate what I believe to be Paula Rego's own drive in painting: to recover repressed, unauthorised or untold stories' (Lisboa, 2003: 18).

My own method not so much entails searching for the arcane or obtuse detail, as engaging with the *obvious* for all its tautological manifestness. If, etymologically, the obvious is that which stands in the way (Latin *ob*: against + *via*: way), that which we stumble upon in our trajectory, then it is also a little like an obstacle in our path, an occluded opportunity. Such an understanding of the obvious is psychoanalytically resonant. For if the aim of psychoanalytic practice is to defamiliarise the manifest, to uncover its buried meanings, then its methods entail an attempt to overcome the obstacle between desire and its object. The obvious, in other words, is the obstacle impeding our access to underlying desire. The relationship between such impediments and desire is not, however, stable or predictable. As Adam Phillips has observed, not only is the obstacle 'used to conceal – to pack up, as it were – the unconscious desire' but, also, 'the desire does not reveal the obstacle, the obstacle reveals the desire' (Phillips, 1993: 85–86). Where we find an obstacle, there we know desire to dwell.

It is with this perception that the obvious, as obstacle, is inextricably twinned with desire that I have undertaken the analysis of the three specimen paintings that follow. And in yoking together obstacles and desire, we are back with the family romance, with its Oedipal plot, as paradigm: '[it] is part of the fascination of the Oedipus story in particular, and perhaps of narrative in general, that we and the heroes and heroines of their fictions never know whether obstacles create desire, or desire creates obstacles' (Phillips, 1993: 87). In its embodiment of female subjectivity, Rego's work exposes how the utopianism of desire meets the normative pressure of social practices, institutions and ideologies. These, while appearing as obstacles, are in effect formative, constitutive of subjectivity itself.

I have selected the three paintings that serve as points of departure for Chapters 2–4 for their iconic exemplarity. As case studies, they are, in a sense, obvious choices. Linking these set pieces to other works made by Rego both before and after them, I track the passionate and paradoxical attachments that characterise female subjectivity in the artist's work. Through the paintings viewed as case studies, each of the three principal chapters tracks a particular aspect of the *Estado Novo*, which serves as the historical anchor to so much of Rego's work. Simultaneously, in each of these chapters I engage with a particular range of psychoanalytic concepts through which, I argue, the works might productively be read.

Notes

1 See for instance Marina Warner's formulation that Rego's narratives spring from 'the *camera lucida* of the mind's eye' (Warner, 2003: 8)

or Memory Holloway's idea that in becoming 'a way of externalizing thought by making it material', narrative for Rego is, in effect, an epistemology (Holloway, 1999: 7). Both Warner and Holloway remove 'narrative' from the empirical moorings that, in many other writings on the artist, bind it to the lived life.

2 Michael Sheringham has elaborated this useful analogy between auto-biography and fetishism, where the small and tangible detail 'which can be dominated and possessed' stands as a substitute for an 'elusive and intangible object of desire' (Sheringham, 1991: 6).

3 The date for the start of the *Estado Novo* varies in different histories. The volume dealing with the regime in José Mattoso's substantial history of Portugal begins with the military coup of 1926 and ends in 1974 (Rosas, 1994). Some historians mark as the starting point 1928 – the year Salazar became Secretary of Finance; others say 1932, the year he took office as leader. 1933 is the year in which the regime was consecrated in a new constitution.

4 Julia Kristeva discusses the 'connivance of the young girl and her mother' as foundational of female subjectivity (Kristeva, 1979: 204–205). Similarly, Nancy Chodorow discusses the periods of prolonged symbiosis between mothers and daughters, whom they do not perceive as clearly Other (Chodorow, 1999: 109).

5 With the exception of Maria Manuel Lisboa's monograph (Lisboa, 2003), Rego has not been the object of any published, book-length academic study. Coming to Rego's work from the field of literary studies, Lisboa's approach is avowedly rooted in the theory and practice of New Historicism, seeking to situate Rego's work in relation to the historical forces that shaped it. Memory Holloway (1999, 2001–02) and Ana Gabriela Macedo (1999a, 1999b, 2001a, 2001b, 2001c, 2003) have dedicated important analytic articles to the artist. The unpublished MA thesis of Ana Nolasco (2004) is a significant contribution to the field, while Teresa Capucho's unpublished MA thesis (2001) focuses specifically on the drawings. John McEwen's monograph (2006) is an important generalised reference work, and Marco Livingstone has written on Rego's work with sensitivity and intelligence (Livingstone 2004, 2007, 2008). Catalogue essays and reviews in the popular press abound. One of Rego's most astute early critics was her late husband, Victor Willing (1971, 1983).

6 Svetlana Alpers observes that, in the study of art and its history, there has been a conflation between the study of Western art and the art of Italy, the one seemingly describing the other: 'Italian art and the rhetorical evocation of it has not only defined the practice of the central tradition of Western artists, it has also determined the study of their works' (Alpers, 1983: xix). Against this tradition, she pits the northern tradition, and in particular that of the Netherlands, which she

sees as an art of describing, as contrasted with the narrative art of the Italianate tradition. Rego, of course, belongs much more firmly in the narrative, Italianate tradition.

7 If John Berger made this clear as early as 1972, in his affirmation that 'men act and women appear', underlining the role of scopic pleasure in securing the female subject's submission to 'the owner of both woman and the painting' (Berger, 1972: 45, 52) it was Laura Mulvey who first cogently theorised the gendering of the perspectival gaze and its cinematographic legacy (Mulvey, 1989). For a discussion of the relationship between the position occupied by the painter and that of the viewer, see Charles Harrison's discussion of the picture plane (2005).

8 The import of this exhibition on Rego has become part of the lore around her work. She more recently has confessed (Rego: in conversation, January 2004) to not have seen the exhibition. Nevertheless, she undeniably felt its effects through discourse, through reports and reproductions in the press.

9 The argument that homogeneity undermines a work's disruptive qualities underpins Benjamin Buchloh's critique of Picasso's move from collage back to painting, and the Futurists' rejection of the collage techniques 'through which they had underlined the interaction of aesthetic phenomena with their social and political context' (Buchloh, 1984: 112).

10 This was the title of an exhibition of figurative painting held at the Tate Gallery in London in 1984.

11 The problems of 'psychohistory' are explored by Saul Friedlander (Friedlander, 1978), while Dominick LaCapra brings to the discipline of history a psychoanalytic understanding of temporality as repetition/change (LaCapra, 1989).

12 In discussions of the nature of meaning in art, the relationship of iconography to semiotics is generally temporalised, or, as Donald Preziosi puts it, 'the former . . . framed as a precursor of the latter, and the latter . . . seen as a more inclusive, interdisciplinary version of the former' (Preziosi, 1998: 228). Indeed if, as Mieke Bal and Norman Bryson point out, the semiotic perspective has long been present in art history in the iconographic studies of scholars like Riegl, Panofsky and Meyer Schapiro, since the 1970s 'semiotics has been engaged with a range of problems very different from those it began with . . .: the polysemy of meaning; the problematics of authorship, context, and reception; the implications of the study of narrative for the study of images; the issue of sexual difference in relation to verbal and visual signs; and the claims to truth of interpretations' (Bal and Bryson, 1991: 174; see also Damisch, 1975).

13 For the specific and local connotations of what he calls 'pictorial events', see Michael Baxandall's chapter 'Piero della Francesca's *The*

Resurrection of Christ', in his *Words for Pictures* (Baxandall, 2003). For the problematisation and 'textualisation' of the very concept of 'context', see Mieke Bal's *Reading 'Rembrandt'* (Bal, 1991).

14   There are many accounts of the relationship between psychoanalysis and art, including important writings by Ernst Kris, Adrian Stokes, Anton Ehrenzweig, Edgar Wind and Marion Milner. Peter Fuller (1980) leans heavily on object-relations theory and social history, but does not provide an account of their encounter. For an interrogation into the question of the 'applicability' and a reading of several important texts, see Kuspit (1993), chapters 26 and 27. An essential contributor to this field is Sarah Kofman (1988). More recently, Griselda Pollock has explored the image in psychoanalysis in terms of Freud's deployment of archaeological metaphors (Pollock, 2006b).

15   For a discussion of the differences between biographism and psychoanalytical criticism, see Mieke Bal's exploration of Louise Bourgeois' *Spiders* (Bal, 2001a: 36–40, 73).

16   Invoking the work of Barthes and Derrida, Schor also cites Michel Foucault's call, in *Discipline and Punish,* for a 'history of the detail' (Schor, 1987: 3). See also Schor, Weed and Rooney, 2003.

17   For a discussion of Freud and Morelli, see Jack Spector (1969) and Richard Wollheim (1973: 177–201). Sarah Kofman argues that, in effect, Freud's method differs from Morelli's, in that Morelli's propulsion towards the attribution of authorship implies that the author is the father of his own works, while Freud sets out to unmask such an alignment between author and work, an alignment Kofman considers 'theological' (Kofman, 1988: 10).

Reading the family romance:
Is there a feminist version?

For we think back through our mothers if we are women. (Virginia Woolf, *A Room of One's Own*)

If there is no longer a Father, why tell stories? (Roland Barthes, *The Pleasure of the Text*)

The myth of Oedipus has loomed large in theories of the desire that animates narrative, the motor behind plots and plotting. Emblematically and rhetorically, in *The Pleasure of the Text*, Roland Barthes asks whether every narrative doesn't lead back to Oedipus. With this question, he explicitly situates the storyteller in a tradition regarded as a kind of paternity, a lineage of fathers and sons. But he also regards the 'staging of the (absent, hidden, hypostatized) father' in the Oedipal plot as designed to whet our appetite for narrative to move forward, 'to know, to learn the origin and the end'. Is storytelling not 'always a way of searching for one's origin, speaking one's conflicts with the Law, entering into the dialectic of tenderness and hatred?' (Barthes, 1975: 47). Thus phrased, Barthes' question exposes the Oedipal paradigm not only as an occasion for narrative, but as *the* narrative occasion, where investigation and its failure are closely braided together as the subject searches for the hidden truth of its own origins.

While it remains questionable that the myth of Oedipus adequately covers all narrative desire, as it is re-told by Freud,[1] it is a compelling model with wide-ranging analytic potential. It is a quest narrative; a crisis-resolution plot in which the sleuthing for obscured origins – following the trail of a 'fading record of this ancient guilt' (Sophocles in Freud, 1900a: 261) – exposes a dramatic truth and its tragic consequences in finely calibrated narrative stops and starts.

It is the validating narrative of psychoanalysis, not only because it allegorically describes the subject's formation, but also because, as Freud recognised, in its very structure of 'cunning delays and ever mounting excitement' (Freud, 1900a: 262), it is paradigmatic of the work of psychoanalysis itself. In the skilful way Freud weaves the story that is to serve as his central trope into the context of its telling and into the unfurling of its theoretical implications, he performs the tenets of psychoanalysis as incremental revelation, a kind of strip-tease of slow exposures. The proairetic code of action (the plot or linear story told in a single temporality) and the hermeneutic code of enquiry (the text folding back on itself in the multiple temporalities demanded by exegesis, and anticipating the resolutions of the action) are, in Freud's account, distinct but interlinked, allowing him to posit, in what was then a startlingly innovative way, the imbrication of narrative and theory.

Paula Rego's work visually formulates Barthes' question, with its Freudian underpinnings. How does one tell a story pictorially, her work asks, and how does its address emerge from, and return to, the family? Rego's work has counted, as one of its abiding concerns, an articulation of subjective tension, Barthes' 'dialectic of tenderness and hatred'. The child's relation to her parents, not only as the first objects of longing, but also as those who were powerful while she was helpless, endows all relationships that Rego examines with a legacy of conflict. It is in the nuclear family – the ideal site of our first loves and inaugural fears – that she quarries the prototype for all other relationships to those to whom we are attached and who hold sway over us.

Her works put to us, then, questions of boundaries: how to be separate but not alienated; how to love without being engulfed by the other; how to exercise duty within the field of the social without being subservient; how, as a woman, to disentangle oneself from one's mother and thus avoid converting history into destiny; and equally, as a woman, how to engage with men without translating them into one's father. Is love a vain attempt to re-experience a fantasised primal satiation? Or is it a social glue binding subjects to other subjects, and, if so, can such attachment, Rego's work asks, be compatible with subjective autonomy?

Crucially, in the way it presents and problematises subjective autonomy, always framed from the point of view of the female subject, Rego's work also interrogates the potentialities of an eman-cipatory project for women. Indeed, it has been appropriated by feminist critics, who have found in it a robust subversion of the tenets of patriarchy. Germaine Greer, for instance, identifies in Rego's early and painterly 'struggle for control of her visual language', an attempt to 'present a violent and subversive personal vision in acceptable decorative terms' (Greer, 1988: 29). Sarah Kent observes that 'by usurping a "masculine" genre – history painting – and harnessing its pomposity and self-regard to rewrite history from a female point of view, Rego not only pays tribute to other women, but highlights her impudent act of trespass and the revitalization of the moribund genre which it achieves' (Kent, 1989: 160). With their emphasis on terms such as 'subversive' and 'trespass', such readings attempt to grapple with how the conflict and violence of the content of Rego's works are contained – or contested – by the formal idiom they deploy and by the genre expectations they generate. These readings are also, no doubt, spurred by the artist's vivid statements of intent: '[m]y favourite themes are power games and hierarchies. I always want to turn things on their heads, to upset the established order, to change heroines and idiots. If the story is "given" I take liberties with it to make it conform to my own experiences, and to be outrageous' (Rego in McEwen, 2006: 138). So the welcome Rego has received from feminists owes itself to an erosion of authority and obliteration of categorical divisions.

It is also based on the way she empowers her female protagonists, with their no-nonsense demeanour and their strong limbs. Rego's allegiance with the lowly and the shunned – with the underdog, in short – is always expressed in the most unvarnished and un-patronising of terms, so that lowliness itself is not moralised as a positive value, but is presented, rather, as a social fact.

All this, it is important to say, is rendered with mimetic legibility. Such accessibility, at least from the mid-1980s on, situates Rego's work in a community of understanding removed from some of the more rarefied, conceptual forms of contemporary expression, and equally removed from the kind of material explorations that, for several artists and critics, links certain art forms with feminism, for instance in the work of Louise Bourgeois or Eva Hesse. Such legibility has meant that Rego's work speaks to a particularly broad public, and if it prompts in some viewers discomfort or rage,[2] it instils in others the sense of a profound complicity with shared ethical values. To many of its feminist viewers, then, Rego's work is the bearer of a powerful message. Indeed, in probing the points of intersection of the public and private spheres, paintings such as *The Policeman's Daughter, The*

Interrogator's Garden and *The First Mass in Brazil* give body to the early feminist rallying cry that the personal is political. In Rego's work, the private sphere is not ideologically neutral, neither is it uniform and consensual. It is, rather, an arena in which psyche, history and ideology intersect. But, perhaps more pertinently, Rego's works not only expose how the ideological is channelled through the intimate, they also narrate bonds of intimacy as in themselves political. They explore, in other words, how relations of authority and struggles for autonomy and agency are hatched into desire and attachment, highlighting the narrative implications of the subject's conflict with the law, and, indeed, pinpointing the subject's very appointment *as* subject in the ideological configuration of the family through which the subject emerges. In short, the principal relational axes in Rego's work – the filial and affinal – are structured by bonds that are, typically, those of the bourgeois patriarchal family with its knotty politics of female subject formation (Figure 5). It is just these relations that are so evocatively described by the Freudian 'family romance.'

In 'Family Romances' published in 1909, Freud examines that which he was soon to call the Oedipus complex. As the teleological principle of subject formation, the structuring premise of gender identification, the field within which the distinction between neurosis and an ideal of normality is drawn, and the place of origin of desire, Freud's Oedipus is not only the 'nuclear complex'[3] of the neuroses, but also the immovable foundation stone of the edifice of psychoanalysis. Its outcome and resolution – ideally, the demolition of the subject's incestuous love for the parent of the opposite sex – organises the child's relationship to its parents and shapes the subject's relations with members of its own and the other sex for the rest of its life. More specifically, the subject's Oedipalisation corresponds to its interiorisation (in Freud's schema as it evolved, effected asymmetrically by male and female subjects) of the father's authority, and the concomitant dwindling of its own status from omnipotence to subjection, theorised as the individual's assimilation of cultural prohibition in the form of the superego. The experience of such interiorisation hinges upon the legibility of maternal and paternal functions necessarily producing not only a triangular relationship, but also the core concept of triangulation as a sine qua non of relationality.

This process occurs as a painfully undergone and always incomplete liberation of the child from the authority of its parents, ideally

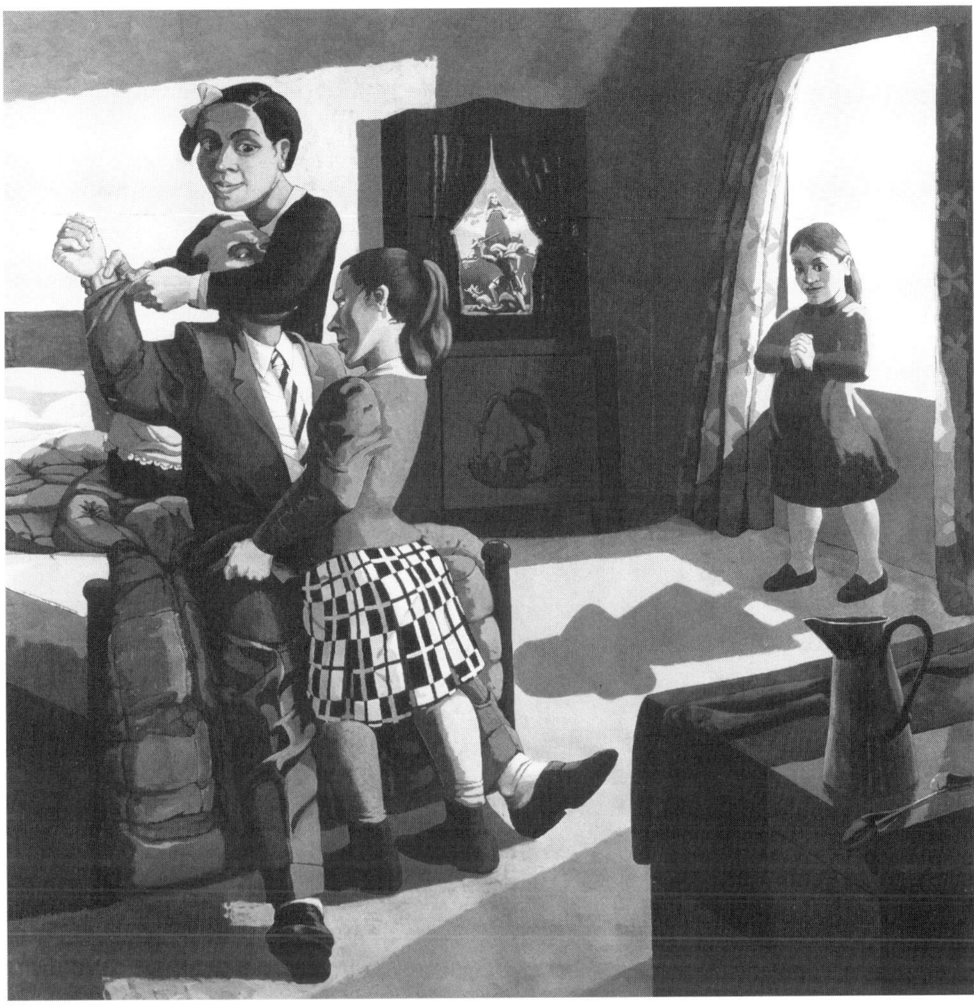

Paula Rego, *The Family*, 1988   Figure 5

producing predictable gender difference and corresponding (heterosexual) desires, whose objects are congruent with the require-
ments of patriarchal transmission. The 'discovery' of Oedipus was
thus the unveiling of the unconscious nature of desire within patriarchy. Here, Freud embeds individual experience in the *socius*, for
the 'opposition between successive generations' of which he speaks
in 'Family Romances' – none other than the Oedipal drama itself –
is a condition for the very 'progress of society' (Freud, 1909: 237).

For Freud, such generational conflict is inextricable from the process of individuation, and is predicated upon disillusionment. The parents, who for the child were once 'the only authority and the source of all belief', gradually fall from grace and are diminished through the labours of comparison as the child 'gets to know other [children's] parents' (Freud, 1909: 237), but, in effect, the debasement of the parents, Freud tells us, is also the result of sexual antagonism and of sibling rivalry for the parents' affection.[4] Simultaneously – and here, as elsewhere, Freud's analysis is centred around the male child – the process of placement and the subsequent substitution of the parents as objects of longing and as sources of authority are accomplished through envy of others of a higher social standing, for instance 'the Lord of the Manor or some landed proprietor if he lives in the country or with some member of the aristocracy if he lives in town' (Freud, 1909: 239).

Originating in fantasy and imagination – such words appear several times in this short text and highlight the importance of the life of the mind in the constitution of the concept of 'privilege' – the family romance is above all a narrative structure. Put another way, it is a narrative representation of how subjective reality is linked to a broader social reality. It exposes the multiple ways in which fantasies of sexual fulfilment, the desire for social status, and the transmission of property converge. In Freud's account, the intersection of social and sexual aspirations crucially marks the point where the ego makes contact with both its individual history and collective experience. The subject's disentanglement from its initial fusional bonds, its passage from family to outside world, is effected through imaginative acts and narrative procedures. Yet Freud's final gambit is to flip the terms of his argument: the debasement of the parents and the consequent fantasy of other origins (the fantasy of having been adopted has the added bonus of sanctioning incestuous fantasies in relation to siblings) paradoxically becomes a nostalgic means of consolidating parental – or, more precisely, paternal – power. For, Freud tells us, the hostile fantasies of these 'imaginative romances' and the desire to replace the parents with 'grander people' are merely disguised recollections of the parents themselves, so that in fact 'the child is not getting rid of his father but exalting him'. Indeed, Freud concludes,

> the whole effort at replacing the real father by a superior one is only an expression of the child's longing for the happy, vanished days when his father seemed to him the noblest and strongest of men

and his mother the dearest and loveliest of women. He is turning away from the father whom he knows to-day to the father in whom he believed in the earlier years of his childhood; and his phantasy is no more than the expression of a regret that those happy days have gone. (Freud, 1909: 240–1)

In this tale of longing for an enchantment now lost, the distinction Freud draws between the fantasy of the father, with his social virtues (noble and strong), and that of the mother with her physical and affective ones (dear and lovely), and his conflation, in the very next sentence, of the terms 'parents' and 'father', is telling and foreshadows the role of the paternal function in Oedipalisation. Now what began as an attempted disentanglement from the family – the 'liberation of an individual, as he grows up, from the authority of his parents' (Freud, 1909: 237) – turns out to be none other than the romance that leads the subject straight back into it. As the genre of historical intrigue, then, 'romance' is the ideologically charged medium through which the family reproduces itself. 'Romance' in this sense is both the love story within the family circle, and the narrative genre that describes it. Like all nostalgics, Freud's idealised subject finds its way back home.

Put in other words, the idealised family romance is a paradigm of the narrative activity through which the subject tells itself. And inasmuch as, for the boy child whose point of view orients 'Family Romances', paternity is 'always uncertain', while maternity is 'most certain' (Freud, 1909: 239), the pursuit of origins, which is also the subject's search for narrative coherence, is a quest for the paternal. The subject later exalts and appropriates this paternal function. 'From this perspective', Dana Heller comments,

> [w]hat Freud invites us to consider are the implicit representational strategies by which the family, as private experience, comes into alignment with romance, or historical fantasy. The family romance is thus defined as the interpolation of the individual *in* patriarchal history and patriarchy *in* individual history. (Heller, 1995: 23)

In short, as a discursive structure in which cultural expectation, subjective experience and narrative processes are intertwined, the family romance is the story that connects the individual subject to a broader, collective history. It is, furthermore, a particular story of imaginings and repetitions, of attachment and release. More specifically, it is the love story that underpins the subject's formation and that shapes both its future libidinal attachments and its relations to authority.

As the means whereby subjects are conservatively propagated, the Freudian family romance constructs paternity as the privileged site of origin and social meaning. In doing so, it invariably and perhaps paradoxically undermines the maternal. For with the mother's status as *certissima*, the maternal function is not so much reassuring in its immutability, as charged with an ambivalent power, for it may come to symbolise the source of a knowledge exclusively hers, the secret of the father's identity. (It is a moot point whether the new technologies of assisted reproduction, together with the altered kinship relations that these have spawned and, not least, the shift in paternal roles offered by DNA testing, have undermined the structuring tenets of the Freudian family romance, or whether the roles defined by Freud remain in place, playing a structural and symbolic role in family dynamics.) Consequently, we have 'the mother figures as a site of potential deception, a betrayal waiting to happen' (Heller, 1995: 32). Where the paternal function stands for narrative coherence, the mother, who can withhold the truth of paternity, may be construed as silent or fraudulent, a hermetic space harbouring the secret of origin and speaking an incomprehensible language. As the source of life, she is also, at worst, an avatar of death.

Similarly, the relation of the offspring to the parents is asymmetrical, depending on the gender of the individual. While the son undertakes an imaginative reinvention of the father, finally to reinvest his authority before stepping into his shoes, the daughter – who in Freud's account has to undergo a more elaborate psychic transformation in order to convert attachment to the mother into desire for the opposite sex – is characterised by an 'imagination' that is 'weak' (Freud, 1909: 238), though surely it would require a titanic imagination to do just that. Indeed, for Freud's female subject, it is a different story altogether. Her positioning within the family is directly related to her negotiation with, and acceptance of, 'castration' as foundational: a condition defined as lack seals her familial fate. It is this lack that, in the Freudian schema, motivates the female subject to wish to fill the void with her father's child.

As object of intense criticism from early on in the psychoanalytic movement, the more literal and anecdotal aspects of castration and its corollary in women's ostensible penis envy have received the revision they deserve. We should certainly reject the more anecdotal or literal aspects of Freud's theory and the naturalisation of its patriarchal premises. But the idea of 'castration' as an a priori condition governing the prohibition that underlies the human being's insertion in culture is already present in Freud, and receives its imprimatur from Lacan. For all its obscurantist jargon, Lacan's re-reading of Freud in the light of Saussurian linguistics contributes a structural order to Freud's notion of castration, a reading that de-literalises Freud. For Lacan, 'castration' describes the subject's necessary severance from a fusional and inarticulate bond with the maternal; a disconnection that positions a speaking, signifying subject in culture at large. Lacan thus attributes to castration a singular symbolic role in introducing all human subjects to culture, to the circuits of language and desire, and, concomitantly, the Phallus loses its mooring in the anatomical (the penis belongs to an individual, the Phallus to the system itself), playing a symbolic role in the signification of desire: it stands for what we all want but cannot have. (While apparently removing biological determinism from his theory, Lacan continues to act as an irritant to some feminists. If the Phallus is both incontrovertible and arbitrary, the fact that Lacan calls the central signifier 'Phallus' simply transfers the patriarchal underpinnings of Freud to a structural dimension.)

But even if we consider 'castration' in this broader sense, there is no escaping the fact that the Freudian family romance, with its absent mother and its mute and unimaginative daughter, is synonymous with women's disempowerment in that field of cultural value and meaning that constitutes the Symbolic Order. It is no surprise, then, that some feminists have repudiated both Freud and Lacan. Others have turned their backs on psychoanalysis in general. This was especially the case with British feminism in 1980s, which tended to overlook or dismiss questions of subjectivity.[5] The work of Juliet Mitchell was a notable early exception. Her essay 'Women: The Longest Revolution' (1966), expanded to constitute *Women's Estate* (1971), initiated a revisionism in social feminism by introducing psychoanalytically based theories of sexuality and gender to a Marxist-based analysis of women's place in relations of production. Her celebrated *Psychoanalysis and Feminism* (Mitchell, 1974) consolidated Mitchell as a major theorist of the possible marriage of psychoanalysis and feminism. She was followed in this path by Jacqueline Rose,[6] together guiding the way to a politicisation of psychoanalytic discourse in theoretical writings of the later 1980s and 1990s, by Judith Butler and Elizabeth Grosz among others.

The traditional indifference of psychoanalysis to issues of class, race and cultural difference, and its proposition of immanent subjects, runs counter to those feminisms that posit multiple, embodied subjectivities and sponsor social change. For to the question emphatically asked by Jacqueline Rose, 'where does the misery come from?'[7] – a question implicit in the issues I address in this book – the traditional psychoanalytic response would always be, in the first instance, that it comes from within (Rose, 1989). While psychoanalysis is not a monolithic discourse, the 'difference' it frequently proposes tends to ignore the political and historical contexts in which subjects emerge. It is precisely in these contexts that such socially based feminist theories of difference situate themselves.

From the perspective of a materialist feminism, then, the starting point of a feminist project would be a politicised wish to explore the specificity of female bodily experience, assumed to have been shaped by class conditions and framed by ideology. At first sight, this appears to be diametrically opposed to a psychoanalytically inflected investigation into the gendered constitution of subjectivity. 'Although psychoanalytic theory has done a great deal to improve our understanding of sexual difference', materialist feminist Rosi Braidotti observes, 'it has done little or nothing to change the concrete social conditions of sex-relations and of gender-stratification. The latter is precisely the target of feminist practice' (Braidotti, 1989: 97–98).

This approach is not confined to feminism alone. In his infamous attack on Freud's abandonment of the seduction theory, Jeffrey Masson charged Freud with turning into a purely psychic misery his female patients' claim that they had been sexually abused.

> By shifting the emphasis from an actual world of sadness, misery, and cruelty to an internal stage on which actors performed invented dramas for an invisible audience of their own creation, Freud began a trend away from the real world that, it seems to me, is at the root of the present-day sterility of psychoanalysis and psychiatry throughout the world. (Masson, 1984: 144)

Commenting on this passage and on the 'grotesque image of masculinity' promoted both by Jeffery Masson and by Wilhelm Reich, to whom she compares him, Jacqueline Rose observes that if the dichotomy between world and psyche appears now as a feminist issue, this is because 'the aggression of the outside world has been stepped up and sexually differentiated, and is now conceived of in terms of seduction, mutilation, and rape' (Rose, 1989: 91). In other words, class alone does not cover the variables of 'misery' that the 'world' has in store: one need not look as far afield as contemporary Afghanistan to see that misery includes all forms of gender-based violence, a euphemism for violence against women. Given the gravity and horror of 'misery' in the social sphere, the scope of a critique like Braidotti's seems narrow. Furthermore, it does not address the more pertinent questions that might, in this context, be asked of psychoanalysis: how does it negotiate the relationship between the public and the private, the social and the psychic? Can its production of knowledge be in any way re-oriented, or is it ineluctably tied to the logic of patriarchy? These questions have steered my exploration of Rego's work.

For Jacqueline Rose, who, like Juliet Mitchell, has argued for the mutual compatibility of psychoanalysis and feminism, one of the strengths of psychoanalysis lies in its account of patriarchal culture as operating through history and across cultures, and it is precisely for this reason that it meets 'a feminist demand for a theory which can explain women's subordination across specific cultures and different historical moments' (Rose, 1986: 90). While acknowledging its existence in the social sphere, Rose asks – as does Judith Butler after her (Butler, 1997) – how that subordination is psychically constituted. Not surprisingly, she articulates her concerns around the question of violence. In countering the allegation of political quiescence against psychoanalysis, she turns the political question on its head, pressing for an acknowledgement of gendered violence as it plays itself out psychically. She therefore asks if the feminist clash with psychoanalytic theory is not, finally, that 'by ignoring the pressing reality of sexual violence, [it] becomes complicit with that violence and hands women over to it?' (Rose, 1989: 92).

Both Jacqueline Rose and Juliet Mitchell represent a psychoanalytic turn in feminism as a bid to override biological determinism. Mitchell's still remains one of the most lucid accounts of the ways in which Oedipalisation is not about a particular instance in an individual narrative, as much as about the individual finding of a place within the culture of patriarchy and its underlying ur-taboo (incest) and kinship organisation (exogamy). Splicing together Freud and Lévi-Strauss, she observes:

> The myth that Freud rewrote as the Oedipus complex and its dissolution epitomizes man's entry into culture itself. It reflects the original exogamous incest taboo, the role of the father, the

> exchange of women and the consequent difference between the sexes. It is not about the nuclear family, but about the institution of culture with the kinship structure and the exchange relationship of exogamy. It is thus about what Freud regarded as the order of all human culture. It is specific to nothing but patriarchy which is itself, according to Freud, specific to all human civilization. (Mitchell, 1974: 377)[8]

While acknowledging that, in Western societies, it is expressed within the specific context of the nuclear family, Mitchell embraces, where many other materialist feminists do not, the universality of Freud's Oedipus, while insisting that the particular forms used to re-describe it are culturally specific. Moreover, in her acceptance of the Lacanian definition of 'castration' as marking the insertion of the individual within culture, she recognises in the Oedipus complex the subject's structural position in relation to desire.

Like Mitchell, Shoshana Felman is concerned with the 'grave misreading' that stems from the misguided identification of Freud as 'the enemy of women'. For Felman, this misconstrues psychoanalysis itself and its 'potentialities for a feminist reflection' (Felman, 1993: 68–69). Felman parses the Lacanian reading of Freud as the discovery in Oedipus not of a universal answer to a question but, rather, of the very structure of a question. For her, as for Juliet Mitchell, considering Oedipus as structural liberates the process of Oedipalisation from a more literal formulation of the gendering of the family triangle. Indeed, it reveals the triangular structure not as simply the biographic geometry of love and rivalry, but as the foundation of the socio-symbolic order of substitutions and alliances in which the subject is positioned. Oedipalisation, then, introduces the process of triangulation as the organising principle of subject formation, a procedure through which the subject is, so to speak, put in its place. For the 'irreducible complexity' (Felman, 1993: 103)[9] and productivity of Freud's paradigmatic schema lie in the way in which its triangular structure transcends particular familial hostilities and passions and, in its implicit taboo on consanguinity, positions the subject also in relation to members of a broader social group, thereby configuring the family as the agency through which an entire socio-symbolic network is elaborated.

Thinking 'castration' as the rupture that heralds the subject's mastery of symbolic representation – and, concomitantly, regarding Oedipus as the *structure* of desire – allows us to frame psychoanalytically women's relation to, and constitution by, discourse. Yet this too has not proved satisfactory to some psychoanalytically informed feminists, who propose, instead, a de-Oedipalised model of the family as the only possible way of spurning patriarchy. 'I am beginning to realize', says Jane Gallop, 'that feminists need to stop reading everything through the family romance' (Gallop, 1992: 239).

Likewise, in urging upon the reader the possibility of a model for what she terms a 'post-family' romance, Dana Heller rightly recognises the family romance to be an already mediated structure bridging the private and the public realms. As we have seen, where the family romance conflates 'sexual identification, familial structure and narrative form' (Heller, 1995: xii), it is underpinned by the notion of the family as the site of intersection of personal identity and the compulsions and restrictions binding the individual to the group. But the family, Heller argues, could be narrated otherwise, and indeed must be thought differently in the case of people 'displaced from their homeland, denied their claims to origin ... and refused participation in the dominant discursive economy to which they are subordinated' (Heller, 1995: 129). For Heller, in other words, the Freudian family romance is culturally specific.

Other feminist arguments against the Oedipal model of the family romance attack its conflation of femininity and subordination, locking women into a role of frequently hopeless longing. They attribute it to Freud's own difficulties in theorising the role of the pre-Oedipal mother. These arguments follow two predominant trends. On the one hand, those renegades of Lacanian theory espousing an *écriture féminine* seek (in vain, I would argue) to forge modes of representation that challenge the Symbolic Order, defining it as a regime in which women may only signify themselves in a language they do not command. First theorised by Hélène Cixous, it is, arguably, a practice of writing on the side of the Imaginary rather than the Symbolic (Cixous and Clément, 1986; Irigaray, 1985, 1993). Invoking carnival, madness or hysteria, they propose fluid forms of signification that, they suggest, are not subject to the logic of the Phallus, but that invoke, rather, the maternal body and the umbilical cut as the founding moment of division and separation. 'Does the father replace the womb with the matrix of his language?' asks Irigaray. 'The family name', she suggests, 'and even the first or given name, always stand at once remove from that most elemental identity tag: the scar where the umbilical cord was cut' (Irigaray, 1993: 14).

On the other hand, there are those feminists whose theoretical foundations lie in the object-relations theories that haul the mother out of the wings (albeit never as a desiring subject detached from her maternal role) and demote the standard Oedipus complex, with its roots in castration anxiety, from its central, organising function. Melanie Klein writes that she cannot agree with Freud's description of castration anxiety as '*the single factor* which determines the repression of the Oedipus complex' (Klein, 1945: 417), locating the latter, instead, in successively earlier points in the child's life. 'If the Oedipal moment begins at this early stage', observe Janice Doane and Devon Hodges in their reading of Klein, 'it must necessarily entail anxieties primarily concerning the mother – and the father only secondarily' (Doane and Hodges, 1992: 11). Such shifts may reflect the historical context of their enunciation: Denise Riley notes that the theoretical disappearance of the father from the picture in the Kleinian-inspired theories of Winnicott, for instance in his BBC broadcast 'What About Father?' of January 1945, as indeed in 'most other psychoanalytic speech' at the time, 'coincided with the social stress – which was indifferent to the actual numbers of absent men – on the vanishing of the father to the [Second World] war' (Riley, 1988: 88). Revisionist arguments within the discipline of psychoanalysis had already occurred amidst Freud's closest disciples, such as Ruth Mack Brunswick's discovery of a neurosis of which the origins were *pre*-Oedipal (1928), or Jeanne Lampl-de Groot's accounts of clinical examples of a negative Oedipus complex in girls,[10] which unsettled Freud's earlier, more symmetrical model of gendering and which substantially modified prevailing views of feminine Oedipal object-relations, calling attention to the pre-Oedipal mother–daughter bond.

Mothers do not feature in Freud's case histories. While he recognised the foundational status of the mother's body as 'the place where each one of us lived once upon a time and in the beginning' and hence as the referent for all that homesickness that goes by the name of love (Freud, 1919b: 245), he was not concerned with maternal subjectivity. His belated interest in the mother was always from the point of view of the child. Freud famously compares the child's pre-Oedipal bond with the mother to the discovery, beneath the surface of classical Greek civilisation, of the prehistoric remains of the Minoan–Mycenaean one, suggesting an identification of the mother with the archaic. 'Everything in the sphere of this first attachment to the mother seemed to me so difficult to grasp', Freud remarks, '– so grey with age and shadowy and almost impossible to revivify – that it was as if it had succumbed to an especially inexorable repression' (Freud, 1931: 226). It is rather extraordinary that that most primal of attachments should have been so repressed and so late disinterred by Freud. But if, from the point of view of Greek culture, the Minoan–Mycenaean one is merely a precursor, for women considering this analogy, Greek culture represented their own erasure, a subjective relegation to greyness and shadowiness. From this perspective – from the perspective of 'Greek' order and meaning – 'it will be at [women's] peril that their prehistory, though it will always be in evidence, will continue to dominate in their lives' (Mitchell, 1974: 110), because women, like men, will have always to contend with, and operate within the bounds of the Symbolic.

Yet from another perspective, the relics of Mycenaean prehistory expose not something shadowy, but rather something that is a culture in its own right. It is the focus on the pre-Oedipal maternal that serves as the point of departure for Julia Kristeva, who, despite her own problematic relation with feminism, provided for some critics in the mid-1980s 'the most formidable literary and psychoanalytic elaboration of maternity . . . available to feminists' (Jacobus, 1986: 145). Following Melanie Klein, and in opposition to Freud and Lacan, Kristeva stresses the import of the maternal function not only on the foundation of subjectivity. Kristeva proposes a maternal discourse that seems – at least at first sight – to circumvent the logic of Oedipalisation. Where in Freud's scheme the subject emerges through its response to a paternal injunction that, with Oedipalisation, is retroactively significant, for Kristeva, the subject's emergence has a previous site in the first splitting within the maternal body. For her, it is the sublimation of the pain suffered through the loss of the mother as primary object, rather than the mastery of the symbolic, that informs poetic language or aesthetic discourse.[11] This strikes me as a more robust model than Irigaray's over-excited privileging of the womb and the navel.

Kristeva characterises by her use of Plato's concept of the *chora*, and by her idiosyncratic use of the term 'semiotic', this earliest manifestation of difference in the pre-Oedipal not-yet-subject. The *chora* is a containing, sensory cavern; a pre-verbal, uterine space of sensation impelled by the drives. Kristeva's 'semiotic', as the raw material of signification, is likewise correlated with the pre-Oedipal drives. She distinguishes this from the space of the Symbolic into which the subject is expelled from maternal plenitude. Yet if, for Kristeva, a pre-linguistic capacity for signification is mapped onto the body in its early contiguity with the mother, because there can be no absolute fusion, the mother's care for the child installs early forms of division and separation that precede the instauration of the Phallus as the mark of the subject's social contract. Leaning on Melanie Klein's research into the pre-verbal expression of the drives in childhood, Kristeva sees in the pre-Oedipal and the non-verbal a signifying disposition of sorts, one that is closer to the primary processes, connecting meaning to the body. Concomitantly, she posits the mother as a representation of the frontier between the corporeal and the mental. As a pre-verbal, mother-bound energy, Kristeva's 'semiotic' is always not only linked to the bodily, but also is potentially transgressive, posing a threat to the homogeneity offered by language and making its presence felt through ruptures in discourse.

From a feminist point of view, the privileging of the maternal semiotic over the paternal symbolic affects the political order of the sign. For if an obsession with mastery of the Symbolic may ultimately be linked, as Benjamin Buchloh links it, to authoritarianism (Buchloh, 1984), then, following Kristeva's formulations, we might expect a feminist avant-garde practice to emerge at the level of the semiotic and the abject. And indeed the practice of many women artists from the late twentieth century onwards has proffered the abject body, the body as frontier or boundary – of which, in Kristeva's view, the maternal body is the epitome – as a potential site of transgression in feminist intervention. It is from this position that Paula Rego's works of the 1960s, with their dilacerations and visceral forms and their emphatic, heterogeneous materiality, might claim a strong position within a feminist genealogy (see Figures 4 and 6, and Plates 5 and 6).

Yet such a convergence between the aesthetic and the political seems, in the last analysis, specious. If Kristeva chooses the semiotic as the source of an emancipatory effect capable of countering authoritative abstractions, she nevertheless concedes that, in the end, there is no choice to be made between the semiotic and the symbolic. Rather, what is called for is an account of their interplay. It is in her later writings that Kristeva more overtly acknowledges the importance of identification with the phallic/paternal as the third term that interrupts the subject's immersion in the Imaginary. Identification with the paternal, Kristeva argues 'which may be called phallic or symbolic, insures the subject's entrance into the universe of signs' (Kristeva 1989: 24).[12] It is the mother's desire

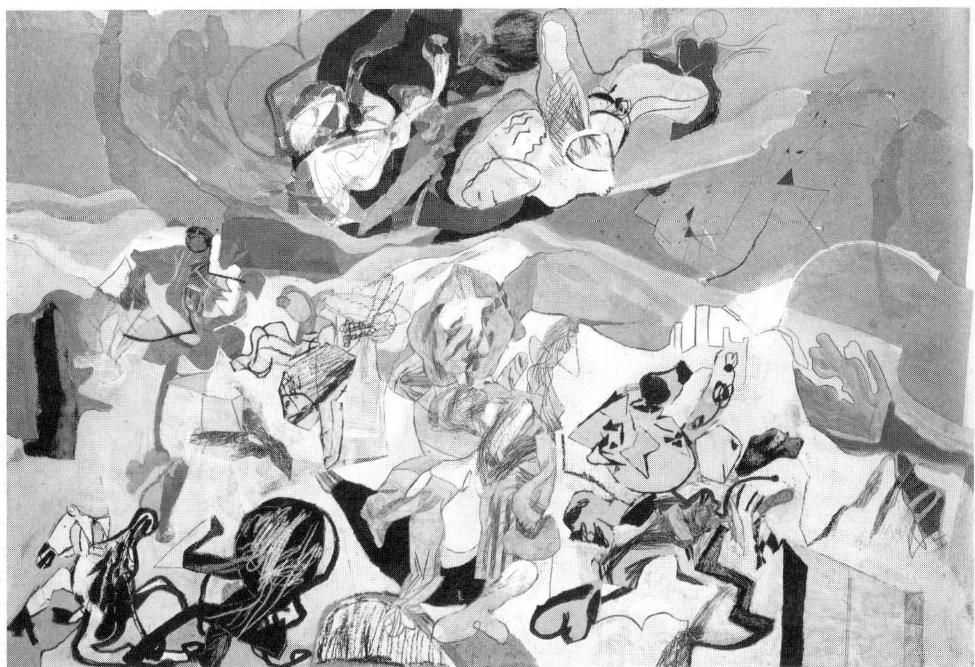

Paula Rego, *Nursery Violence*, 1963–64   Figure 6

for another (and the child's identification with this desire) that pries open a space between child and mother. The father as an object of maternal desire, is, in other words, the place from where the discourse of the Other issues as a pre-condition of symbolic representation.

However abstractly these arguments are put, in the last analysis Kristeva's position holds in place a family romance where the 'maternal' and the 'paternal', as positions, play traditional roles. If the paternal at times stands for a structural position – the third term – at other times Kristeva confirms an absolute dichotomy between father and mother, implicitly confirming anatomical destiny, in a scheme that, as with Freud and Lacan, regards the phallic as the standard. Moreover, in implicitly confirming anatomical destiny by her lyrical overvaluation of pregnancy, Kristeva undermines the purely symbolic value of the Phallus. For her, the mother–daughter bond is fraught, their 'connivance' marred by the fact that Oedipalisation will always re-insert the girl in the patriarchal family, while vexing her relations to both sexes. This means that 'a girl will never be able to re-establish this contact with her mother . . . except by becoming a mother herself . . . or through a homosexuality which is in itself extremely difficult' (Kristeva, 1986: 204).

Kristeva's view is, I would argue, compatible with the Freudian/ Lacanian position. Contrariwise, a focus on mother–daughter relationships as opposing the patriarchal Oedipal plot has been a governing strategy for numerous psychoanalytic feminists. In her influential object-relations account of the psychological and social reproduction of mothering, Nancy Chodorow foregrounds maternal identity and the mother–daughter bond in relation to the ideological norms framing the family as institution. Underlining the difficulty many mothers experience in regarding their daughters as separate, Chodorow proposes that it is a sense of union and continuity with her mother that informs the girl's Oedipal crisis. If, for Freud, boy children may continue to look to women for love but the girl must learn to look elsewhere, for Chodorow, the girl develops an Oedipal attachment to her mother as well as to her father, an attachment that is built upon, rather than replacing, 'her intense and exclusive preoedipal attachment to her mother and its internalized counterpart'. In her view, then, the female subject never abandons the mother 'as an internal or external love object, even if she does become heterosexual' (Chodorow, 1999: 127).

Such theoretical re-orientation of the family romance within the field of psychoanalysis has had repercussions outside of it, particularly in literary studies. Mary Jacobus has brilliantly endeavoured to redress Freud's failure with regard to the representation of the maternal, exploring signifying practices that might short-circuit the Oedipal family model. She introduces us to scenes of reproduction that do not conflate feminine desire with conception. A feminist analysis of the role of maternity, she suggests, might examine woman-to-woman relations that 'threaten the father's installation as the regulating term of sexual arrangements' (Jacobus, 1986: 143). Like Kristeva, Jacobus stresses the importance of the pre-Oedipal and, like Chodorow, she underlines the narrative potentialities of mother–daughter bonds in a bid to reverse the hierarchy defining both mother and daughter roles as secondary in the Freudian picture, although, strictly speaking, maintaining the Oedipus complex as a referent confirms its centrality.

Similarly, Marianne Hirsch inverts the Oedipus myth underpinning the family romance, foregrounding instead the 'other woman', the mother, in relation to the 'other child', the daughter (Hirsch, 1989: 2). While maintaining the Freudian family romance as a point of reference – and leaning on Kristeva, Irigaray, Cixous and Chodorow – Hirsch reframes its terms and treats both motherhood and daughterhood as *story*, as 'narrative representation of social and subjective reality' (Hirsch, 1989: 10). Spurning Freud's choice of Oedipus as paradigmatic of subject formation (or, as she puts it, of 'human maturation in the context of familial structures'), Hirsch, like Irigaray, explores the mythic potential of other figures, such as Electra, Clytemnestra and, especially, Antigone:[13] figures that embody different forms of individuation and socialisation for female subjects, performed through alternative kinship and narrative patterns. (Such formulations tend to ignore the fact that Freud used the Oedipus myth because it most approximated the familial model he was trying to describe, not because he was arbitrarily trying to find a classical myth onto which to append his theory.)

If such writing literalises a feminist nostalgia – a longing for the primacy of woman-to-woman bonds – it also reveals that only in their dialectic can the feminism of equality (the social model) and that of difference (the psychoanalytic model) be mutually resonant. Julia Kristeva's essay 'Women's Time', published in 1979, was important in its analysis of three 'generations' in feminism and their formulations of equality and difference. The first two generations might be represented by socialism and Freudianism respectively. The first generation, campaigning for women's rights in the social and political sphere, aimed to dislocate women from a mythical, cyclical time, and to give them a place in the linear time of history. The second generation, especially after May 1968, was essentially concerned with symbolic realisation. But the third is an imagined generation, one that is not so much a temporality as a signifying *space* enabling the co-existence of all three generations in the same historical time. Kristeva thus eschews the Lacanian Woman 'with a capital "W", possessor of some mythical unity' (Kristeva, 1986: 207) in favour of the specificity of women's experience, situating feminism not as reconciliation but, rather, as marking a crisis in representation.

However, while other theorists and practitioners have urged for the elaboration of signifying systems outside the rule of the Phallus, with its concomitant fetishisation of the art object, Kristeva remains convincingly bound to the workings of the Symbolic Order. Her formulation of the generationally reproduced mother/daughter bond, while taking into account the semiotic space defined by the maternal, finally acknowledges both Oedipalisation, and the symbolic status of castration. For Kristeva, the 'connivance of the young girl with her mother' is equated with

> her greater difficulty than the boy in detaching herself from the mother in order to accede to the order of signs as invested by the absence and separation constitutive of the paternal function. A girl will be unable to re-establish this contact with her mother – a contact which the boy may possibly rediscover through his relationship with the opposite sex – except by becoming a mother herself … her eternal debt to the woman-mother [makes] a woman more vulnerable within the symbolic order, more fragile when she suffers within it, more virulent when she protects herself from it. (Kristeva, 1986: 204–205)

If Paula Rego's work highlights the 'virulence' of female subjects as they attempt to protect themselves against the injunctions and strictures of the Symbolic Order, they do so, I shall attempt to show in the following chapters, by operating within that same order.

A feminist definition of maternal culture may well want to lean on Kristeva's concept of the semiotic as a locus of effective feminine subversion of paternal law. But what Kristeva's writing itself reveals is the inextricability of the bond between the semiotic and the symbolic. For, crucially, like Lacan's Imaginary, the semiotic exists not only prior to the symbolic, but alongside and inseparably from it. Indeed, following Kristeva, I suggest that it is impossible to imagine a pure semiotic discourse, one that exists entirely outside of the Symbolic Order, without relying on that very order to articulate it. Resistance, in other words, must be phrased in a voice that can be heard.[14] How that voice might be articulated is the question addressed by Paula Rego's turn towards a more homogeneous narrative space and a more naturalistic form of mimetic figuration in the second half of the 1980s.

Notes

1 The term 'Oedipus complex' first appeared in Freud's writings in 1910 (Freud, 1910b: 171), but he had already touched on the subject briefly in a letter to Fliess in 1897 (Freud, 1892–99: 265).

2 While most see Rego as a 'woman's painter', Maria Manuel Lisboa sees in her work a strategy to lure male spectators, springing a trap on them in order to then punish them with the real content of her work (Lisboa, 2003: 12).

3 Freud speaks of Oedipus as the 'nuclear complex' in a footnote added in 1920 to *Three Essays on Sexuality* of 1905 (Freud, 1905b: 226n).

4 In her revisionist reading of Freud, Juliet Mitchell argues that sibling relationships have been repressed in his nuclear model. 'When a sibling is in the offing, the danger is that the hero – "His Majesty the Baby" – will be annihilated, for this is someone who stands in the same position to parents (and their substitutes) as himself' (Mitchell, 2000: xi). See also Mitchell, 2003. Rego has little interest in exploring sibling relationships. A rare exception is *The Cadet and his Sister* (1988), a painting which, in dealing with the opposition between sexual ignorance and knowingness, has strong incestuous overtones.

5 See, for example, Barrett and McIntosh, 1982.

6 Together, Juliet Mitchell and Jacqueline Rose edited *Feminine Sexuality: Jacques Lacan and the École Freudienne* (Mitchell and Rose, 1982), each writing an important introduction. Rose's essay 'Femininity and its Discontents', first published in the *Feminist Review* in 1983, acknowledged that 'outside of the work of Juliet Mitchell for feminism', there had been a 'fairly consistent repudiation of Freud within the British Left' (Rose, 1986: 89n). Rose's essay 'Where Does the Misery Come From?' reveals her nuanced views on the possibility of mutual enrichment of politically and psychoanalytically informed feminisms (Rose, 1989).

7 The title of Rose's important essay, as she announces at the outset, comes from the question Wilhelm Reich 'placed at the heart of his dispute with Freud in a conversation with Kurt Eissler in 1952'. Reich observes that while Freud 'developed his death instinct theory which said "[t]he misery comes from inside"', Reich 'went out, out where the people were' (Reich, 1967: 42–43, quoted by Rose, 1989: 89).

8 For a reading of Lévi-Strauss's positioning of the incest taboo in the context of semiotics and of Freudian and Lacanian psychoanalysis, see Silverman, 1983: 178–180.

9 Like Shoshana Felman, Christopher Bollas addresses the question of what is complex about the Oedipus complex in his essay 'Why Oedipus?' (Bollas, 1992: 231ff.)

10 A negative Oedipus complex would be one in which the girl's libidinal object was the mother, and her sexual rival the father, rather than vice versa. See Freud's acknowledgement of the importance for his rethinking of theories of femininity, of the work of Jeanne Lampl-de Groot, Ruth Mack Brunswick and Helene Deutsch in his imaginary lecture 'Femininity' (Freud, 1933: 134–135). Sarah Kofman sees Freud's allusion to these women psychoanalysts as strategic (Kofman, 1985: 18). Similarly, Irigaray engages with Freud and subjects 'Femininity' to minute scrutiny (Irigaray, 1985: 13–129). In turn, Jane Gallop points

to the blind spot in Irigaray's reading of Freud's text, which renders it more phallocentric than it is (Gallop, 1982: 57–60).

11 See Kristeva's essay 'Stabat Mater' reprinted in Kristeva, 1987: 234–263, and her *Black Sun* (Kristeva, 1989).

12 Julia Kristeva proposes an 'imagined partner' that is neither the mortifying mother, nor the 'symbolic stallion'; someone who is 'more-than-a-mother' and who 'can obtain for me the major gift [the mother] was never able to offer: a new life' (Kristeva, 1989: 78–79). Here, as Doane and Hodges observe, Kristeva restores the father, while remaining careful 'to mitigate his power'. He is no longer the Oedipal father, but they find, nevertheless, that 'this new and improved father does not prove especially liberatory for women' (Doane and Hodges, 1992: 66).

13 Both Luce Irigaray and Judith Butler see Antigone as a figure of rebellion, throwing Oedipally based kinship relations into disarray, threatening the paternal order of the state. Antigone, then, is the mythical figure par excellence that offers herself for feminist recovery, an alternative to the Oedipal familial model. See 'The Eternal Irony of the Community', in Irigaray, 1985: 214–226, and Butler, 2000. See also Pollock, 2006a.

14 Jacqueline Rose makes this point in 'Julia Kristeva – Take Two' (Rose, 1986: 144–145). Judith Butler's quarrel with Kristeva rests on this very premise, that '[h]er theory appears to depend upon the stability and reproduction of precisely the paternal law that she sought to displace' (Butler, 1993b: 165).

Romancing the father:
The Policeman's Daughter

> The daughter submits to the father's rule, which prohibits the father's desire . . . out of the desire to seduce the father by doing his bidding and thus pleasing him. (Jane Gallop, *Feminism and Psychoanalysis: The Daughter's Seduction*)

> However necessary it may be to isolate the body for analytic purposes, the body in question is not a hypostatized object, still less a simple biological mechanism of given desires and needs acted on externally by controls and enticements, but a relation in a system of liaisons which are material, discursive, psychic, sexual, but without stop or centre. It would be better to speak of a certain 'bodiliness' than of the 'the body'. (Francis Barker, *The Tremulous Private Body*)

A description

It is hard to think of a work that more clearly exemplifies the notion that 'the body is our general medium for having a world' (Merleau-Ponty, 2002: 169) than Paula Rego's *The Policeman's Daughter* of 1987 (Plate 1). The lived body serves not merely as a passive instrument of sensations, but as the vessel through which the condition of subjectivity meets the world, and that subjectivity is shaped, as this painting makes amply clear, by the individual's placement at once in the context of its family of origin and, more broadly, in the social body at large, with all its pressures. For in *The Policeman's Daughter* the body of the protagonist described by the title is clearly the site of intersection of public and private domains, of the networks linking state and family.

As in the companion piece *The Soldier's Daughter*, painted shortly before (1987; Figure 7), the title frames a relation of kinship: not

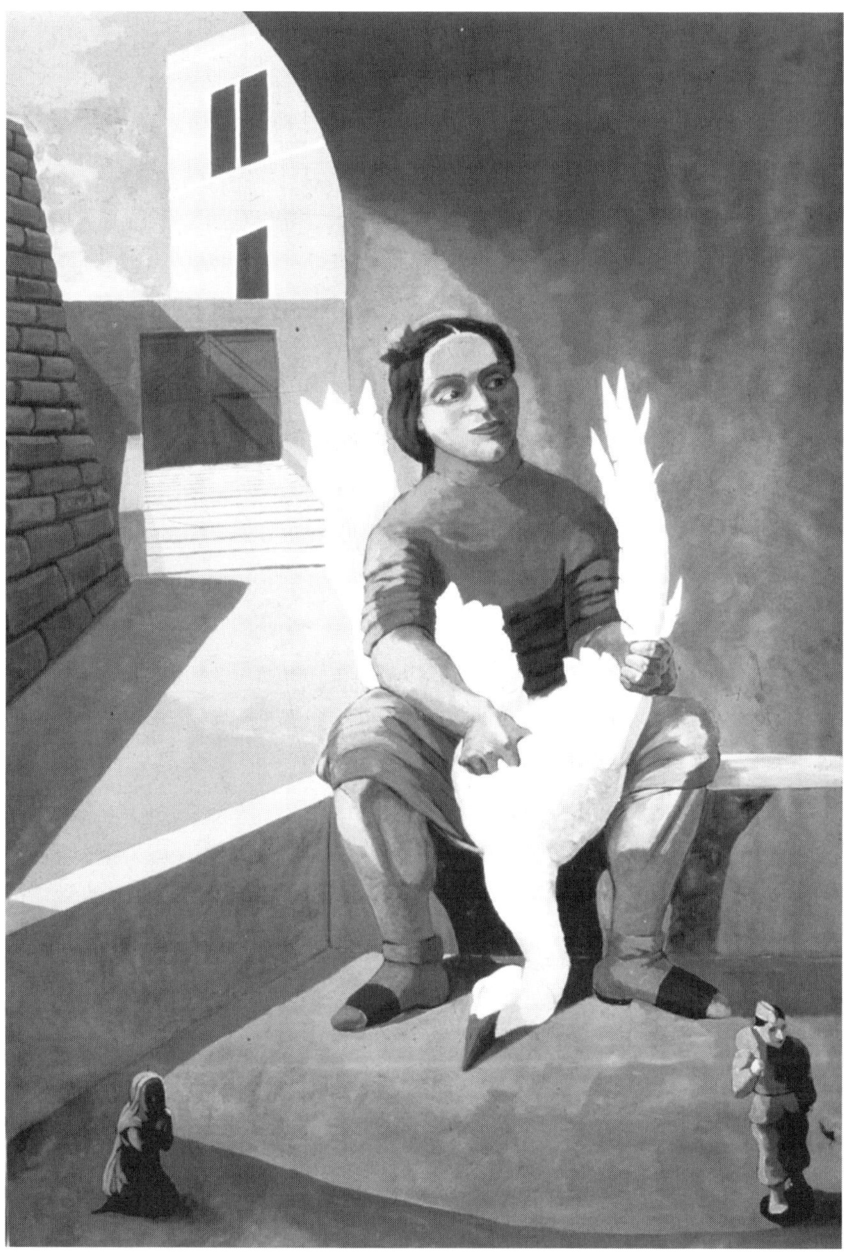

Figure 7   Paula Rego, *The Soldier's Daughter*, 1987

the contiguous relationship of a child and its mother, but the more mediated relation of child and father: a relation in effect condemned to the substitutive logic of the symbol. For by bestowing upon the child his name rather than his body, and by interceding with his authority to interrupt the closed circuit of the mother–child dyad, the father (or the father's name) polices the family boundaries and oversees the child's move from a seamless, unstructured state to subjectivity and to the social world that is its corollary. But the price for the subject's capacity to make meaning is her subjection to a law that is not her own. That, at least, is the logic of patriarchy.

It is also the logic implicit in the Freudian model of subjectivity in the family romance. So what exactly, in this context, is Rego's painting telling us about female subjectivity? Is the model of subjectivity posited by Freudian theory and played out in patriarchy affirmed or resisted? How do we read the relation here between the female subject and the power represented by her absent father on the one hand, and between the father and the state in whose name he publicly exercises authority on the other?

Of indeterminate age, the girl or young woman is contained in a room where she polishes a jackboot belonging, we infer from the title, to her father. The geometry of the room converges upon her vigorous body, packed into a sleeveless white dress. Her placement in the corner of the room underlines her estrangement from the public sphere in which her father's power is exercised. One white-shod foot is planted firmly on the ground, the other is tucked under her on the chair, remaining all but invisible under the folds of her dress and making her position at once more precarious and more purposeful. She seems simultaneously sprung for action, and comfortable where she is. The high neck of her dress lends an austere note that throws into relief the muscular power of her bare arms; its sharply cinched waist emphasises her voluptuous body and allows the skirt to fall into ample, sculptural drapes. In her aspect, an avowed sexuality and available health are channelled into an act of apparent obedience. Her flesh is rendered with emphatic brush marks carving form out of the flat, opaque acrylic paint. Her right shoulder is articulated violently: flattened out to meet the picture plane, it pins the girl's gestures down squarely within the visual field. As if gutting a fish or stuffing a turkey, her left arm is expertly rammed, elbow-deep, into the erect boot to hold it stiff; the right arm exerts its force, polishing with a tightly scrunched white rag, its fleshy volume labial against the phallic boot. Her eyes are downcast in concentration, but her firm chin and pursed lips, though intent on giving nothing away, reveal the disdain beneath her brisk compliance. The painting is replete with images of penetration: the arm in the boot, the absent right leg which can only be pressed into the secret flesh under the dress; the chair disappearing into the skirt-like drop of the tablecloth.

What we first notice here is that the painting is temporally removed from the time of its utterance, taking us back to the years of Rego's childhood in the 1930s and 1940s. In Rego's paintings from the mid-1980s on, the clothes and hairstyles are redolent with such pastness: the pinafores and frocks – with their embroidered or smocked bibs, gathered skirts and neat collars – evoke the garb of urban girls dressed for parties, or prettied-up representations of the traditional costumes of rural Portugal in postcards or films of the 1930s and 1940s.

In the pristine setting of an unadorned room, the father's boot on the clean tablecloth is striking as matter out of place. Where most works that Rego made around this time – for instance *Snare* (1987) or *The Cadet and his Sister* (1988) – include objects that are metonymic or metaphoric props advancing and expanding the narrative, here there are no ornaments, no pictures on the wall, no flowers or toys of any description. The only pieces of furniture we see are the corner of the table with its plain, draped cloth, and the imposing brass-studded chair, recollected from Rego's parents' dining-room in their holiday home in the fishing village of Ericeira; a chair that Rego identifies as Indo-Portuguese. The paneless window gives onto the Atlantic Ocean, which would be somewhere along the coast north of Lisbon, a coastline to which Rego frequently returns in her paintings. It bears hints of the construction of Portuguese identity through its maritime history and iconography, but it is also infused with autobiographic connotations. For it was along this coast that Rego's parents had two homes: the principal one in Estoril, and the holiday home in Ericeira.

The Rego family moved into the villa in Estoril in 1938 when Paula was three years old. About twenty kilometres north of Lisbon on the coast, Estoril, like neighbouring Cascais, has long been inhabited by the wealthy bourgeoisie and is home to many English expatriates. Built on the slope of a hill, the Regos' home commands a view over the rooftops of Estoril to the Atlantic. Paula Rego lived in this house from 1938 until she left Portugal for England in 1951, first attending a finishing school in Kent, and then, in 1952, the Slade School of Art in London. The house has remained in the family's possession and, since her mother's death in November 2001, belongs to the artist.

The fishing village of Ericeira lies north of Estoril and Cascais. Its coast appears in paintings such as *The Dance* and *Departure,* both of 1988. Rego's grandfather bought the land for a *quinta* in Ericeira strip by strip over a long period, and the house was built some time around 1908. It was there that the artist and her parents spent the summer holidays of her childhood, and it has remained an enchanted place in her memory. Between 1957 and 1962, after she was married to Victor Willing and their three children were born, they lived in the house in Ericeira, having converted the barn into a studio. After that, it remained a holiday home until they vacated and sold it in 1979.

Drawn in simple perspective, the room in *The Policeman's Daughter* scarcely contains the large girl. The foreshortening of the window, the angle of its ledge, the relationship of verticals to horizontals, follow no systematically geometric precept. Rather, the window is tilted in such a way as to ensure that we glimpse a view of the still surface of the ultramarine ocean outside. On the far shore, we see a tiny, bright glimmer. This nail-paring of light on the horizon is the *punctum* of the painting: it is the place where its surface tears open to reveal, as the bright, unattainable point in the distance, a longing, a glimpse of ineffable loss.

It is evening or night and the harsh light flooding the room seems to be less the work of an irrepressible moon than an intrusive search-light beaming into the enclosed space from the window. The white beam picks out the girl's thick left arm, her left cheek, her white-swathed lap, hip and left leg. This leg, like that of the chair, casts a stark, silhouetted shadow on the ground. A cat, partially blotted out by the sooty shadow, stretches up against the wall without reaching the window ledge. Family pet or witch's familiar, the cat is unable to take in the view, perhaps mimicking the girl's entrapment. Like the luminous speck on the horizon, the animal's body – its alert little ears and its precarious motionlessness – contains all the listlessness that properly belongs to the girl. Here is a picture of an apparently irre-mediable breach between inside and out, between world and psyche.

The father's trophy

In the intimacy of a domestic space, a hierarchical structure that begins with the state, whose agent the father is, inaugurates a chain of relay that reaches down to the most subaltern of family members, the daughter. In her subservience, we see not so much coercion as complicity, an accommodation to, or interiorisation of, the law. Yet this subjection is unsettled by the distaste on the young woman's face, a hint of resistance to the power metonymically represented by her father's jackboot. How, this painting asks, within the conservative logic of patriarchal transmission, within the social and familial reproduction of regulated subjects, can resistance take place?

This painting might be compared to a later work in pastel, where the father is also symbolically represented by an object, though now metaphorically rather than metonymically. In *Snow White Playing with her Father's Trophies* (1995; Plate 7), a fleshy young woman, dark-haired, dressed, as the policeman's daughter is dressed, in white and sporting a childish, shiny pink hair-bow, sits on an arm-chair holding in her lap – in effect between her parted knees – her father's hunting trophy, a huge stag's head. The animal head gazes at the spectator with opaque indifference. The girl rests one podgy hand on her knee, the other holds with proprietary pleasure the stag's antlers, which, branch-like, thrust up to touch the framing edge of the painting. Sullen and snarling, relegated to diminutive background status, the slim stepmother (we recognise her as such from another work in the same series, *Snow White and her Stepmother*) sits demurely on the floor. The confrontation of these two irreducible physiognomic types, the heavy and the slim, also appears in other works by Rego, most notably in *The Fitting* (1990), where, with the seamstress at her feet, a lumbering debutante displays her dress to a petite and pinched mother. The contrast between these two physical types highlights a relational dynamic between mothers and daughters and points to an irreconcilable rivalry at the heart of the constitution of Rego's female subjects.

While in *The Policeman's Daughter* the father–daughter link is privileged, in *Snow White Playing with her Father's Trophies*, it is the triangular formation of the family itself that is explored. For, the painting suggests, if the specular relation of a maternal placeholder and a daughter seems to offer the possibility of a female-to-female connection that circumvents paternal legislation – a circuit of identification outside of the Symbolic Order – this potentially complicit relationship is sundered by the daughter's Oedipal desire and by the jealousy in the (step)mother that that desire occasions and mobilises. This desire, if we are to believe Freud – and the painting sets us up for such a belief – is the *outcome* of the girl's enlivening to sexual difference and to her burgeoning sexuality. In Freud's version, the girl's rude awakening drives a wedge between her and her mother. In the *Snow White* story, the substitution of the mother by an interloping stepmother only serves to sharpen the crisis of authority and replacement inaugurated by the girl's emergent sexuality, which, for Freud, is figured as the knowledge of a lack.

Indeed, in Freud's elaboration of the Oedipus complex as structural to subject formation, the female body is, for both boys and girls, represented as lacking. This is notoriously central to Freudian theory and forecloses the possibility of a woman considering herself to be anything other than incomplete. To continue with Freud's Oedipus: in the boy-child, the mere possibility of suffering a disempowering mutilation is realised through his first sighting of the woman's body. Registering the female genitalia as lack makes the loss of his own penis imaginable and with this, 'the threat of castration takes its deferred effect' (Freud, 1924b: 176). In this founding scene, while the boy, unable to believe his eyes, first disavows the woman's lack, he insistently remembers it, and this repeated recollection 'forces him to believe in the reality of the threat which he has hitherto laughed at' (Freud, 1925: 252). The fear of reprisal that is materialised in the female body and grasped retrospectively, brings to an abrupt and violent halt the boy's desire for his mother. Freud notes that

> in boys, the [Oedipus] complex is not simply repressed, it is literally smashed to pieces by the shock of threatened castration . . . its objects are incorporated into the ego, where they form the nucleus of the super-ego . . . In normal, or, it is better to say, in ideal cases, the Oedipus complex exists no longer, even in the unconscious; the super-ego has become its heir. (Freud, 1925: 257)

In the idealised course of events that Freud describes, then, the boy-child's incestuous desire is exploded by a sanction made visible. Within the matrix of a normative heterosexuality, in a process that will enable him eventually to transfer his initial libidinal attachment to the mother onto another woman, the boy becomes identified with his father. With the demolition of Oedipal enchantment, paternal authority is internalised and, importantly, in the form of the super-ego, the male subject assimilates not only a personal injunction but also a cultural prohibition. In the mutual imbrication of paternal and social value, the subject acquires a designated position in the patriarchal family (for now, as the son), and also a history of being human, articulated through the incest taboo.

As we have seen, the assumption implicit in the logic of Oedipalisation – that children will identify with the parent of the same sex and desire the parent of the opposite sex – frames the family romance as the symbolic process through which these roles are both imaginatively narrated and positioned for naturalisation. As an outcome of his successful Oedipalisation, the male subject will recognise himself in the mirror of the reigning ideology. He will, in Kaja Silverman's words, 'find himself "at home" in those discourses and institutions which define the current symbolic order in the West, and will derive validation and support from them at a psychic if not at an economic social level' (Silverman, 1983: 141). In this Lacanian parsing of the process of Oedipalisation, the subject's insertion into the Symbolic Order designates its binding by the terms of social and linguistic contracts and its assimilation of triangulation as defining its own position within culture. For the importance of Lacan's Oedipus resides in his conceptualisation of triangulation not simply as a narrativisation of an inaugural rivalry, but as the geometry of the individual's emergence as a subject. The Symbolic is thus, as another Lacanian, Shoshana Felman, puts it, 'the differential situating the subject in the *third position*' (Felman, 1987: 115, italics in the original). The 'third position' – that of the law, of language, of ideology – is the site and source of both desire and the prohibition of desire, the place from which not only the Other addresses the self, but also from which the self is addressed *as* Other.

This split, self-alienated subject – a subject comprehending itself through the position of the desire of another – is the product of a symbolic breach that goes by the name of castration. If Freud's more literal 'castration complex' and the concomitant 'penis envy' have been the objects of feminist rage, their translation into symbolic currency by Lacan is crucial to an understanding of the instauration of difference as a condition of the formation of subjects in culture, engendering that subject and granting it a position in relation to desire. But Lacan makes explicit what had been implicit in Freud: in patriarchy, the Phallus initiates an order of exchange in which women are figured as objects. Wives and daughters are placed in a chain of relay between men; daughters *become* wives as an effect of such an exchange. This is the order of patriarchy as a condition of culture. This becomes emblematic in the agon between Snow White and her stepmother.

Returning to the letter of the Freudian text: while the Oedipal drama in the male subject is inaugurated by a deferred apprehension of the significance of castration, the formation of the female subject is a very different story, and it is centred on a special relationship with the body. It is founded upon the *consummated* fact of castration that is represented by the female body itself, compared to the boy's fear of 'the possibility of its occurrence' (Freud, 1924b: 178). In a much-cited passage, Freud elaborates:

> There is an interesting contrast between the behaviour of the two sexes . . . when a little boy first catches sight of a girl's genital region, he begins by showing irresolution and lack of interest; he sees nothing or disavows what he has seen . . . It is not until later, when some threat of castration has obtained a hold upon him, that the observation becomes important to him. . . . A little girl behaves differently. She makes her judgement and her decision in a flash. She has seen it and knows that she is without it and wants to have it. (Freud, 1925: 252)[1]

In this instantaneous acknowledgement of lack, 'not having' turns into a desire that is resolved by the mediating function of pregnancy. For Freud follows his observation of the girl's penis envy and the concomitant 'wound to her narcissism' by announcing that the desire for the penis is sublimated into the desire for a child. His account of femininity is thus formulated entirely in Oedipal terms. The girl

> gives up her wish for a penis and puts in place of it a wish for a child: and *with that purpose in view* she takes her father as a love-object. Her mother has become the object of her jealousy. The girl has turned into a little woman . . . *Whereas in boys the Oedipus complex is destroyed by the castration complex, in girls it is made possible and led up to by the castration complex.* (Freud, 1925: 254–256, italics in the original)

The Freudian formula for female desire casts women as rivals to one another, and re-routes the female subject back home. She will therefore

> choose her husband for his paternal characteristic and be ready to recognize his authority. Her longing to possess a penis, which is in fact unappeasable, may find satisfaction if she can succeed in compensating her love for the organ by extending it to the bearer of the organ. (Freud, 1940: 194)

In this substitution, paternal authority is, of course, acknowledged. Through her desire, the female subject does nothing short of taking her assigned place in the chain of transmission. It is here that the Freudian scheme is congruent with patriarchy: in the maternal function that transforms her from girl to woman, the female subject is the vessel through which fathers pass their names and their property down to sons. For Freud, then, the female Oedipus complex is a conservative force, ensuring the sustained idealisation of the father. In 'The Dissolution of the Oedipus Complex', he puts it in the following terms:

> In my experience, [the girl's Oedipus complex] seldom goes beyond the taking of her mother's place and the adopting of a feminine attitude towards her father. Renunciation of the penis is not tolerated by the girl without some attempts at compensation. She slips – along the line of a symbolic equation, one might say – from the penis to a baby. Her Oedipus complex culminates in a desire, which is long retained, to receive a baby from her father as a gift – to bear him a child. (Freud, 1924b: 178–179)

So while the constitution of the male subject sees the Oedipal fixation 'smashed', the female subject, idealising procreation, is represented as unable to move beyond Oedipal desire and is thus tied to a psychic economy in which the father remains central.

Inviting a reading through a Freudian lens, *Snow White Playing with her Father's Trophies* presents a metaphoric reification of the girl's Oedipal desire in the stag's head with its proud and clearly phallic antlers. Could we say that she knows that she is without it and she wants to have it? The 'father's trophy' is here excised, detached from any integral body. As a fragment and a fetish, it is a monument to what once was whole. This vestige has become the plaything of the girl, her own trophy, a souvenir of conquest. The girl's classic achievement – to have 'turned into a little woman' – triumphs in the domestication of the phallic signifier. In both displaying and playing with her trophy, this Snow White embodies the male dread of *vagina dentata*, of female sexuality as maiming, mortifying. And indeed, if the decapitated stag's head stands in for the father/husband, the painting also suggests that the only good father/husband is a dead one. 'Marriage is a kind of winding-sheet, isn't it?' Rego has rhetorically asked (Macedo, 1999a: 14).

In this play of signifiers, the stag's antlers simultaneously stand for and undermine paternal authority. Traditionally, alluding to horns in the popular lexicon of physical gestures in Portugal (as in numerous other European cultures) and in the mocking verbal term *cornudo* ('horned') indicts men as cuckolds. This association between stag and betrayed husband is made by Jean-Jacques Grandville, the nineteenth-century French illustrator and draughtsman much admired by Rego, in two satirical drawings dated around 1830: *Actaeon Changed into a Stag by Diana* and *The Evening Shadows Make Objects Grow*. In the first, a stag-headed Actaeon interrupts Diana as she sits in the bathroom with her feet in a tub, accompanied by a cringing suitor; in the second, the horns on the stag-husband's head are magnified in his shadow, there for all to see.

The etymology of 'cuckold' links it to the cuckoo's habit of laying its egg in another bird's nest. As a crisis of legitimate genealogical succession, cuckoldry signals the failure of patriarchy. For if patriarchy depends on the legitimacy of the bond between a father and his progeny, then cuckoldry, as its vexation, affects not only material inheritance but also the symbolic legacy of the father and the privileges that accrue through it. In patriarchy, to be a cuckold's child is to be, in effect, no one at all. Cuckoldry also sees the male subject's Oedipal drama (the mother's possession by another) aggravated by the nightmare of public exposure. For if the experience of sexual betrayal is to be thought of as 'cuckoldry', then derision or laughter is a necessary ingredient. The *cornudo* is one who is seen to be ridiculous; traditionally he is the 'last to know'. This epistemological failure is not regarded as a source of compassion, but is rather thought to reveal the man's own failing. Nothing can so readily recall the vulnerability and disempowerment of the boy at the moment of the dissolution of the Oedipus complex as such a public display of the loss of love's object as loss of potency.

In diverse contexts, the derisive terms for the deceived husband as weak or pathetic invoke a horned animal: *cornudo* in Portuguese, *cabrito* (little goat), or *cabrón* (big goat), in Spanish. While on the one hand the horned animal is frequently registered as a symbol of male potency (in verbal expressions such as 'horny' or 'old goat'), Alison Sinclair points to a possible source of horn symbolism as the visual sign of domestication. She quotes Cirlot's link of the *cornudo*'s horns to those of the ox, which represents castration, sacrifice and persistent toil (Sinclair, 1993: 40). Others have seen in the cuckold's horns allusions to the 'horns' of the moon or to the woman as agent of the Devil. Natalie Zemon Davis recounts a neat verbal transposition in French between *conard* (fool) and *cornard* (horned one, cuckold) in sixteenth-century France (Zemon Davis, 1975: 161). In short, the image of the horned animal is embedded in a cross-cultural network of contradictory significations where new meanings emerge from old signs. But one thing is for sure: to be thus horned is to endorse the instability of male signifiers and the precarious power of male potency.

In *Snow White Playing with her Father's Trophies*, the father's trophy is also that which betokens his betrayal. Instead of the traditional Freudian female subject slipping into her role of 'little woman' as a result of her own castration, the girl's position in the Oedipal triangle is here one of greater, if ironically avowed, empowerment, as she possessively holds the stag's head. In 'becoming a little woman', she has triumphed over her (step)mother in the seduction of the father, and, at the moment of acknowledging her victory, she mocks the father for the very power that privileges him. She exposes, in other words, the betrayal that demotes him from his position as custodian of patriarchal law. The girl whose father's horned trophy is her plaything casually reveals the limits of patriarchy where the policeman's daughter does not, for she announces the ultimate inability of the father/husband to lay claim to offspring in anything but a name.

No dirty laundry

For Paula Rego, a pictorial narrative is ratified by its rendering of specific settings from childhood, and the country of her birth has remained insistently present in all her work: 'My paintings have never been about anything else' (Pinharanda, 1999: 2), she once affirmed. However, it is not only the settings that evoke Rego's childhood in Portugal, but also the bodies themselves, and in particular the female bodies. Robust and often stocky, they announce and reiterate an image of women as survivors: earthy, practical, capable. Such bodiliness always treads a fine line between specificity and typicality. That typicality can slide into stereotype is amply illustrated in give-away observations in some appraisals of Rego's work: 'Portugal is everywhere in her work', writes Simon Hattenstone, 'in the indigo skies, in the Catholic icocnography, in the women with big bottoms and muscular thighs' (Hattenstone, 2009: 24).

The relationship between generality and specificity is one Rego takes very seriously. Her love of drawing from life – of close attention and minute observation, an intimate relationship between eye and hand – stems from a profound belief that it is only in tapping the idiosyncratic and unique that a work can make a statement that reaches out more broadly. 'I think the more specific, the more general it is. You can only touch lots of people if it is specific', she tells Marco

Livingstone (Livingstone, 2007: 198). Empathy, surely, resides in recognising in that specific otherness something that is like myself.

The model for a large number of these women has been Lila Nunes, the young woman who, in the 1980s, had nursed Rego's bedridden husband, Victor Willing, who died in 1987. For Rego, it is Lila who 'gives punctuation to all the work. She brings it down to earth and makes it real' (in conversation). With Lila occupying the position of principle model, an important mechanism was brought into operation. By being, like Rego herself, a Portuguese woman in London, and, moreover, by sharing some of Rego's physical attributes, Lila was able to serve as a screen for Rego. The screen metaphor is particularly apt, for Lila simultaneously shields Rego from the embarrassment and confessional excesses of pure autobiography, and her body acts as a surface upon which Rego projects herself. So Lila was to become much more than Rego's favourite model: actor and conspirator, she is also ventriloquist's dummy, cross-dresser and, finally, the artist's alter ego. Hers is the body that performs the artist's intentions, desires, conflicts, staging various identities and epitomising 'Portugueseness'. 'With Lila, I'm looking all the time, but it's a means to an end', Rego has observed.

> The fact that she's Portuguese helps. I can only do something if I connect it to Portugal. Because my basic experience is there – my early youth experience. So if I manage to relate things to something of my experience in Portugal as a child, some connection there, then this triggers off my imagination so that I can cope with the stories. (Rego: in conversation)

Rego's reiterations of stories that invoke childhood have become part of her verbal and visual narrative of self: the most cursory glance at her work reveals how important the construction of childhood experiences has been in the production of her images. While in innumerable published interviews she has talked about storytelling in terms of the tales issuing from the mouths of women who cared for her as a child, the broader cultural narratives that informed her are equally pertinent.

If Lila's specific body enacts a generic bodiliness that links it to Portugal in the late 1930s and 1940s, the clothes she wears reinforce this connection. In the staging of a character and its accoutrements in the studio, the dresses – which the artist carefully selects as a theatrical director might choose the costumes for a play – operate as signifiers of pastness, locating the figures somewhere between the memory of dressing-up and role-playing in childhood, and the evocation of Portuguese traditional rural garb and its cultural representations in postcards, prints or school books, constituting an ideologically based narration of nation.[2]

Rego has dressed the *Policeman's Daughter*, as indeed Snow White in *Snow White Playing with her Father's Trophies*, in white. In addition to the overarching significance of white in the West – the colour of baptism, of communion, of marriage – the fictional time of the painting points to a more particular association for the signifier 'whiteness'. The film *Aldeia da Roupa Branca* – literally meaning 'the village of white linen' – directed by Chianca de Garcia, had its first screening at the Tivoli Cinema in Lisbon on 2 January 1939. Starring the popular stage and film actress Beatriz Costa, the film portrayed – in comic, picaresque style and in romanticised detail – the life of a fictional Portuguese village on the outskirts of Lisbon and its inhabitants (*saloios*), who grow vegetables and do the laundry for city-dwellers. The film's subtext is a conflict between tradition and modernity: two families are business rivals, until one of them buys a truck in order to transport the clothes more efficiently into the city.

Although modernisation (the purchase of a truck) seems positively valued, the film more insistently stresses the traditional values associated with a ruralism that is presented as morally and physically salubrious, while the modernity of the city brings corruption (drinking, smoking) in its wake. Made during the first decade of the *Estado Novo*, the film represents the countryside as a site of pastoral innocence, of abundance and carefree joy. Village life runs smoothly; conflict emerges and is resolved, and we are shown the efficacy of the modern solution absorbed and integrated into the ahistorical life of the countryside. Work is without tedium or fatigue, undertaken with pleasure and song; leisure time is the picture of social harmony, positively valorising poverty as a foil to urban decadence and self-indulgence. It goes without saying that the film in no way exposes the appalling effects of poverty in Portugal at the time it was made.

The film opens with a scene of washerwomen by the river, singing as they pummel sheets, underclothes, aprons and other such familiar fetishes of domestic purity, leaving them to dry in the sun. Images of white linen punctuate the film. Washing and laundering reinforce the mythology of rural life as antidote to, and purification of, the urban diseases: cosmopolitanism and industrialisation.

The association of soap with moral hygiene is not unique to Chianca Garcia's film. One of the well-known mottos of the Salvation Army, founded in 1865, is 'Soap, Soup and Salvation'. Anne McClintock has shown how the advertising of soap such as Pears in Victorian England served to bring the empire home, to domesticate it and make it also for and about women. Discussing the commodity fetishism of soap and its advertising, McClintock observes how, before the late nineteenth century, 'clothes and bedding washing was done in most households only once or twice a year in great, communal binges, usually in public at streams or rivers' (McClintock, 1995: 210) such as we see in Chianca de Garcia's film. Discussing the visibility of soap in Victorian England, McClintock examines its ideological role:

> Soap did not flourish when imperial ebullience was at its peak. It emerged commercially during an era of impending crisis and social calamity, serving to preserve, through fetish ritual, the uncertain boundaries of class, gender and race identity in a social order felt to be threatened by the fetid effluvia of the slums, the belching smoke of industry, social agitation, economic upheaval, imperial competition and anticolonial resistance. Soap offered the promise of spiritual salvation and regeneration through commodity consumption, a regime of domestic hygiene that could restore the threatened potency of the imperial body politic and the race. (McClintock, 1995: 211)

Similarly, it is the image of the political regime that Beatriz Costa is laundering in *Aldeia da Roupa Branca*. Furthermore, the iconography of women laundering in the river (*lavadeiras*) continued for decades to represent a grass-roots image of Portugueseness, for instance in Pedro Homem de Mello's melancholy poem *Povo que Lavas no Rio* (literally, 'o people, washing your laundry in the river'), set to wrenching music by Joaquim Campos as late as 1962. In the film *Aldeia da Roupa Branca*, it is not so much the commodity consumption of soap that offers a promise of spiritual regeneration, as the myth of hygiene and rurality represented by laundering and by whiteness itself.

In the most literal sense, such myth-making is a form of appropriation and naturalisation of values. Its matter-of-factness − what Roland Barthes called 'depoliticised speech' − masks an operation whereby a text is surreptitiously made to express the dominant values of a given historical moment through the deployment of signifiers that appear to be neutral. Myth belongs not to individuals, but is, rather 'chosen by history' (Barthes, 2000: 110) and then mimicked in diverse cultural expressions. It presents itself, in other words, as non-ideological, factual. Such appropriated motifs are not only pressed at the service of existing ideologies in cultural artefacts such as film or painting, they may also be simultaneously performed and constructed by them. The signifying density of the policeman's daughter's white dress at once exposes and vexes the naturalising potential of such mythical utterance, reinforcing the work's allusion to a particular historical and political context.

The historical and political context

In Rego's work, the home, as a hierarchically constructed space and a site of intimate violence, is the stage upon which history is performed. Maria Manuel Lisboa urges that, in all her work, the artist makes history central, 'while simultaneously effecting that two-way translation ... whereby the remote historical process becomes available through the transformative medium of day-to-day human relations' (Lisboa, 2003: 5–6). It is from the atmosphere of political repression of Salazar's dictatorship, institutionalised in the *Estado Novo*, that her protagonists address us.

When António Oliveira Salazar took up the Finance portfolio in 1928, Portugal was a predominantly rural country on the periphery of the world economy. In 1938 – the year when *Aldeia da Roupa Branca* was made – it was still common for women to launder in rivers. Manuel Braga da Cruz outlines five principal phases of the *Estado Novo*, of which the second, third and fourth are of relevance as referents in Rego's work (Braga da Cruz, 1988: 38–47). The first phase corresponds to the military dictatorship (1926–33); the second to the construction of the *Estado Novo* (1933–45); the third to the image changes in the regime consequent to the defeat of Nazism and Fascism (1945–61); the fourth pertains to the increased isolation of the regime during the Portuguese Colonial Wars in Africa (1961–68); and the last phase is marked by Salazar's retirement from office and the apparent liberalisation effected by his successor, Marcelo Caetano (1968–74). The regime was toppled in the 'Carnation Revolution' on 25 April 1974.

After the assassination of the last king of Portugal and his son in February 1908 (Rego's painting *Regicide* of 1965 [see Figure 4] is an allusion to this event) and after the subsequent republican overthrow of the constitutional monarchy in October 1910, Portugal saw the instauration of its First Republic. It was under the aegis of republicanism that the symbols of nation were promulgated: a new flag, a new anthem, and a newly nationalised school curriculum. However, the country remained politically unstable. A military coup in May 1926 announced the demise of parliamentarism. It had become clear that the promises of the Republican Revolution had not been kept; the economy was in permanent crisis; the republican factions were in constant conflict; emigration to Brazil and North America was rife. The process of transition from the military dictatorship to Salazar's 'authoritarian corporative republic', institutionalised in the constitution of 1933, was one of the most politically agitated in Portuguese modern history. It has frequently been noted that Salazar's success resided in his capacity to unify this politically splintered country and to transform the multiple right-wing factions into a single right, permitting him to exercise complete control over the state.

In April 1928, António Oliveira Salazar, then aged thirty-nine, an avowed Catholic and a Professor of Law from the University of Coimbra, was invited to take up the finance portfolio. By the end of the following year, he had issued an ultimatum: the government had to choose between saving the economy under his aegis, on the one hand, and supporting the liberal republic and its old parties and alliances without the help of his financial acumen on the other. Even republican conservatives opted for the assurance offered by Salazar. In granting Salazar what was effectively a power of veto on all future ministries and control over the country's income and expenditure, the president, General Óscar Carmona, sealed the country's fate.

With his stringent economic reforms was born the myth of Salazar as 'finance wizard' or 'finance dictator'. His aim was to foment self-sufficiency through the protection of the national market, including the revenue from the colonies in Africa, which were to gain independence only after the collapse of the *Estado Novo* in 1974. The desire for insularity was symbolised in the difficult period beginning in the late 1950s by the slogan '[a nation] proudly alone' (*orgulhasamente sós*). In December 1931, the National Political Council (*Conselho Político Nacional*) was created as the institutional context for the new constitution, drawn up by Salazar while he was still Minister of Finance. On 5 July 1932, Salazar took office as President of the Council of Ministers. Shrewdly, he was not only anti-liberal, but also opposed the radical right, wishing to attract support from the so-called centre, and in particular from within the constituency of the party that he launched in 1930, the conservative National Union (*União Nacional*). As the institutional expression of Salazarism, this was to be the country's only official party until 1974, organised from the top down.

Reserved and unassuming, Salazar nevertheless pursued a strategy of paternalist supervision. His talent as a leader would lie not only in his economic policies, but also in his capacity for rejoining the country's dispersed forces and keeping them under the control of the state apparatus. His policies were marked by anti-parliamentarianism, anti-liberalism, anti-Communism and – like Italian Fascism – corporativism, but also by a fervent adherence to Catholicism. After the political, economic and social chaos of the first two decades of the century, his rise to power met with the consensual approval of the country's elites, tired of the chaos and inflation that had marked the Republic.

Salazar's Catholicism and his background in law militated against an adherence to totalitarianism, which, as a divinisation of the state, he saw as anti-Christian. 'The Fascist dictatorship', he announced, 'tends to a pagan caesarism, to a new state which knows no legal or moral limitations, that marches ahead towards its objective without any tribulations or obstacles . . . the Portuguese New State, on the contrary, cannot and will not flee from certain moral limitations and considers these indispensable as marking the boundaries of its reforms' (Salazar, 1945: 71). This theoretical demarcation of a position apart from Fascism and Nazism helped secure Salazar's political survival after the end of World War Two.

The relationship of Salazarism to Fascism has been the topic of keen historiographic debate,[3] and it is generally agreed that the *Estado Novo*, with its cultural and political roots in social Catholicism, does not conform to the Fascist prototype properly speaking, although 'fascist' is now the shorthand term used for it in popular speech. The year 1936 marked the beginning of the regime's most overt fascistisation, which was to last until 1945. The need to establish a more assertive symbology of nation was to a large extent a response to the destabilising effects of the Spanish Civil War. Under the aegis of the Ministry of Education, the *Mocidade Portuguesa* (Portuguese Youth) – a form of political socialisation for the young – was founded. It had links, such as exchange programmes, with the *Hitlerjugend* in Germany, but this lasted only until the outbreak of World War Two. In 1937, the *Mocidade Portuguesa Feminina*

(Portuguese Female Youth) was founded. In addition to these youth movements, Salazar now also authorised the founding of a militia, the *Legião Portuguesa* (Portuguese Legion), as well as setting up a women's organisation of Fascist inspiration under the supervision of the Ministry of Education: the OMEN (*Obra das Mães para a Educação Nacional* (Work of the Mothers for National Education), an initiative of women from the upper echelons of the bourgeois elite.[4] In the same year, the *Secretariado de Propaganda Nacional* (Secretariat of National Propaganda) was founded under the influential directorship of António Ferro. The propaganda machine of the *Estado Novo* was now firmly in place.

In addition to state control of the economy and an offensive against organised workers' movements, Salazar curtailed all forms of public assembly, instituting the persecution of political dissent, censorship of the press, and control to be exercised over the appointment of all civil servants. Two of his main concerns were, not surprisingly, education and the reorganisation of the police force. The political police was the backbone of the regime. First known as PVDE – the *Polícia de Vigilância e de Defesa do Estado* (Police for the Vigilance and Defence of the State), in 1945 it was renamed PIDE (*Polícia Internacional e de Defesa do Estado* – International Police for the Defence of the State).[5] This name is to this day engraved in Portuguese collective memory as an emblem of the regime itself. The pall of fear cast by the political police was aimed at cowing even the most recalcitrant opposition, although, in effect, the history of opposition is as long as that of the regime itself.

Notoriously, education was the most assiduously monitored ideological state apparatus. Ideological control of education progressively closed in on teachers and students alike. Teaching in each subject was honed down to a single, authorised textbook: these, today, are invaluable sources for the official iconographies and ideology of the time. Everything, right down to the decoration of the classrooms, was supervised by the state. The dictatorship reinforced, through its control of education, an ideal of moral purity based on manual and agricultural labour. Furthermore, the monitored contents of education spawned an official version of Portuguese history, one that aggrandised the role of a few select national heroes. Above all, education was Christianised in accordance with the values of a subservient and ideologically controlled Catholic Church, inculcating the virtues of Christian compliance and obedience in its programme of nation building. School was seen not only as a fertile ground for citizen building, but also as a 'sacred workshop of souls' (*sagrada oficina de almas*).

The effects of education were intended to percolate through to the very heart of the institutions of home and family. As early as 1932, the Minister of Education drew up a policy that emphasised the family as a social cell: respect for authority and hierarchy within the family reiterated micro-discursively what was seen as a governing principle of sociality. At its most intimate, the regime's corporativism favoured the family over the individual. Indeed, for Salazar, the family was the natural aggregate through which individuals came to exist, the cohesion of the family serving as a model for the political and social order of the nation. Suffrage was limited to the corporativist representation of the family by its hierarchic head and 'boss' – the *chefe de família* – as placeholder rather than as individual citizen. Usually, though not universally, this meant the father. Women's right to hold public office was generally conceded in the case of widows, divorcees, or women whose husbands were away in the colonies.[6]

As has already been noted, unlike many other authoritarian regimes, Salazarism embraced the traditional ideology of Catholicism, reinstating the alliance between the state and the church that the constitution of 1911 had severed. Although the Catholic church had no formal authority, Salazar sealed the moral link between church and state by signing a concordat with the Vatican in 1940. Salazar's motto *Deus, Pátria, Família* (God, Fatherland, Family) binds together religion, land, state and family cell. 'When the family is undone,' Salazar announced, 'the home is undone: links of kinship are dissolved and men face the State as isolated, estranged, unprotected beings' (Salazar, 1945: 133–134). The family was regarded not only as the vessel of godliness, but also as the seat of transmission, sociality and cohesion: an organised, efficiently functioning, hierarchically structured social and political unit, reproducing in miniature the chain of command of the state, with each member holding an assigned position and a concomitant code of conduct. In the figure of the father, the authoritarian state had its representative in the home: the father's political, moral and economic position, in other words, resounds in his paternalistic relationship to the rest of the family. Like Fascism, in other words, Salazarism attached itself to the already rooted structures of patriarchy.

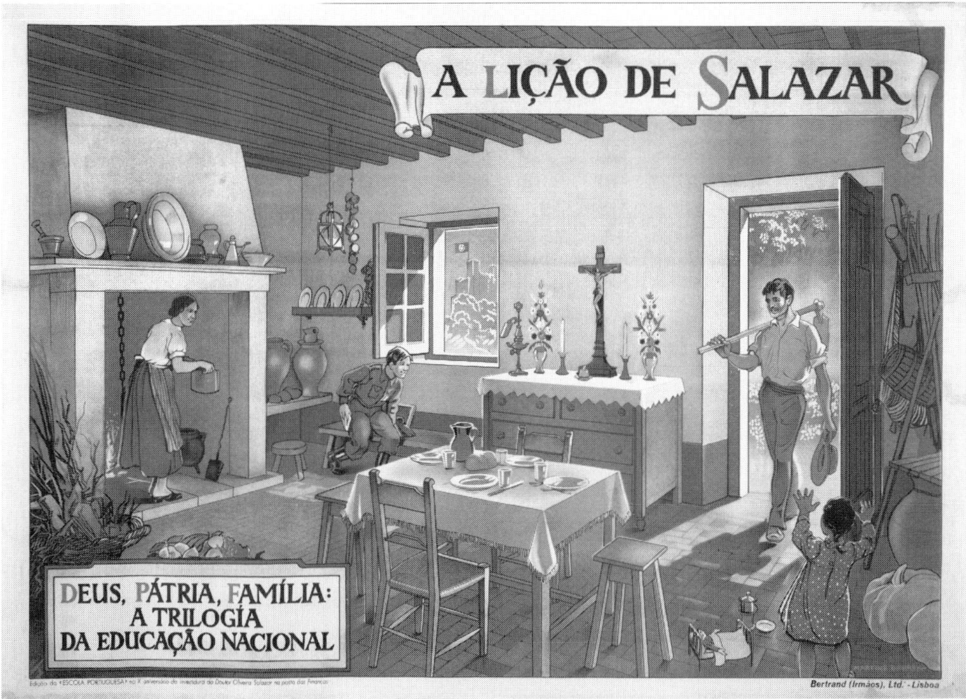

Jaime Martins Barata, *Salazar's Lesson*, 1938   Figure 8

In 1938, to celebrate the tenth anniversary of Salazar's investiture as Minister of Finance, the government sponsored an educational project consisting of a series of seven didactic paintings by Jaime Martins Barata, under the general rubric *Salazar's Lesson* (*A Lição de Salazar*). Copies of these images not only made their way into the official textbooks used at school, but were also hung on classroom walls even in the most decrepit schools. These images show a sanitised country running on oiled wheels, and a well-adjusted, cheerful and productive population enjoying the fruits of the *Estado Novo*'s projects of public works and confirming its status as the capital of its Empire.[7]

The words *Deus, Pátria, Família: A Trilogia da Educação Nacional* ('God, Fatherland, Family: the Trilogy of National Education') are inscribed on one of these seven images constituting Salazar's 'lessons', transporting us into an idealised home, a humble abode where each character plays a hierarchically assigned role (Figure 8). Through such a harmonious image of family life, the nation itself is construed as co-operative and operational. The world represented here is at once patriarchal, rustic and Christian. Central in the scene is a large crucifix flanked by two lit candles, transforming a chest of drawers into an altar. On the table, which is set for a family meal, bread and wine not only advertise the abundant produce of the soil but also symbolically represent the incorporation of Christianity through the Eucharist. The home microcosmically reflects an ordered social, political and economic world: a meal is simmering on the stove; through the illuminated doorway, the head of the household, the father – larger than any of the other figures – cheerfully crosses the threshold that separates outer world from inner sanctum, bearing the instruments of his agricultural labour. It is a threshold that only he negotiates. The mother, whose place is over the stove, works at keeping the domestic economy going and forging the conditions for the man's agency in the public sphere.

Fascinatingly, Salazar drew an analogy between running the country parsimoniously, and the strict economic measures of a good housewife. Being a good housewife was the highest value for a woman, and the epitome of productive industry: 'never has there been a good housewife who hasn't had a lot to do' (Salazar, 1934: 201). Though, in truth, economic circumstances often obliged women to work outside the home, and cheap female labour continued to be common in Portugal, *Estado Novo* ideology stressed the importance of woman's domestic role: '[i]n countries or places where married women compete with men for work', Salazar proclaimed, 'in the factories, in the workshops, in offices or in the liberal professions – the institution of the family, for which we have fought as the cornerstone of a well-organised society, threatens to fall into ruin' (Ferro, 1933: 133).

In the print by Martins Barata, two children welcome their father home, the little girl raising her arms in delight, the little boy rising respectfully from his chair. The boy is dressed as a *lusito* – the lowest rank of the *Mocidade Portuguesa* – as if preparing to embrace the manly duties and responsibilities he will eventually own: the chain of transmission has been initiated. Through the window, we glimpse a castle, symbol of Portugal's heroic history and a sustaining image for its present imperial glory; a past harnessed to legitimise the values of continuity, tradition, Christianity and, in effect, of Nation itself, represented by the fluttering Portuguese flag.

This family, then, is the bedrock and emblem of a functioning society, with its status emanating from the unassailable moral authority of the father. Such authority was also transmitted by capital means: excluded from the representation is a more literal visualisation of the importance within the family of corporal punishment, considered always important in a good education. Education, which was to take on the functions of paternal authority, worked to reinforce these values. In 1931, at the opening of the Tenth Congress for the Protection of Children (*X Congresso de Protecção à Criança*), the Minister of Justice defined the aim of education as being 'to twist, to prune, to cut down, to oppose, to crush' (quoted in Mónica, 1978: 273).[8]

To have and to be

'To twist, to prune, to cut, to oppose, to crush': Freud might thus have described the paternal function represented by the superego. Looking at Paula Rego's *Policeman's Daughter*, one sees within this humble abode a pruned and ideologically shaped daughter playing her part in the family hierarchy, undertaking a homely and daughterly task. In doing so, she identifies with the maternal in facilitating masculine agency in the public domain: she is polishing her daddy's boot. Apparently, she performs the Salazarist desideratum of women's domestic and, concomitantly, political subordination. Ideology and the superego work together to produce a compliant little woman, honed and subjected not only to father and state, but also, if one views the work through a Freudian prism, to a psychic regulation of the norm: she does what she does because she knows she has to. Is this a painting about feeling safe under the authoritative wing of the father and paying the price for such security? Or does she feel that by accepting the father's authority she can have a part of it? The question this painting asks is: does the female subject it represents identify with paternal authority or spurn it? What is the role of the superego in the representation of this particular subject? More broadly, what role does identification play?

In psychoanalytic terms, identification plays a crucial role in the formation of subjects. It is a form of incorporation, the 'assimilation of one ego to another one', or of traits of one ego into another, so that, in a significant way, the constitution of the subject is founded on the relics of relationships with others, or, in the language of psychoanalysis, object relations. Identification is, for Freud, tied up with the question of Oedipalisation and the instatement of the superego that is its outcome, because of course, in the ascription of a fixed gender identity, the subject has had to identify with either the maternal or the paternal: to be *like* the mother or the father. So: the structural consequences of Oedipalisation bring identification to the fore.

In 1910, the year that Freud first adopted the term 'Oedipus complex' (Freud, 1910b: 171), Freud wrote, apropos Leonardo da Vinci's homosexuality: 'The child's love for his mother cannot continue to develop consciously any further... The boy represses his love for his mother: he puts himself in her place, identifies himself with her, and takes his own person as a model in whose likeness he chooses the new objects of his love' (Freud, 1910a: 100). What we see here is an intense maternal love transformed by identification. For, in order to compensate for the need to abandon the object of his affections, Freud's Leonardo identifies with that object – *becomes* the object – enabling him to enjoy someone like himself as his own object choice: he loves boys, just as his mother loved him.

Although the two may coincide, Freud differentiates between object choice and identification. The difference between them might be summed up as the opposition between 'to have' and 'to be'. 'If a boy identifies himself with his father, he wants to *be like* his father; if he makes him the object of his choice, he wants to *have* him, to possess him. In the first case his ego is altered on the model of his father; in the second case that is not necessary' (Freud, 1933: 62). While having the object is the aim of desire, identification results from an assimilative, cannibalistic relationship with the other that Diana Fuss very nicely describes as a 'detour through the other that defines the self' (Fuss, 1995: 2–3). However, the distinction between the attachment to an object and identification is, like many Freudian concepts, not stable, and in different writings, mother and father respectively take on the role of the first object of attachment or identification. In both *The Ego and the Id* (1923) and in the later *New Introductory Lectures on Psycho-Analysis* (1933), Freud makes it clear that object choice and identification co-exist or are even indistinguishable in the small infant. Indeed, 'it is . . . possible to identify oneself with someone whom, for instance, one has taken as a sexual object, and to alter one's ego on his model' (Freud, 1933: 63). It is, in other words, possible to have an attachment to the father, and simultaneously to incorporate the paternal agency as an identification.

As we have seen in Freud's comments on Leonardo, if identification is a form of mastery by incorporation, the condition for such an identification is the annihilation of the object: to swallow an object means to possess it, and yet to have lost it. Identification is, then, a form of compensation, of substitution. Late in his life, Freud put it succinctly thus: 'If one has lost a love-object, the most obvious reaction is to identify oneself with it, to replace it from within, as it were, by identification' (Freud, 1940: 243). Importantly, however, in *The Ego and the Id* – Freud's seminal theorisation of the subject's first passionate attachments – he observes a similarity between this identificatory structure in the 'normal' (rather than pathological) character and what he had earlier discussed as the defining characteristics of melancholia (Freud, 1923: 28).

Freud's allusion in *The Ego and the Id* to 'Mourning and Melancholia' (Freud, 1917b) makes explicit the relationship that had been implicit in the Leonardo essay, between identification and loss: to identify with someone means to have already lost them. In 'Mourning and Melancholia', Freud clarifies the distinction between getting things over and done with in mourning, and the inability to do so that characterises melancholia. He outlines the ways in which, owing to its reluctance voluntarily to let go of a libidinal object, the subject converts loss into identification, thus possessing the object it can no longer have, as if to say: 'I have lost you, but if I become you, I can continue to have you.' But he makes it clear that however dilated the work of mourning, this clinging to the object is temporally bound: '[t]he fact is . . . that when the work of mourning is completed the ego becomes free and uninhibited again' (Freud, 1917b: 245). It is, he proposes in *The Ego and the Id*, on the remnants of such losses – on the ruins of the id's attachments – that the ego is built. *Wo Es war, soll Ich werden*: 'where id was shall ego come to be' (Freud, 1933: 80). In this famous dictum, a connection is acknowledged between a founding loss and the constitution of the ego itself, and, in the breach, an innate otherness installs itself. That otherness corresponds, in Lacan's reading of Freud, to the 'discourse of the Other' (Lacan, 1957: 171–172), the language that precedes the subjects and shapes it. We shall soon return to this idea, and to how that discourse of the Other might otherwise be defined not only as language, but also as ideology.

Wo Es war, soll Ich werden: Lacan also explores the ambivalent and shifting operations of 'having' and 'being' in this strange excentricity of the self. If, as we have seen, it is the paternal injunction that assigns a role to each placeholder in the family romance, it is that same paternal edict that 'signals to the subject that "having" only functions at the price of a loss and "being" as an effect of division'

(Rose in Mitchell and Rose, 1982: 40). The subject is not only characterised by its belatedness, but is also always divided and always in mourning. Moreover, in the formation of the superego, loss plays a double part: the superego is formed as a response to object loss, and equally as a response to the fear of the loss of an organ.

How would such an idea fall on female ears? It follows, for Freud, that without a penis to lose, the female subject should be destined never to have a fully developed superego (Freud, 1924b: 178). As Kaja Silverman drolly observes, 'the missing superego functions as the moral equivalent and "consequence" of the missing penis' (Silverman, 1983: 145). If this reinforces women's difference, highlighting the otherness of 'Woman', it does so by underlining this final humiliation: women's moral subservience to men: 'The male sex', Freud tells us, 'seems to have taken the lead in all . . . moral acquisitions; and they seem to have been transmitted to women by cross-inheritance' (Freud, 1923: 37).

Paradoxically, it might be to some feminist advantage to accept Freud's own claims that the female subject should be destined never to have a fully developed superego. The stunted superego, in other words, might be considered a triumph over the restrictive mandates of patriarchy. Nevertheless, to modern ears, Freud's claim is untenable. Yet, on closer reading, we see that a speculative instability marks Freud's position, here as elsewhere. Countering the famous assertion that 'anatomy is destiny' (Freud, 1912b: 189; 1924b: 178), Freud's introduction of the human being's innate bisexuality sees women and men shaking free biological determinism. In 'Some Psychical Consequences of the Anatomical Distinction Between the Sexes', he observes:

> I cannot evade the notion . . . that for women the level of what is ethically normal is different from what it is in men. Their super-ego is never so inexorable, so impersonal, so independent of its emotional origins as we require it to be in men. Character-traits which critics of every epoch have brought up against women – that they show less sense of justice than men, that they are less ready to submit to the great exigencies of life, that they are more often influenced in their judgements by feelings of affection or hostility – all these would be amply accounted for by the modification in the formation of their super-ego. (Freud, 1925: 257)

This extraordinary statement is followed by an equally extraordinary caveat:

> We must not allow ourselves to be deflected from such conclusions
> by the denials of the feminists, who are anxious to force us to regard
> the two sexes as completely equal in position and worth; but we
> shall, of course, willingly agree that the majority of men are also
> far behind the masculine ideal and that all human individuals, as a
> result of their bisexual disposition and cross-inheritance, combine
> in themselves both masculine and feminine characteristics, so that
> pure masculinity and femininity remain theoretical constructions of
> uncertain content. (Freud, 1925: 257–258)

Moreover, girls may diverge in the way they construe their biological sexual difference from boys, varying in the degrees of passivity and activity, feminine and masculine identification: psychological femininity is not obligatorily the consequence of female biology, but is, rather, one of the ways in which girls react to genital sex difference.

Yet what are we to make of the fact that, while undermining the notion of biological determinism, Freud returns repeatedly to the materiality of the biological body: the penis, the breasts, the mouth, the anus? His vacillation turns his theories into works-in-progress: teasing and frustrating models flexible enough to be used to support conflicting arguments. Freud's theorising of the superego incorporates a central ambiguity with regard to the formation of male and female subjects, and with regard to the subject's relationship of both desire and identification – 'to have' and 'to be' – first with the parents, and then with the introjected paternal agency, the superego. It seems to be this ambiguity that *The Policeman's Daughter* performs.

That strict taskmaster

Two distinct topographies emerge in Freud's writing. In the first, the significant distinction is between the Unconscious, Preconscious and Conscious, while in the second, Freud identifies the three psychic agencies – id, ego and superego – that have now entered our common parlance. The superego, Freud tells us in *The Ego and the Id*, 'occupies a special position between the ego and the id. It belongs to the ego and shares its high degree of psychological organization; but it has a particularly intimate connection with the id.' But it is the fact that the superego is 'less firmly connected with consciousness' that constitutes the 'novelty which calls for explanation' (Freud, 1923: 28). It is, in other words, in the unconscious that social regulation takes hold. The spatial metaphors that Freud deploys in discussing the second psychic topography are fluid and undergo continual realignment as Freud attempts to secure the parts played by passion, reason and moral judgement. Thus we are told that the ego is attached to consciousness, which is the 'surface of the mental apparatus' (17); that 'the ego does not completely envelop the id' (Freud, 1923: 24); that in the relationship of id to superego the 'lowest part is transformed to the highest part of the human mind' (Freud, 1923: 37); and that 'the super-ego is always close to the id . . . It reaches deep down into the id and for that reason is farther from consciousness than the ego is' (Freud, 1923: 48). What Freud proposes, in all these metaphors, is an interpenetration of the three psychic regions rather than their visualisation as distinct, vertically arrayed archaeological strata and a proximity between superego and id.

The id is the most archaic, irrational, unconscious part of the self: it is driven by the pleasure principle and enjoys no contact with external reality. The ego, however, is more complex and not altogether coherent. It is not so much a substance as an 'organization of mental processes' to which 'consciousness is attached' (Freud, 1923: 17). But it is also 'reason and common sense' (Freud, 1923: 25). It is porous to, and dependent on, sensory perceptions and is thus, importantly, 'first and foremost a bodily ego' (Freud, 1923: 26), a remnant of, and witness to, the intensity of sensations accumulating on the site of the child's body. Its contact with reality famously renders it 'a frontier creature' (Freud, 1923: 55) mediating between the id and the world. Indeed, through its need to test reality, the ego persuades the id to renounce the objects that have proved inaccessible to it; yet the ego itself is a residue of, and monument to, those relinquished attachments. There can, therefore, be no such thing as an entirely newly made, inaugural subject, independent of the introjected fragments of other subjects, especially from the world of the infant's primary caregivers. In bearing the residues of past attachments – the ruins of the id's lost objects – the ego is a kind of cemetery.

While the ego is closest to 'the surface' and 'to consciousness', both the superego and the id are embedded in the unconscious and are structurally interrelated. In being close to the id, Freud tells us, the superego 'can act as its representative *vis-à-vis* the ego' (Freud, 1923: 49). The form in which the id is presented to the ego is therefore paradoxical, for while it is connected to the drives, it only becomes manifest by negation, as prohibition. Slipping through the net of psychic control in dreams, parapraxes and jokes, the id remains unknown except through its domestication by the superego. The superego is therefore not only the psychic representative of paternal authority; it is also, as we shall later see, the remainder of the very passions it has censored. The subduing of the id by the superego conforms to the norms that constitute not only civilisation, but – again as we shall shortly see – also ideology. It is, then, as a strict taskmaster that the superego hails the ego.

In *The Ego and the Id*, Freud oscillates between the affirmation, on the one hand, that the superego is an internal substitute for paternal authority once the subject's desire has been barred by 'castration', and on the other, the affirmation that it stems from a form of identificatory attachment that occurs prior to castration, prior to Oedipalisation. For while, in the main text, Freud insists on the importance of the father as the authoritative locus of identification, his footnotes characteristically expand and make the argument more ambiguous. So in the body of the text, we read that behind the superego, or ego ideal as he calls it here, 'lies hidden an individual's first and most important identification, his identification with the father in his own personal prehistory', in the footnotes he wonders if '[p]erhaps it would be safer to say "with the parents"; for before a child has arrived at a definite knowledge of the difference between the sexes, the lack of a penis, it does not distinguish in value between its father and its mother' (Freud, 1923: 31). Certainly, Freud submits, an infant does not distinguish between its father and its mother on grounds of gender, but rather on grounds of bodily proximity and the structural and structuring roles of nurture and discipline. This then renders extremely problematic the role of both parents as gendered prior to the Oedipus complex, while similarly vexing the relation between object choice and identification.

The relationship of the superego to object choices on the one hand, and to identification on the other, is disturbed by what Freud calls 'the constitutional bisexuality of each individual' (Freud, 1923: 31). Freud draws a four-way grid of possible identifications and object choices (male with female and male with male, female with male and female with female), positing the subject as the locus of complex intersections of identifications and object choices. In the classic version of the Oedipus complex, the boy child finds the prototype of his object choice in the mother, and identifies with the father. With the dissolution of the Oedipus complex, the mother must be abandoned as an object choice. This, Freud tells us, may result either in an identification with his mother (whose outcome as we saw in the case of Leonardo da Vinci, could be a homosexual object choice) 'or in an intensification of his identification with his father' (Freud, 1923: 32) leading to an object choice of a female like his mother.

An analogous situation occurs with the little girl, who is obliged to abandon her father as object choice, and who could thereafter either identify with the father or with the mother. Although we are 'accustomed to regard the latter outcome as more normal' (Freud, 1923: 32), the inverse consequence of the Oedipus complex is sufficiently frequent to warrant Freud's attention in a discussion of the formation of the superego. 'It would appear, therefore,' he observes, 'that in both sexes the relative strength of the masculine and feminine sexual dispositions is what determines whether the outcome of the Oedipus situation shall be an identification with the father or with the mother' (Freud, 1923: 33). And, most significantly, 'one gets the impression that the simple Oedipus complex is by no means its commonest form, but rather represents a simplification or a schematization which, to be sure, is often enough justified'. But closer investigation 'usually discloses the more complete Oedipus complex, which is twofold, positive and negative, and is due to the bisexuality present in children' (33).

Reading the range of possibilities offered by Freud, one is struck by the extent to which identifications are unstable and incomplete, leaving identity unmoored, never as totalised as in Freud's model of ideal Oedipalisation. Such theorisation also clearly vexes the certainty of women's moral inferiority and puts paid to accusations of biological determinism, also leaving various theoretical avenues open to the compatibility between feminism and Freudian theory. And, finally, it leaves the relationship between pre-Oedipal identification and object choice inconclusive. Examining this conundrum, Diana Fuss asks how it is that, if identification is the outcome of the ego's response to an object-cathexis, 'Freud can claim elsewhere that identification precedes object-cathexis? If identification *is* an abandoned object relation, then how can it simultaneously be the *precondition* for an object relation?' (Fuss, 1995: 47). The chronology that links object choice and identification forms a knot that Freud does not untie.

Yet while the superego inherits this paradox, it remains incontestably the site of an operation of censorship and regulation, acting as the psychic delegate of a cultural norm. The picture Freud gives us, then, is of an entirely incoherent self: a self composed of incorporated fragments of other subjects; flexible masculine and feminine object choices; unstable gender identifications; an ego that lives on a borderland that it uneasily patrols, and a superego that behaves like a tyrant that, while indecisive, nevertheless compels subjects to identify conservatively with the representations supplied by their culture.

It is true, I am here

Famously, Louis Althusser defines the operation whereby individuals feel compelled to identify with the representations authored by their culture – those representations that collectively constitute ideology – as interpellation. It seems that interpellation best describes the pre-condition of the subject in *The Policeman's Daughter*, a subject that Rego has been at pains to depict in careful detail. For it is of the essence, in the artist's work from this time on, that the viewer should grasp the structure of social and personal relations that the work conjures. Interpellation, as expressing a shift from violence as a means of suppression to ideology as a tool of repression – a tool through which the subject becomes self-regulating, in particular in the context of the small social unit that constitutes the family – provides the heuristic device best suited to describe the the articulation of the social and the psychic in Rego's work from the late 1980s on.

Interpellation is the procedure through which subjects experience as natural the scenes where ideology has done its work. Like Barthes' notion of mythical speech, ideology functions surreptitiously. Althusser's founding scene of subjectivity acknowledges the ways in which people recognise not only themselves and one another, but also reality itself through ideology. But not only is an interpellated subject a subject *in* ideology; also, Althusser makes it clear that there is no other way to be a subject; that being ideologically situated defines the subject-position itself. His account is therefore one of a subject that is necessarily a product of the discourse of the Other; a subject addressed by an order that precedes it. Althusser's subject, then, like Freud's and especially like Lacan's, is always late.

In Althusser's formulation, the 'I' comes into existence 'as a human child in a world of adult thirds' (Althusser, 1971b: 193) through an address produced by a hypothetical cultural agent, an address to which the subject is unwittingly but inevitably drawn. It is in this exchange that power, censure and – most importantly – ideology are internalised. In his celebrated example, Althusser refers to this address, this 'hey, you there!' by a policeman to someone on the street, as the hailing, and its successful outcome when the person turns around to face the call as interpellation. With this process of hailing and response, the identity of the locutionary object is defined. In the spatialised figure of a turn to face the call,[9] the individual both finds a face for the law and perceives herself as compromised, assuming a fixed position in relation to it. From this ideologically prescribed location, the turning individual confirms her identity, and in doing so is both subjected and subjectivised, responding: 'It is true, I am here.'

It is clear that in this scheme, subjects and objects are closely interlinked in an infinite chain: the subject is divided between its roles as calling and called, speaking and spoken. To be a subject, then, is to be *subjected* to a prior system of meaning and value. This is why, for Althusser, interpellation not so much introduces the subject into ideology as defines the subject as 'always-already' *in* ideology. Interpellation, then, undercuts the notion of an independent and free subject, 'short circuiting that subject's potentially subversive desire by establishing inside it a self-disciplining fixation' (Barker, 1995: 54). It is precisely such a 'self-disciplining fixation' that characterises the Freudian superego as the precipitate of Oedipalisation. Ideology is therefore to the Althusserian subject what the superego is to the Freudian subject. The two models are entirely compatible: with interpellation as a function of ideology and the superego as its agent, the subject is positioned in a complex constellation of social alliances (family, peer-groups, professional hierarchies, the state) in which desire and the law prohibiting desire are regulated from within the subject.

Yet while Althusser's concept of interpellation is congruent with the Freudian superego, his metaphor of the subject turning to face the policeman's call makes it possible also to argue that the subject is interpellated – situated in ideology – prior to Oedipalisation. For without such positioning in relation to the law, how would that call be recognised at all? In effect, Freud had already anticipated such a conundrum. Here we find ourselves up against the question of first causes that vexes the discussion of identification and object choice for Freud. For, indeed, in the acquisition of the rudiments of language – in the articulation of first signifiers like 'want', 'no' or 'mother', – the individual is already enmeshed in a network of significations (desire, refusal, family) that acquire their meaning and value from a wider cultural field. Judith Butler gestures to this paradoxical temporalisation of interpellation, asking why the call from a cultural agent should elicit the turning around, which implies the self-ascription of guilt, and why, in turn, the formation of subjectivity within ideology should be compromised by such a sense of culpability or, at least, responsibility. Importantly, her interrogation leads her to examine the seminal paradox of Althusser's formulation: how is one to theorise this turning around which both defines subjectivity and occurs at the moment prior to subject formation? (Butler, 1997: 107).

This paradox in the formation of a subject that must be identified *as* a subject in order to emerge as such, is analogous to Freud's assertion in *The Ego and the Id* that identification with the father occurs prior to Oedipalisation. However, one could argue with Freud that the full extent of these meanings is only apprehended retrospectively with the internalisation of cultural norms. For the subject as one-who-is-subjected, enjoined to self-regulation without external coercion, the family functions as an ideological state apparatus (Althusser, 1971a). This is the conceptual matrix in which we are 'from the beginning "always-already" . . . appointed as subjects'. Such a context, which at its most intimate is represented by the family, is, by definition, always ideologically shaped: our earliest ideas about what constitutes a family are thus value laden even if, later in life, we come to reject these assumptions. But while for Althusser, the family is an ideological construct, in Freud's and Lacan's formulation, the universality of the Oedipus complex erases the ideological from the picture. For them, in producing the incest taboo, the Oedipal experience is concomitant with culture itself. As the individual cannot transcend or bypass the Oedipal configuration, patriarchy is the necessary condition in which the acculturated subject finds itself.

Reading *The Policeman's Daughter* alongside the Freudian family romance and together with Althusser allows us to see how the apparently inevitable or 'natural' has nevertheless already been appropriated by ideology. For the family in *The Policeman's Daughter* – absent from the field of representation but everywhere implicit in the painting – reproduces an existing cultural order through the appointment of a subject in sexual difference. Such a reading takes into account the Oedipus complex and its heir, the superego, as performers of interpellation, producing subjects whose desires are congruent not only with patriarchy, but also with Salazarism. Considering *The Policeman's Daughter* through the overlapping filters of interpellation and Oedipalisation, we see that rather than being ahistorical and invariable, the body in the family is a body that is immersed both in ideology and in history, sexually differentiated in a particular and idiosyncratic way and armed to take its place in a chain of cultural transmission. For Althusser, as for Salazar, the policeman would be a typical – perhaps, alongside educators and priests, *the* typical – cultural agent of interpellation, incorporating and representing the dominant ideology through identification with an institution that enforces the law.

One might ask, looking at *The Policeman's Daughter*, where the jackboot, metonymic representation of the father, metaphoric representation of the state, has been; what it has kicked or squashed, what has stuck to it, what abject history is invisibly stamped upon its smooth surface, and with what powers, therefore, the obedient daughter is complicit. She exudes distaste, even defiance, but she is doing her duty. The implicit question here concerns the status of resistance: whether it is possible for the policeman's daughter to resist the ideologies of both Salazarism and patriarchy, without also attesting to their power. For the viewer, this raises a very particular problem: how to identify a critique which affirms, despite itself, the very thing it opposes, or, contrariwise, how to pick out of the affirmation of power a reaction to it. There is no simple resolution to this conundrum, but the question itself is important. If *Snow White Playing with her Father's Trophies* stages a mockery of patriarchal continuity, the political position of *The Policeman's Daughter* is more ambiguous.

This is a question that may also be productively framed in Foucaultian terms. In his avowedly anti-psychoanalytic view of power and subject formation, Michel Foucault affirms that power always produces resistance, that 'points of resistance are present everywhere in the power network' (Foucault, 1978: 95), so that the disciplined subject is also one who is always theoretically capable of exercising the liberty to oppose. '[A]side from torture and execution, which preclude any resistance,' he notes,

> no matter how terrifying a given system may be, there always remain the possibilities of resistance, disobedience, and oppositional groupings. On the other hand, I do not think that there is anything that is functionally, simply by its nature, absolutely liberating. Liberty is a *practice*. So there may be, in fact, always a certain number of projects whose aim is to modify some constraints, to loosen, or even to break them, but none of these projects can, simply by its nature, assure that people will have liberty automatically. (Foucault, 1984: 245)

It is in this sense, as an automatic guarantor of liberty, that resistance seems to be a taken-for-granted desideratum of some feminist theories. Yet examining Foucault's notion of power in her study of the ways in which injury has become the basis for political identity, feminist political theorist Wendy Brown flatly and more realistically observes that resistance *per se* 'goes nowhere in particular' and 'has no inherent attachments' (Brown, 1995: 49). She further points out that not only do disciplinary institutions and discourses confound emancipatory narratives, but that when a psychoanalytic account is added to the picture, when 'discipline becomes the stuff of our desire', then 'we may be seen not simply as lacking the desire for freedom, but desiring our very own subjection' (Brown, 1995: 19). In the policeman's obedient daughter, we see a female subject whose bodiliness announces these warring yet mutually collusive factions of the self.

The vulture

The preparatory sepia ink Study for *The Policeman's Daughter* (Figure 9) presents a different picture from the finished painting. The tense cat was preceded by a toy fort, making the connections to Salazarist iconography more explicit (the old military fort at Ericeira – Forte de Mil Regos – appears in the background of another painting of around the same time, *The Dance*). The cat in the painting, however, heightens the mood of unease as the static fort cannot do. In the sketch, the legs of the table are entangled with those of the chair. In the painting, pictorial economy has been purchased at the expense of realism: the tablecloth drops to the ground covering the table legs, and only one chair leg is now visible. The visible chair leg is more substantial than those in the sketch, and now, in its ornate profile, it carries more precise period allusions to the type of Indo-Portuguese chairs Rego remembers from her childhood. In thrusting up from the ground and meeting the place where the girl's bent leg is folded under her dress (and here again, for the sake of economy, there is no hint of a foot hidden within the draped folds), the chair leg itself seems to have an aggressive, phallic charge, almost impaling the girl.

The biggest change from sketch to painting is in the girl herself. In the sketch, she is much younger, more unambiguously compliant. She is also less robust, less assertive, less sexy, less *knowing*. Where, in the painting, her upright posture and stiff neck suggest distaste

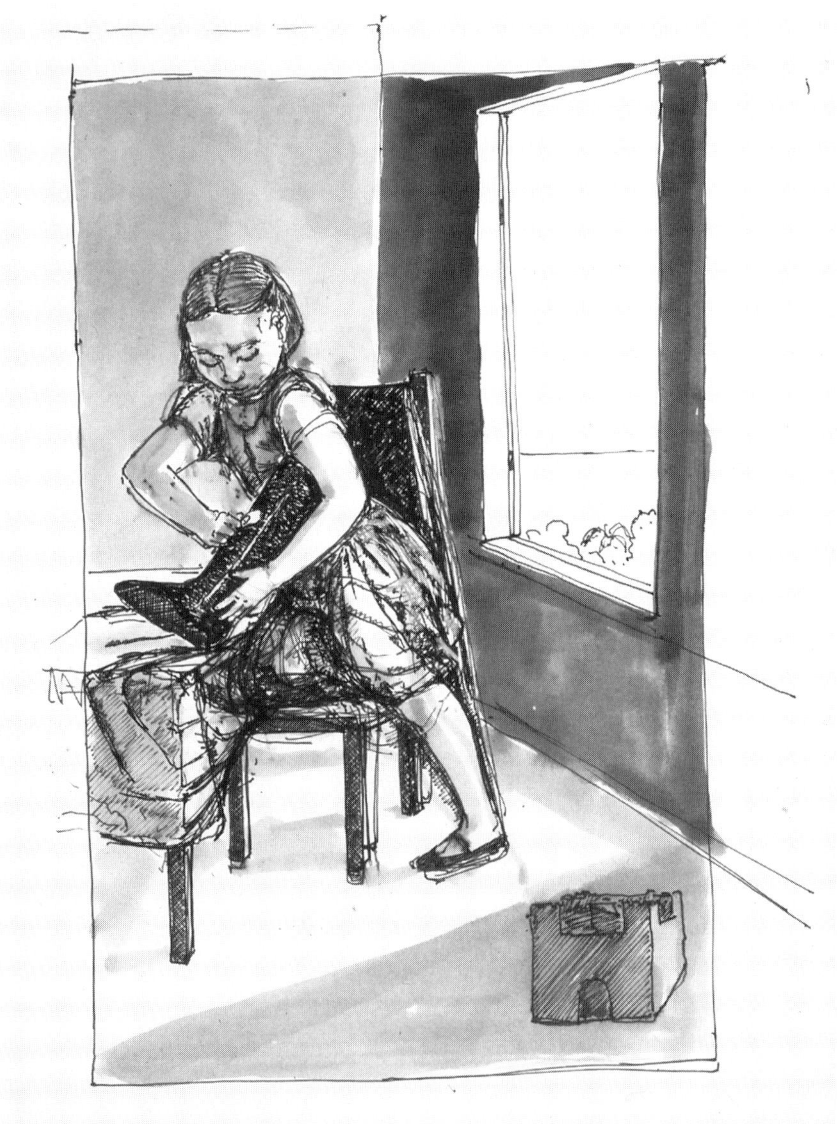

Figure 9   Paula Rego, Study for *The Policeman's Daughter*, 1987

and hostility, in the sketch she is bent over her task in unwavering concentration and dedication. Rather than thrusting her arm into the boot, she cradles it with one arm while polishing it with the other. The gesture is mimetically maternal. The painting, in other words, embodies an ambiguity absent from the sketch. What has happened between the sketch and the finished painting? Rego's words are startling:

> *The Policeman's Daughter* comes from *The Soldier's Daughter* – from the goose: the goose [in the former painting] was transformed into the girl in *The Policeman's Daughter.* I related that goose to the vulture in Freud's essay on Leonardo. The goose becomes the girl. But also, there's that photograph by Mapplethorpe of fist fucking. I had Vicky model for *The Policeman's Daughter* and she was cleaning the boot and then I remembered the Mapplethorpe photo and I said 'put your arm in it like that'. (Rego: in conversation)[10]

The link between Mapplethorpe and Leonardo sharpens the ambiguous gender identification and the sadistic eroticism of Rego's protagonist. Let us see how.

In a celebrated footnote added in 1919 to his 1910 essay on Leonardo – one of his earliest published references to narcissism and his first extended analysis of a manifest case of homosexuality – Freud famously discusses the figure of a vulture embedded in the composition of the later version of Leonardo's *Virgin and Child with St Anne.* He writes:

> A remarkable discovery has been made in the Louvre picture by Oskar Pfister, which is of undeniable interest, even if one may not feel inclined to accept it without reserve. In Mary's curiously arranged and rather confusing drapery, he has discovered the *outline of a vulture* and he interprets it as an *unconscious picture-puzzle.* 'In the picture that represents the artist's mother, *the vulture, the symbol of motherhood,* is perfectly clearly visible . . .' Pfister continues: 'The important question however is: How far does the picture-puzzle extend? If we follow the length of cloth, which stands out so sharply from its surroundings, starting at the middle of the wing and continuing from there, we notice that one part of it runs down to the woman's foot, while the other part extends in an upward direction and rests on her shoulder and on the child. The former of these parts might more or less represent the vulture's wing and tail, as it is in nature; the latter might be a pointed belly and – especially when we notice the radiating lines which resemble the outlines of feathers – a bird's outspread tail, whose right-hand end, *exactly as in Leonardo's fateful childhood dream* [sic], *leads to the mouth of the child, i.e. of Leonardo himself.* (Freud, 1910a: 115–116, italics in the original)

Pfister's analysis is significant to Freud because it retrospectively confirms Freud's speculations in the body of the text. Freud uses

Pfister to bolster his own theory of the origins of Leonardo's homosexuality in a childhood fantasy (a dream for Pfister becomes a fantasy to Freud) of a vulture that descended upon him in his cradle, and that, in Leonardo's words 'opened my mouth with its tail, and struck me many times with its tail against my lips' (Freud, 1910a: 82).[11] Notwithstanding Freud's now famous mistranslation of *nibio,* meaning not a vulture but a kite,[12] Freud notes the ubiquity of the symbolic coding of 'tail' – *coda* in Italian – as penis, and rapidly comes to the conclusion that Leonardo's account is a fantasy of fellatio transported back to the period of infantile suckling, the pleasure of which 'doubtless remains indelibly printed on us' (Freud, 1910a: 87). So the fantasy of fellatio is also a memory of the engulfing pleasure of being suckled, where the mother, in a reading legitimated by Pfister, is also a vulture. The maternal is devouring and threatens the child with annihilation.

For the link Freud establishes between Leonardo's homosexuality and his relationship with his mother, the mistranslation is essential. Indeed, Freud supports his theory by arguing that Leonardo must surely have been familiar with the association in ancient Egyptian legends between vultures and mothers: the single (female) sex of the vulture and the myth of her insemination by the wind, was 'seized on by the Fathers of the Church' (Freud, 1910a: 90) as an analogy for the Virgin Birth.[13] The veiled presence of a vulture in Leonardo's double portrait of maternity would therefore, Freud argues, not be random, reflecting Leonardo's unconscious identification of the vulture with his mother. This, for Freud, confirms the conclusions Leonardo would have drawn from his own youth when, as an illegitimate child, he was brought up for the first five years of his life by 'his poor, forsaken real mother' (Freud, 1910a: 91)[14] – in other words, like Jesus, as a child of a single mother. The vulture leads Freud to the phallic mother, with all the advantages she offers of an undivided love, and is used to sustain his speculation of Leonardo's identification with the fatherless Christ child in his own paintings.

Clearly misguided as an art historian (though also making no aesthetic claims), Freud misreads or ignores the more obvious contextual evidence, not least that offered by Leonardo's other work, using select details to support a theory already in place. Yet his study of Leonardo remains a brilliant conceit, serving to explore the nature not of art but of passive homosexuality. Freud's theory also underlines the ambivalent nature of maternal love. Leonardo experiences his mother's caresses as overwhelming, simultaneously loving and threatening, especially when combined with his father's absence:

> his mother's tenderness was fateful to him; it determined his destiny . . . The violence of the caresses, to which his phantasy of the vulture points, was only too natural. In her love for her child the poor forsaken mother had to give vent to all her memories of the caresses she had enjoyed as well as her longing for new ones; and she was forced to do so not only to compensate herself for having no husband, but also to compensate her child for having no father to fondle him.
> (Freud, 1910a: 116–117)

Here, Freud knots together loss and mourning with identification: mother and child each represent the lost father to the other. He continues: 'So, like all unsatisfied mothers, she took her little son in place of her husband, and by the too early maturing of his erotism robbed him of a part of his masculinity' (Freud, 1910a: 117). For Freud, that stolen part of Leonardo's masculinity is his heterosexuality: the clarity of a sexual orientation and gender position that, ideally, result from Oedipalisation.

Freud thus reveals the child to be caught between an indifferent paternal agency and an excessive maternal investment. With nothing to bar maternal seduction, Leonardo oscillates between replacing the father by imitating paternal indifference (his renowned coldness) on the one hand, and possessing the mother by imitating her possession of him on the other. Just as she loved a little boy, so he will love little boys. This narcissistic solution also allows the son to be faithful to his first love, the mother, by turning away from all other women. In the absence, then, of a punitive paternal agency to intervene between the child's and the mother's mutual incestuous desire, a fateful maternal kiss reveals Leonardo's precocious heterosexual maturity as too threatening. Thus trapped in an impossible sexuality, Leonardo is seen by Freud as an example of failed masculinity. In this failure, Freud identifies the tragedy of Leonardo's personal life and in its sublimation, the origin of his genius, but also the cause of the frequent incompletion of his works.

As we have seen, Freud's reading tells us more about Freud's theories than it does about Leonardo. Contemporary readings highlight all that is irresolute and troubled in Freud's monograph. Leo Bersani, who sees much of Freud's work as articulated around a process of theoretical collapse, brilliantly underlines the instability of the Freudian subject positions outlined in the Leonardo essay. He notes how in the vulture fantasy,

> Leonardo is at once being nursed and nursing; he is both being kissed and being nursed by his mother; it is Leonardo's own penis which the vulture-mother thrusts into his mouth; and the bird is at once the mysterious, loving mother and the child experiencing, in flight, the sexual satisfaction of his desire to be sexually satisfied. In these self-shattering fantasies, Leonardo is nowhere except in a certain readiness always to begin again his experimental representations of how and by what he has been shattered. (Bersani, 1986: 44)

Bersani reads Freud against the grain in order to produce alternative scenarios of kinship relations and, concomitantly, of sexuality. He proposes a psychoanalytic model which de-Oedipalises the father, replacing the 'paranoid nature of Oedipal sexuality' – the subject's persecution by paternal authority – by a structure where the father might duplicate, rather than repudiate, maternal love. Even if we reject such queer readings, Bersani's speculations highlight the complex and productive play of representations inaugurated by a traumatic precocity, and the sublimation and transformation of two forbidden impulses – of incestuous and homosexual libidinal energy – into creative and intellectual energy.

Jacqueline Rose uses Freud's Leonardo essay to make an important general point about Freud: she notes that not only is most of his monograph 'addressed to the artist's *failure*, that is, to the restrictions and limitations which Leonardo himself apparently experienced in relation to his potential achievement', but also that 'Freud takes failure very seriously' (Rose, 1986: 225). She is referring to the failure to produce the unambiguous gender identity and heterosexual desire that are, ideally, the outcome of Oedipalisation. 'It is often forgotten', she notes, 'that psychoanalysis describes the psychic law to which we are subject, but only in terms of its *failing*' (Rose, 1986: 232). Indeed, in his reiterated assertions of human bisexuality as the norm, Freud undoes the very law he wishes to instate. Rose thus observes that

> [t]he rest of Freud's writing shows that sexual difference is indeed such a hesitant and imperfect construction. Men and women take up positions of symbolic and polarised opposition against the grain of a multifarious and bisexual disposition . . . before recognising

its continuing and barely concealed presence across the range of normal adult sexual life. The lines of that division are fragile in exact proportion to the rigid insistence with which our culture lays them down; they constantly converge and threaten to coalesce. (Rose, 1986: 226–227)

A later lithograph, *Loving Bewick* (Figure 10), from the *Jane Eyre* series (2002, Rosenthal, 2003: n° 205) reiterates the formal arrangements of this duo. The allusion is to the engraver of natural history Thomas Bewick's *The History of British Birds* (vol. 1, 1797; vol. 2, 1804), mentioned in Charlotte Brontë's book, where, fascinated by the prints in Bewick's book, Jane notes how '[e]ach picture told a story; mysterious . . . yet ever profoundly interesting: as interesting as the tales Bessie sometimes narrated on winter evenings. . . With Bewick on my knee, I was then happy: happy at least in my way' (Brontë, 1996: 14–15). Bewick's book, in which Jane Eyre loses herself, is interesting both to Brontë and to Rego because it acts as an enabler of narrative: it prompts and encourages imaginary meanderings, storytelling. The vulture from Rego's *Girl Swallowing a Bird* (1996) – and indeed, Bewick's *Alpine Vulture and Crested Vulture* – are replaced by a huge, rapacious-looking pelican, gingerly inserting the tip of its beak into the girl's mouth as if to feed her, a gesture she receives with 'eucharistic rapture' (Warner, 2003: 9).

Three more drawings, all dated 1999, contain related motifs. Loosely executed in the rapid, fluent pen and ink strokes and watercolour washes that characterise the more intimate of Rego's drawings, they are notebook sketches of an improvisatory nature. Two of these drawings, both titled *Love* (Figures 11 and 12), portray a woman and a vulture at moments of seduction and embrace. The third, *The Dybbuk* (Figure 13), contemplates the eponymous character from Jewish folklore, a malevolent spirit of a dead person that has transmigrated into the body of a living person. Rego pictures the *dybbuk* in an image of violent oral expulsion and incorporation: first a bird is disgorged with apparent difficulty from the mouth of a winged female figure (the malevolent spirit emerging from the body of the deceased sinner), and then, itself winged, forces its beak into the mouth of its host body. These works together expose love not only as the violent intrusion of the Other, but also as cannibalistic identification. To love, they suggest, is to confront an Other that is by nature strange, and make it not so by incorporating it, thus also bringing strangeness in. But they also intimate, as Freud had done

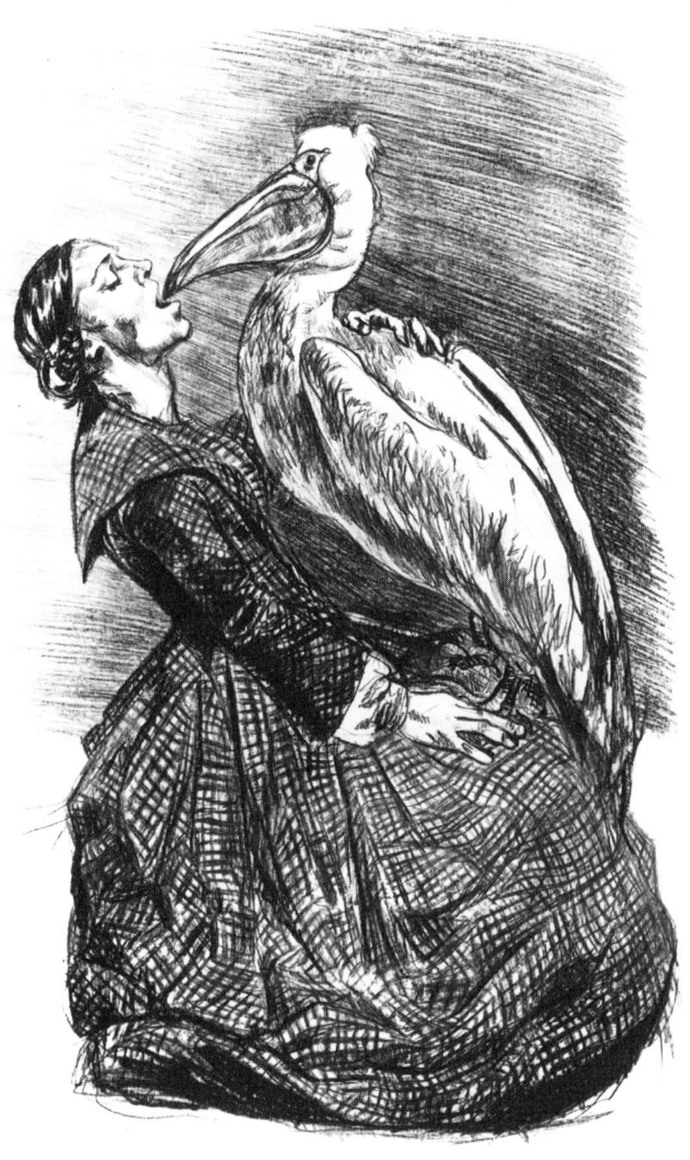

Figure 10   Paula Rego, *Loving Bewick*, 2000–01

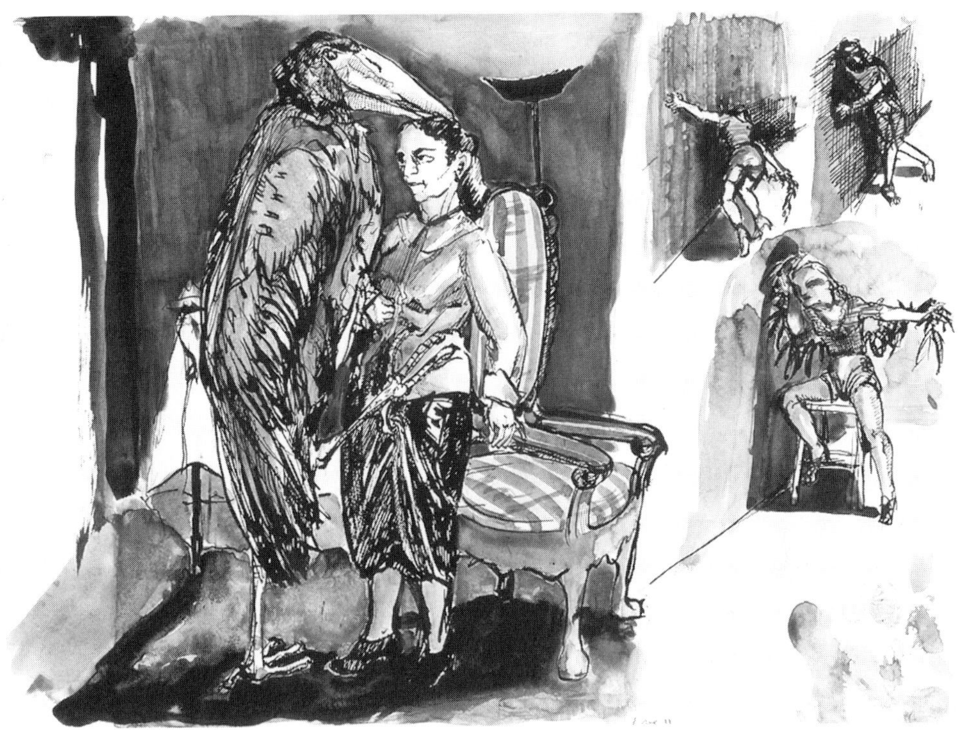

Paula Rego, *Love I*, 1999   Figure 11

in his account of Leonardo's fantasy, an analogy between fellatio and maternal nurturing. Indeed, if they align love with an incorporation of the object, they also evoke in love the masochistic desire for an aggression of which phallic penetration is the most acute instantiation.

The girl polishing her father's boot in *The Policeman's Daughter* has, Rego tells us, emerged out of *The Soldier's Daughter*. In this earlier painting, we see a girl sitting in the courtyard of a soldiers' barracks, plucking a dead goose wedged into her body, just as the vulture is fitted into the body's of St Anne and the Virgin in Pfister/ Freud's diagram of the Leonardo painting. Foregrounding the figure that traditionally lurks in the wings, 'the cook in the kitchen plucking feathers' (Rego in Mackenzie, 1991: 15), Rego invokes the private domain of women preparing the stage upon which History is played by male agents. Like the jackboot in *The Policeman's Daughter*, the goose is a symbolic substitution for the father invoked by the title of the painting. Held between the girl's parted knees, just as Snow

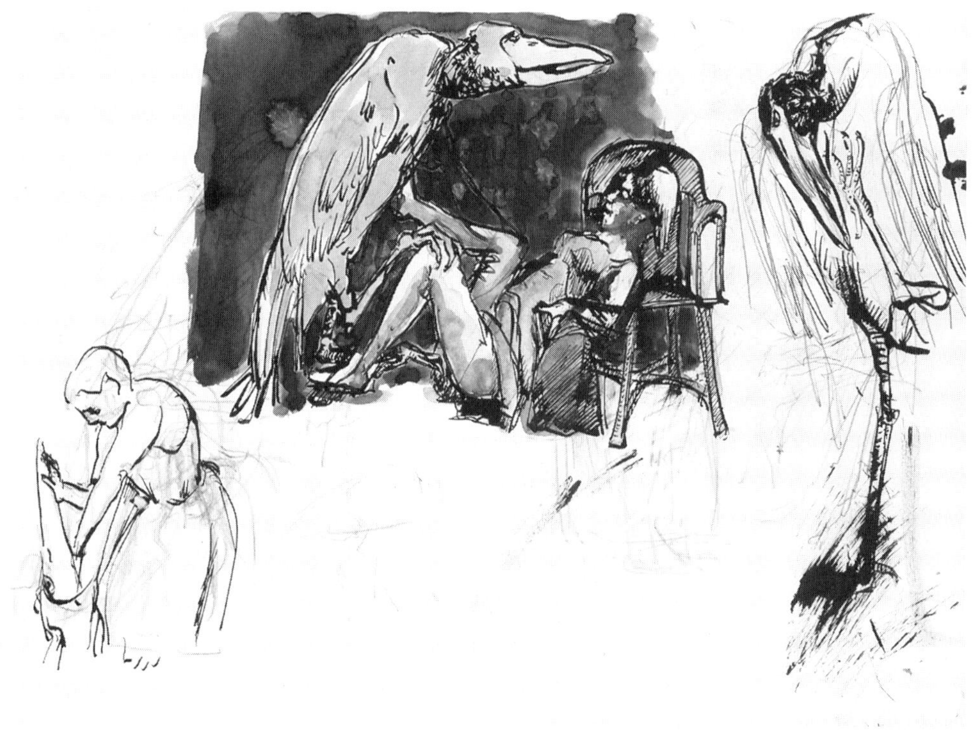

Figure 12   Paula Rego, *Love II*, 1999

White was later to hold the trophy of a stag's head, the goose is not so much domesticated as violently controlled. Here, too, fatherliness is equated with deadness: the long, phallic neck has been wrung and hangs limp, leaving the lifeless head twisted on the floor. The supple white curve described by the bird's corpse is evocative of innumerable eroticised representations of *Leda and the Swan*.

In her excellent analysis of *The Soldier's Daughter*, Maria Manuel Lisboa discusses the homology of goose and swan, reminding us that the swan was the disguise used by Zeus, exercising his *droit de seigneur* over Leda. Lisboa traces the long term consequences of this rape and of the progeny that was its consequence (Helen and Clytemnestra), observing that 'the tenor of these stories, seen from one angle, is the pitting of man against woman, or husband against wife, in betrayal and death, and the unleashing of conflicts at home and abroad'. This opposition, Lisboa suggests, is metaphorically staged by the props in the foreground of the painting, the toy figures playing out a conventional drama in miniature

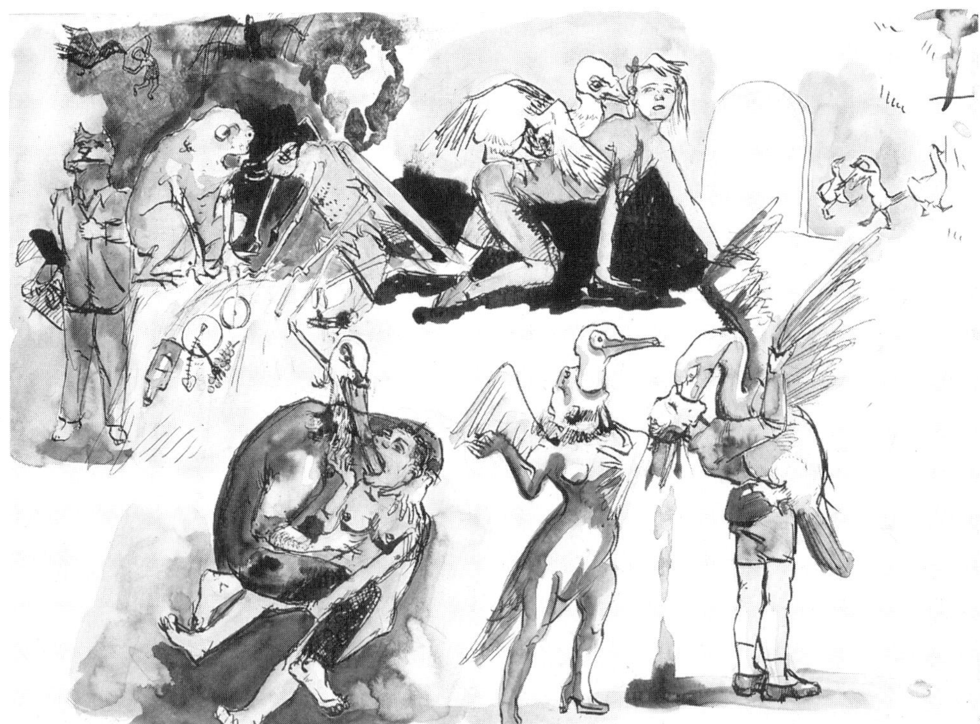

Paula Rego, *The Dybbuk*, 1999   Figure 13

scale: a departing soldier and a woman kneeling in prayer. 'The
scenario conjured up by these two figures is clearly that of the
archetypal "men must work and women must weep" plot', Lisboa
observes (2003: 81–84). Such a plot gains more specific currency
in the contexts invoked by Rego's painting: not only of the exemplary idealised family promoted by Salazarism, but also of the
Portuguese Colonial Wars in Africa, to which I shall return in the
next chapter.

In the passage from *The Soldier's Daughter* to *The Policeman's
Daughter*, the goose, Rego has told us, becomes the girl. In this
transit, the dead father is resurrected in an identification through
which the (phallic, dead) goose becomes the white-clad girl: what
is externally lost is internally recovered through identification. In
a single move, the girl absorbs the father she has lost and is not
only slotted into an assigned daughterly position as an Oedipalised
subject, but also, paradoxically, made to identify not with the sex to
which she has been assigned, but with the Other.

In *The Soldier's Daughter*, in her left hand the girl firmly grasps a wing; her right fist is deeply embedded in the flesh and feathers of the bird. If we read the dead goose as alluding to the traditional representations of Zeus who, disguised as the swan, raped Leda, *The Soldier's Daughter* must be seen as a work that inverts the traditionally gendered relations of brutality and helplessness, a work that in effigy pays sexual violence with immense aggression. This is confirmed when, from one painting to the next, the fist fucked goose becomes the fist fucking girl. In an extraordinary elision and collapse of active and passive roles, of desire and identification, of violator and victim, genders are exchanged and with them, not only is revenge meted out, but also the certainty of object choices is dissolved. Furthermore, one might say that in the passage between Leonardo and Mapplethorpe, identification by oral incorporation (the vulture's wing beating in the child's mouth) has been replaced by incorporation through anal penetration.

In Freud's scheme, the discovery of the anal phase of psychic organisation precedes the oral and the phallic phases: as Diana Fuss puts it, 'Freud's famous theory of the three partial drives [oral, anal and phallic] makes its dramatic entry onto the psychoanalytic stage arse backwards' (Fuss, 1995: 85). While in principle related to particular organs, the drives as Freud describes them tend to co-exist and to be dynamic and porous in the adult; perversion, with regard to 'correct' organ use, is more a question of *degree* ('exclusiveness' or 'fixation') than of *kind* of sexual activity. Thus it is that while in the case histories of the Wolf Man and the Rat Man, anal intercourse is constitutive of homosexual eroticism, in his early *Three Essays on Sexuality*, Freud asserts that a predilection for anal intercourse 'by no means coincides with inversion' (Freud, 1905b: 105). Rather, surprisingly, it owes its origins 'to an analogy with a similar act performed with a woman' (Freud, 1905b: 152). What we have here, then, is a model of subject formation and of sexuality that is shot with violence and riddled with contradiction. Rather than slotting unproblematically into an assigned gender position, we see the Freudian subject as doomed to ambiguity. Its relation to the law of desire condemns it to failure; its objects and identifications slide away from resolution.

Published in 1923, Freud's essay *The Ego and the Id* is the most explicit exposure of this fundamental uncertainty, where each child experiences both a positive and a negative Oedipus complex, in turns identifying with *and* repudiating the desired *and* the rival parent. Read together, *Leonardo da Vinci and a Memory of his Childhood* and *The Ego and the Id* present an unstable picture of our desires and their objects. Yet it must be said that, however arbitrary our objects are, we are, as subjects, obliged to distinguish between inner and outer objects, between the real and the psychic. Freud had observed in his *Three Essays on Sexuality*, and implied in 'Family Romances', that the finding of an object was always in fact a re-finding, a reiteration of the child's first attachments. However, subject formation – the individual's acculturation – forces us to choose between incest and incestuous fantasy, between murder and murderous desire.

The Policeman's Daughter offers us an image of the female subject positioned to make this distinction. As I have shown, we are dealing with a 'typical' female subject both within a specific historical and political context, and within patriarchy at large; one whose compliance with both father and state plays a mediating role in a chain of transmission. Her expression of disdain cannot counter the pressures (of the intertwined forces of ideology and superego) within her. However, reading through the combined filters of Leonardo, Mapplethorpe and Freud, we are invited to acknowledge a more complex web of object choices, incorporations and identifications, troubling the clear-cut assignment of positions described by the Freudian family romance.

For the well behaved girl, all primped and pruned and ready to play her ideologically honed role, anal penetration becomes the ultimate form of domination, and of subversion. Maria Manuel Lisboa reads this painting as staging a symbolic revenge against father–daughter incest, as an inversion of the customary (gendered and generational) relation between violence and helplessness (Lisboa, 2003: 83). She places, in other words, the protagonist squarely in a political discourse. Contrariwise, following Jacqueline Rose, I have attempted to throw into relief the ways in which the distinction between outside and inside – politics and psyche – speciously polarises 'us as women' as 'either pure victim or sole agent of our distress' (Rose, 1989: 98). Rose asks

> what could be the understanding of violence which, while fully recognizing the historical forms in which it has repeatedly been directed towards women, none the less does not send it out wholesale into the real from which it can only return as an inevitable and hallucinatory event? How can we speak the fact that violence moves across boundaries, including that of sexual difference, and not only in fantasy. (Rose, 1986: 106)

In *The Policeman's Daughter*, I have found an operation of the dialectic between outside and inside, performed as the relationship between history and ideology on the one hand, and the desires and imperatives that underpin the family romance on the other.

Finally, a word must be said about the part that language plays here. As significant verbal associations come to be embodied and performed in dreams, so here the policeman's daughter materialises a play of visual and verbal signifiers. In Portuguese, the word for 'polish' – as in 'to polish a boot' – is *engraxar*. Its colloquial meaning is something like 'to be obsequious', or, more crudely, 'to brown-nose'. Another expression for this would be *lamber botas* – as in English, to lick someone's boots. The metaphors are all abjectly bodily: nose, anus, tongue. One hand polishes – massages, licks, assuages; the other is rammed up the father's boot. The verbal evocation here is aggressive: the Portuguese insult *vai levar no cu* (literally 'go take it in the arse') springs to mind. The obedient daughter is one whose bodiliness is the site where both the law and resistance to it are interiorised. In *The Policeman's Daughter*, such a tension is both embodied and performed. It is as if the left hand violently opposed what the right hand was doing, but both knew they were doing the right thing. With repeated, regular, brusque and practical strokes, the right hand is servicing the father; the left hand – traditionally identified with subversion – is aggressively gesturing 'up yours!'

Notes

1   The paradox of course is that in order for the girl to perceive her body as the site of a lack, the phallus has to have had prior significance.

2   Homi Bhabha seeks to define the relationship between nation building and the role of narrative, where the 'political rationality of the nation' might be depicted as a form of narrative. This relativises, contextualises and contests 'the traditional authority of those national objects of knowledge – Tradition, People, the Reason of the State, High Culture' that are frequently invoked in attempts to locate the nation within a historical continuum (Bhabha, 1990: 2–3).

3   For an excellent analysis of the relation of Salazarism to Fascism, see Costa Pinto, 1995. Like many other historians, Costa Pinto thinks that Salazarism was influenced by, but does not coincide with, the Fascist prototype and its totalitarian turn in the 1930s. A key text – the first in which Salazar's *Estado Novo* was discussed in any depth outside Portugal – is Hermínio Martins' essay 'Portugal' (Martins, 1968). Martins dis-

cusses Salazar's roots not in Fascism, but in the Portuguese movement *Integralismo Lusitano* – Lusitanian Integralism – influenced by the *Action Française* and a Maurrassian loathing for demo-liberalism. Manuel Lucena considers Salazar a 'fascist without a Fascist movement' (*fascista sem movimento fascista*) (Lucena, 1976: 27).

4 Simon Kuin notes that OMEN had far less social and political import than its Italian correlate, the *Opera Nazionale per la Maternità e l'Infanzia* because it was more difficult for the state to exercise direct control over the family than over larger social cells such as the school. However, the demagogy of the ruling ideologues insisted on the importance of the family for the propagation of their values; furthermore, it is not necessary for the state to have direct influence on the family for idealised family values to be reproduced (Kuin, 1993: 555). Irene Flunser Pimentel has done important, exhaustive research on OMEN and on the female youth movements (Pimentel, 2001, 2007b).

5 Under international pressure, after World War Two, several Portuguese institutions were given more sanitised, neutral names. In 1945, the *Secretariado de Propaganda Nacional* (Secretariat of National Propaganda) was renamed the *Secretariado Nacional de Informação, Cultura Popular e Turismo:* National Secretariat of Information, Popular Culture and Tourism.

6 In 1931, women gained partial suffrage and conditional eligibility for the National Assembly, and in 1934 the conditions were slightly altered. The opposition feared what both the regime and the Catholic Church believed, that the female vote would favour Salazar and sponsor both higher morale and a more vigorous re-Christianisation. The restrictions on female suffrage were only lifted in 1976, after the fall of the regime. For the rights of women under the *Estado Novo*, see Pimentel, 2001: 30–32.

7 Not coincidentally, 1938 was also the year in which the Minister of Public Works, Duarte Pacheco, proposed ambitious and utopian new projects for roads, monuments, bridges and schools. Hermínio Martins notes that Portugal's attempt to develop an imperial consciousness through various official policies enjoyed only a modicum of success. Martins, 1968: 332.

8 Maria Filomena Mónica quotes the popular punning adage 'Quem dá o pão, dá o pau' – literally 'he who gives bread also gives the stick' – based on the homophony between the words 'bread' (*pão*) and 'stick' (*pau*) (Mónica 1978: 273).

9 For a brilliant analysis of the figure of the turn in interpellation, see Butler, 1997: 106–109.

10 See also Bradley, 1997: 22.

11 '. . . que un nibio venissi a me e mi aprissi la bocca colla sua coda e

molte volte mi percuotesse con tal coda dentro alla labbra.' Quoted in an editor's footnote (Freud, 1910a: 82).

12 Following Peter Gay's biography of Freud, Diana Fuss suggests that in 1923 Freud was informed of his mistake by Pfister, but refused to make any significant alterations to the Leonardo paper (Fuss, 1995: 88).

13 Meyer Schapiro argues that to re-examine its 'manifest content by ordinary textual study' in the context of Leonardo's other drawings and notes, and of contemporary associations within the broader culture, would reveal the kite to be a bird of destiny, an omen of fortune or genius (Schapiro, 1956: 151–155). Any association between 'vulture' and 'mother' would of course also be eradicated.

14 Twice in the text, Freud refers to his 'poor, forsaken' mother. Leonardo's father married one Donna Albiera, but the marriage remained childless. When Leonardo was five, he was taken, so to speak, under his stepmother's wing. It is the existence of 'two mothers' that Freud reads into the double maternity of Leonardo's *Virgin and Child with St Anne*.

Men don't make passes at
women with moustaches:
The Interrogator's Garden

3

> The powers of the weak – to curse and criticize – set limits on the power of the strong – to coerce and ordain. (Victor Turner, 'Flame, Flow and Reflection')

> Within the physical events of torture, the torturer 'has' nothing: he has only an absence, the absence of pain. In order to experience his distance from the prisoner in terms of 'having', their physical difference is translated into a verbal difference: the absence of pain is a presence of world; the presence of pain is the absence of world. Across this set of inversions pain becomes power. (Elaine Scarry, *The Body in Pain*)

Violence turned in

It is common knowledge that children who have had violence or abuse visited upon them frequently, in adulthood, become perpetrators of violence and abuse. This shift from passive victim to active agent is psychically staged for each individual as the transit of violence from id to superego: the repressive agency of the superego is, in Freud's account, nourished by the id's violence that it controls. But it also, in sanctioned conditions, re-enacts it.

As we have seen, the tripartite configuration of Freud's second topography – the distinction between id, ego and superego – cannot be simply mapped as geological strata of increasing depth. The superego is, in important ways, closer to the id than to the ego of which it is a part. Apparently at odds, the id and the superego are in effect interdependent: paradoxically, the id's operations can only be apprehended through the agency of the superego, which acts as the id's delegate vis-à-vis the ego. The superego, then, incorporates the id's own violence, and, in constituting conscience, punitively turns this aggression against the ego. In the relationship of id to superego, Freud tells us, raw aggression is disciplined and repressed, and in this process, the 'lowest part is transformed to the highest part of the human mind' (Freud, 1923: 37). To be repressed, in other words, is to be civilised. So: it is not simply that the superego counters violence with violence. It is also that, in the name of civilisation, it takes on the aggression of the drives it restrains. 'Inside the child', observes Jacqueline Rose, 'is a degraded relic of the father's authority' (Rose, 1993: 205). If, then, the effect of the dissolution of the Oedipus complex and the consequent institution of the superego is the domestication of the subject, this occurs through a reflexive movement, a violent subjective turn that incorporates the injunctions of an-other. In the subject's entry into the Symbolic Order, an injurious address is inseparable from subjectivity itself.

This has both political and psychic implications. Between self-determination and subjection, the self forges its agency through being implicated in the relations of power it also seeks to oppose. Put otherwise, it is not simply that the subject's internal police is as violent as the violence it aims to control, but that these are two sides of the same coin: discipline is most effective when its subject and object are one and the same. But the Freudian superego is not only a censorious agency: it also incorporates an ideal. In his paper 'On Narcissism: An Introduction' of 1914, Freud linked the formation of an ego ideal to the subject's longing for its own lost narcissism, noting how the child had created an ideal by projecting its primary narcissism onto the parents. But by the time he wrote *The Ego and the Id* in 1923, this projected, narcissistic ego ideal had given way to an ideal that the subject garnered from its primary caregivers. Such an ideal is, Freud suggests, congruent with the values of the culture at large.

Already in 'On Narcissism', Freud stresses that that the ego ideal has 'a social side: it is also the common ideal of a family, a class, a nation' (Freud, 1914b: 81). It is this communal – indeed, civilisational – ideal of rectitude, serving as the measure against which the ego is judged, that emerges in the later paper. In effect, what we witness, then, is a shift in orientation of the ego ideal from narcissistic projection to an idealisation that is nothing short of Oedipal. So, in *The Ego and the Id*, Freud tells us that the ego ideal is

> the heir of the Oedipus complex, and thus it is also the expression
> of the most powerful impulses and most important libidinal vicissi-
> tudes of the id. By setting up this ego ideal, the ego has mastered the
> Oedipus complex and at the same time placed itself in subjection to
> the id. (Freud, 1923: 36)

With its source relocated, the ideal paradoxically enjoins the subject
both to be and *not* to be like the parental model (Freud, 1923: 35).[1]

But there is more: in the passage from narcissistic ego ideal to
a parentally or paternally inspired, conscience inducing superego,
there occurs an eruption of extraordinary violence. The harshness
of the superego is never so emphatic as in Freud's radical observation that it is the gathering place for the death instincts, which he
defines as the drive towards organic equilibrium and inertia. 'How
is it', Freud asks in this seminal work, 'that the super-ego manifests
itself essentially as a sense of guilt (or rather, as criticism – for the
sense of guilt is the perception in the ego answering to this criticism)
and moreover develops such extraordinary harshness and severity
towards the ego?' (Freud, 1923: 53).

He finds his answer in the link between the ego, the superego
and melancholia. As we saw in the previous chapter, Freud observes
that certain features that he had earlier attributed to melancholia
are, in fact, constitutive of what he calls 'character' in general. One
of those features is the ego's setting up of its lost objects inside
itself in an identificatory substitution. The other is the fact that in
melancholia the conscience, 'one of the major institutions of the
ego' (Freud, 1917b: 247), splits off and turns against the rest of the
ego. In 'Mourning and Melancholia' (Freud, 1917b), Freud had
expressed a hunch that this split off critical agency might be autonomous, but he does so without naming it. When, in *The Ego and the
Id*, he revisits this passage, he identifies that agency as the superego.
First he makes the connection between melancholia and 'character'
explicit; and then he recognises in this connection something that
he had previously identified in *Beyond the Pleasure Principle* (Freud,
1920), but that he now chillingly speaks of as 'a pure culture of the
death instinct' (Freud, 1923: 53). The death instinct, then, finds
itself lodged in the superego.

This is an astonishingly dark picture of a subject under the sway
of its own violence:

> If we turn to melancholia first, we find that the excessively strong
> super-ego which has obtained a hold upon consciousness rages

> against the ego with merciless violence, as if it had taken posses-
> sion of the whole of the sadism available in the person concerned.
> . . . What is now holding sway in the super-ego is, as it were, a pure
> culture of the death instinct, and in fact it often enough succeeds in
> driving the ego into death, if the latter does not fend off its tyrant in
> time by the change round into mania. (Freud, 1923: 53)

Harsh taskmaster, parental and cultural ideal, inducer of conscience, internal tyrant, gatherer of death instincts: these are
astonishingly severe images for a constitutive part of the self. Such
metaphors for the superego are hardly compatible with laughter.
(Put otherwise, one might say that there is nothing funny about
torture.) And yet, Freud suggests that such violence can be warded
off by 'mania' – by a kind of carnivalesque, perhaps hysterical fes-
tivity. The ego might fend off its own torment, might escape being
victimised by that despot, the superego, by turning depression into
mania.

It is to the superego that Freud returns in his short paper
'Humour' of 1927. In his succinct account of the operations of
humour, which he links to the advent of the ego and the triumph
of narcissism, Freud surprisingly figures the superego as a solicitous
and somewhat condescending parent who consoles and protects its
child, the ego. It is not only that humour makes suffering endur-
able, but – in this perverse and scandalous inversion – that the very
agent of suffering is transformed into the *agent provocateur* of laughter. It is these two apparently incompatible views of the superego as
vigilante and consoler that are invoked in Paula Rego's painting *The
Interrogator's Garden* (2000).

Women and men

In *The Interrogator's Garden* (Plate 2) a heavyset inquisitor sits on a
chair, half turned toward the viewer, gloved hands upon a pitchfork
that rests in the ample lap. The garden to which the title alludes is
comically represented by a disconsolate, pruned pot plant in the
foreground, and some strange bursts of flower behind the interrogator. In the background, through an open doorway, we glimpse a
bleak beach.

In her politicised reading of Rego's work, Maria Manuel Lisboa
reads the desolate beach settings that appear in Rego's paintings
from the 1980s on as allusions to the Portuguese maritime history
of Atlantic expansionism. Indeed, to this day, the construction of

national identity holds dear a myth of the 'Discoveries' as foundational, suggesting a melancholy attachment to an object long lost but never fully mourned. However, the beach settings seem to carry a more generalised connotation of longing, distance and Portugueseness. The importance of autobiographical triggers, in Rego's work, as mnemonics for the past cannot be emphasised strongly enough. She loves the Atlantic coastline of Estoril and Cascais where she spent her childhood, while nostalgically associating the beach at the fishing town of Ericeira to her family's holiday home.

The interior space of the room in which the interrogator sits is plainly divided by a horizontal line demarcating dark wall from grey floor on the left side of the painting. The back wall is split into two uneven vertical sections. The work is made in pastel, and its vigorous marks tighten around the interrogator's head and body, but break into looser hatchings as the viewer's eye moves from foreground to background, as if mimicking the focus of vision itself, homing in on the human subject. To the right, the brightly lit exterior is shown through a doorway. Its bottom edge is obscured by filled bin liners and unruly plants, from which an occasional flower bursts forth irrepressibly. This rectangle demarcated from the larger space of the work is ambiguous, for we are left uncertain as to whether it is, indeed, a door, whether a painting-within-a-painting, or whether a mirror reflecting an action taking place in the space that we occupy as viewers. Such devices – whether doors or pictures or mirrors – recur in Rego's work: *Time – Past and Present, The First Mass in Brazil* and *After 'Marriage à la Mode' by Hogarth* are all examples. These are pictorial devices with a long history in Western painting, whether underlining the paradoxes of painterly illusion by opening out onto a world of potentially infinite regress, or playing with various levels of identity and reality. Usually, they provide iconographic clues to the principal scene. Through this opening, we catch sight of a young woman in underwear stepping into or out of a large bin bag, similar to those that contain the garden detritus strewing the floor behing the interrogator. She is more faintly sketched in than the interrogator, rendered in economic, wispy marks.

In the context of the emblems and kitsch paraphernalia of authoritarian power, the garden detritus in the sealed bags becomes eerily suggestive of body bags, situating the interrogator plainly within a discourse of power and violence. As a ready metaphor for victimisation and sacrifice, a lamb with its back foot attached to a ball of string is strapped to the chair with a menacing black belt. A white feather – traditionally, a symbol of cowardice – completes the picture. The representation of a human body surrounded by emblems ironically recalls the Renaissance and Baroque traditions of picturing saints along with the symbols of their martyrdom, or the representation of allegorical figures accompanied by conventional motifs culled from a pre-existing iconographic lexicon, such as Cesare Ripa's *Iconografia*. Reading the image through the emblems, one might say that the ascription of cowardice to the interrogator plays directly against his power to tether, entrap and hold hostage.

The moustachioed interrogator is seated on a chair, positioned comfortably and confidently, head facing us squarely, body turned at an angle so that one knee butts into our space, while the other is shown in profile. The torso is slumped, the thick legs set apart, feet planted firmly on the ground. The interrogator has found a pompous sartorial solution appropriate to both horticulture and bullying cross examination. The contrast between a benign activity like gardening (an activity that, like art, represents civilisation itself) and the violence of interrogation (as a breach in the codes of shared, empathic, civilised humanity) highlights what Hannah Arendt has famously termed the banality of evil: not so much its immersion in the workings of an ordinary, humdrum quotidian, but its incapacity for critical thought.

The interrogator's generic military costume consists of a pair of khaki shorts, a camouflage jacket and a Sam Browne strapped across the chest. When I first discussed this work with Rego, she claimed that she had wanted to dress the interrogator in the uniform of the *Mocidade Portuguesa*, the Portuguese para-military youth organization founded in 1936. The uniform, however, is not similar to that of any of the ranks of the *Mocidade Portuguesa*, which the artist later depicted in *Madame Lupescu Has Her Fortune Told* (2004; Figure 14). At a later date, Rego said this uniform has nothing to do with the youth organisation: 'Mary Magdalene in the triptych *Martha, Mary, Mary Magdalene* (1999) is the closest to the *Mocidade Portuguesa*', she observed (Rego: in conversation). A tiny figure wearing the uniform of *Mocidade Portuguesa Feminina* also appears in the foreground of *War* (2003).

The interrogator also sports a pair of stiff, bright red gardening gloves. But for their camp high heels, the heavy black boots seem ready for military action, but they also look sufficiently robust to

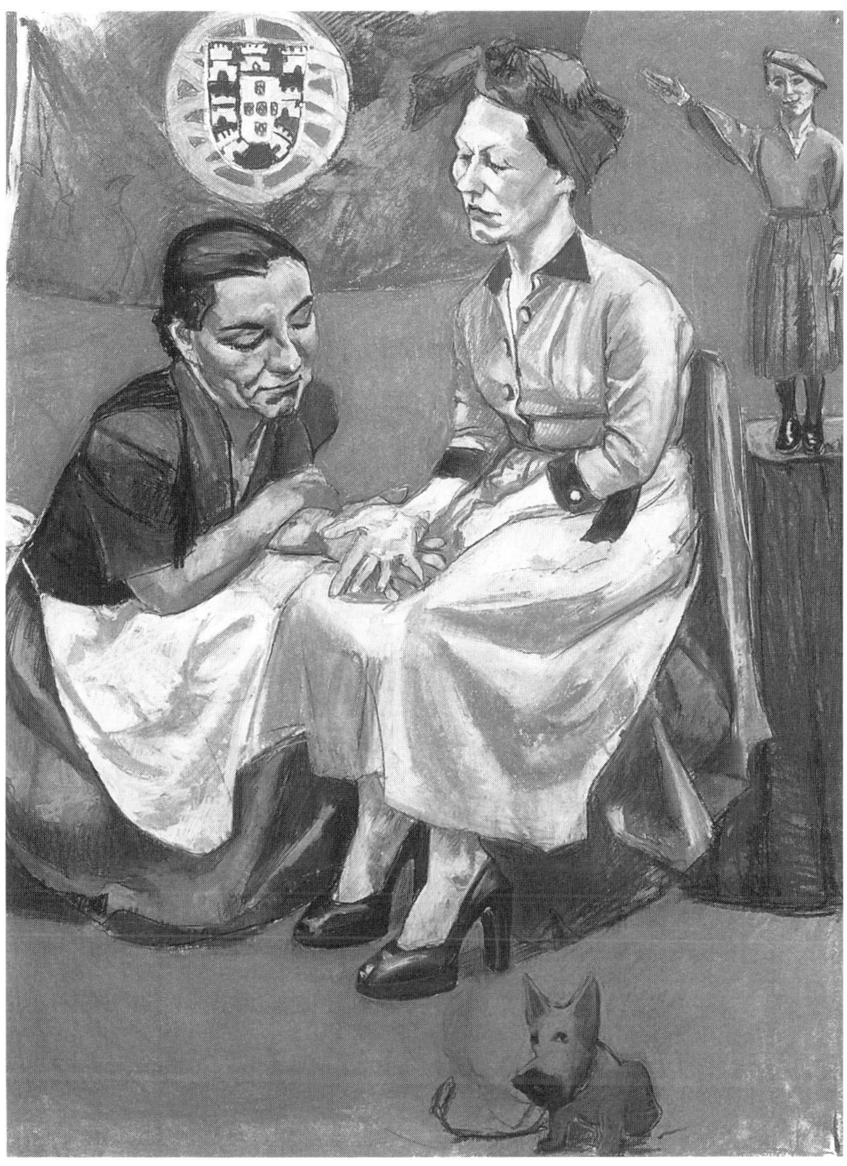

Paula Rego, *Madame Lupescu has her Fortune Told*, 2004   Figure 14

be waterproof: good enough for gardening, they are also protective of anything unsightly through which the swaggering inquisitor might have to tiptoe. Under the high, peaked military cap, the interrogator's expression is assured, smug. Beneath the black pencil moustache, the mouth smirks.

The interrogator is a woman.

Here is how Rego describes the genesis of this painting:

> I was asked by the Foundation for the Victims of Torture to do something for them to sell, and I was told this story about a girl who was arrested. It's a terrible story; she was saved because her uncle bribed the guards to dump her in a binliner on top of a lot of other things in the rubbish. This is the sort of thing that happens with people who are tortured for political reasons, they are dumped in the rubbish. This girl was saved because she was dumped alive and able to get out of there. I thought 'that's what I'm going to do, I'm going to do this Interrogator's garden where he is just looking after his flowers.' So I thought 'what fun, Lila, you dress up as an inquisitor', so she got all padded and I went out to buy the gardening gloves and all that, and there she is.

'So this is a sort of comic tragedy', the interviewer observes. 'Yes, sort of piss-taking if you like', the artist responds (King, 2001: 12).

An attack against privilege and authority by 'taking the piss' is, of course, one of the usual aims of satire; and the use of status or gender inversion as a form of symbolic redress is a standard ploy of rituals of reversal such as traditionally take place on Carnival or Midsummer's Night. But there is something that baldly shocks in the casual delight ('what fun') linked to the psychic and political connotations of interrogation and torture.

Although the events of Abu Ghraib will have advertised the extent to which such cruelty is not necessarily gender specific, the reversal of gender expectation must be seen, in the context of Rego's work, as partaking of a conscious strategy of subversion: 'my favourite themes', she has commented, 'are power games and hierarchies. I always want to turn things on their heads, to upset the established order, to change heroines and idiots' (McEwen, 2006: 138). Such subversive intent, aiming to mock men and empower women, is clearly feminist in orientation. But in what way can the empowerment of *The Interrogator's Garden* be considered feminist? And what plea can Rego's work in general make for feminism?

Feminism has had a role to play in the disciplinary self-critique of art history. Its claims for artistic practice have been articulated around several, at times contradictory, key issues. The appeal for equality (a feminism which concentrates on historical and sociological factors such as labour conditions or exploitation) is opposed to a psychoanalytically inflected feminism of difference. These two orientations – equality and difference – have generated divergent strains of theory and practice. Schematically put, they tend to correspond to different historical moments: clearly, the feminism of difference depends on the prior labour of the feminism of equality. These, in turn, have also spawned quite distinct methodologies for the theorisation of feminine subjectivity, methodologies that are further unsettled by the claims of other liberatory practices or discourses, such as those of class or race or sexual orientation; positions that, for some artists especially in the 1960s and 1970s, overtake feminism as the dominant discourse.

But with all their divergences, the various forms of feminism as theory and practice have generated an enabling discourse around female agency within culture. Feminism sponsored, in the first instance, a retrospective reconstruction of a historical lineage by disinterring the work of practitioners who had operated outside of the canon, asserting the importance of the representations of women *by* women. As early as 1971, with Linda Nochlin's justly famous essay 'Why Have there been no Great Women Artists?', this kind of redressing of the canonical imbalance already seemed naïve: Nochlin was intent on revealing the conceptual limitations of the question itself, recasting its terms (such as 'greatness' or 'genius') in relation to the social institutions that sponsor them (Nochlin, 1991).

Feminism has granted women a voice, and, in doing so, it has also sponsored a consciousness of how authorship is gendered. Deconstructing the ways in which sexual difference is naturalised in art, cinema or advertising; dissecting the economy of vision and reconfiguring the traditional gendering of viewer and viewed; insisting on the insertion of art into broader social contexts and its ensnarement in signifying systems and institutions in the public sphere; promoting self-consciously gendered forms of intervention: all of these can be said to have been part of a feminist critical and operational agenda from the mid-1970s.

The more psychoanalytic concerns of feminist art practice could be described as disrupting the consolation offered by those female bodies that, from the Renaissance to our present day, have been depilated and ornamented, neutralised and aestheticised. Jacqueline Rose has convincingly argued that aesthetic perfection is reassuring because it erases violence. Most importantly, it disavows castration, or the fear of it, by denying imperfection and incompleteness. Beauty makes us momentarily forget loss. For

Rose, then, a feminism articulated within the visual field disrupts the image of plenitude offered by the phallic mother (the woman fantasised as both maternal and complete, i.e. possessing a penis) and disturbs the very opposition between male and female that 'any image seen to be flawless is serving to hold in place' (Rose, 1986: 232).

Rego's large, discomfiting girl-women are bulky and anything but pretty. Their assertive, clumsy bodiliness evokes odours, hair, blemishes. In this refusal to picture the svelte, the cool, the beautiful – their refutation of a fantasy of seamless, uncontaminated physicality – these images refuse to comply with fetishistic disavowal. Following Rose, I would argue that to counter beauty with it opposites, its discontents, is to trigger or challenge castration anxiety. In never appeasing this anxiety through covering up the ugliness or the loss, these girl-women serve as constant reminders of the potential undoing that forms the kernel of such anxiety. An argument such as Rose's, I am suggesting, would frame Rego's figurations as confrontationally feminist.

Rego has frequently stated that the desire for revenge in effigy colours much of her work ('my work is about revenge, always, always' (Tusa, 2001: 10)) – a desire, in other words, for a redemptive self-purging. The specificity of such revenge is, however, quickly overridden by an immersion in the working process. 'I sometimes do work for revenge, but that very quickly vanishes and becomes something else; it's only just a kick start. And I lose myself in what I'm doing, in the work' (Rego: in conversation). Indeed, the 'piss taking' of Rego's work remains more ambiguous than that of political lampoons. The anger it performs is at once private and collective. 'I feel politically strongly about women', she has affirmed. 'I think that the world is becoming more of a man's world again. As a woman who is a painter, I think there is a story to tell that has not been told before' (Blyth 2003: 47).

So, if she is operating within a feminist framework, why has Rego made this podgy little tyrant a woman? Whom is she mocking here? And is this burlesque or parody like or unlike carnivalesque reversal; like or unlike the acerbic humour of political lampoons? To mock repressive authority is the legacy of a long lineage of satirical artists. But how does *The Interrogator's Garden* square with such a project? For, despite its subversive humour, the intimidating image of an interrogator as a moustached woman provokes discomfort: there is contained, outrageous violence in this unexpected gender reversal upon which the work's political impact hangs.

Violence embodied: body as narrative

As many of her exegetes have recognised, violence has always been at the heart of Rego's pictorial endeavour. Her earliest work is playfully satirical. But the mordant observation of human behaviour is traversed by empathy (and sometimes pathos) that is not always compatible with the more vitriolic eighteenth- and nineteenth-century satirical work she admires, such as Rowlandson, Gilray, Hogarth, Grandville and Daumier. While the chunky figuration of the paintings Rego made as a student at the Slade School of Art in London bears traces not of William Coldstream, who was then its director, but of Portuguese Neo-Realism,[2] the themes and quirky humour of her juvenilia marry the Portuguese kitchen or farm yard with the London street. Not for her, then, the Portuguese Neo-Realist romance with agricultural labour: she preferred to capture spivs or soldiers and their tarted up girlfriends; servants in the kitchen or blue-collar workers lunching; tourists out on the town ostentatiously ignoring the poor; the well-heeled bourgeoisie at leisure; girls fighting in the school playground; or a Cockney Pearly Queen. From 1960, however, the subject matter becomes more consistently identifiable with Portugueseness, more visceral and violent, and also more overtly political.

The paintings of 1959–61 and the collages of 1960–66 (see Plates 5 and 6, and Figures 4 and 6) satirise the brutality of both Salazar's and Franco's regimes. But they also render violence explicit in the emphatic physicality of their facture. Under the sway of Dubuffet and *Art Brut*, Rego's paintings and drawings of the early 1960s evince an immediacy and directness of attack that brings with it something of the aggression of the nursery. Paradoxically, the works of greater abstraction seem to enable the expression of a more violent, wittier critique, invoking Jarry, Miró and Picasso of the 1930s. Cut and torn, pasted and scribbled, the dispersed and fragmented images of Rego's collages from this time are bound together by audaciously painted grounds that slip around, behind or over the forms, embracing and containing them. The activities of cutting, tearing, gluing, vigorous over-painting and scribbling register an extreme physicality, materialising the almost painful pressure of the artist's hand.

Such material evidence of violence gave way, in the prolific, fluent brush drawings of the early to mid-1980s and in the denser paintings of the late 1980s, to violence explored iconographically. In works that span several stylistic shifts, Rego explicitly pictures an aggression at the heart of the family: the conflicts inherent in incestuous desire; the repressed, murderous impulses that underlie nurturing; the hostility underpinning politeness. What we see in these works is that civilisation is not only purchased at the cost of instinctual renunciation, but that in their sublation, those instincts also repeatedly return to breach the fabric of human relations.

As we have seen, psychoanalytically, the question of where violence comes from is a vexed one. In response to Jacqueline Rose's assertion that Freudian psychoanalytic practice and theory has privileged sex over violence (Rose, 1988: 121) and that the emphasis of the sex drive over the death drive has aestheticised psychoanalysis (Rose, 1993: 144), Mignon Nixon points out that this stress has tended to reinforce a gendered division, where the opposition between masculine aggression and feminine passivity is naturalised. A model more closely based on Melanie Klein's writings than on Freud's, she argues, might allow for the realignment of these variables and a reconfiguration of the relationship between aggression and sexuality. The significance of the Kleinian model resides in the formulation that aggression is 'not a function of sexual difference', but is rather 'structural to all subjectivities' (Nixon, 1998: 301). But, as we shall see, it is not only in Melanie Klein's work but also in Freud's late work that aggression plays a central and organising role in a human nature that is characterised as frankly lupine. In *Civilization and its Discontents* (Freud, 1930), paradoxically, although it is derivative of the death drive, aggression is alloyed to Eros and destructiveness is constitutive of sexuality.

Rego's *Dog Women* of 1994 (see Plate 8), her first series of large works in pastel, exposes such an interlocking of violence and sexuality. In these images of lone female bodies, violence is not something that is exercised by certain bodies over others. Rather, it is incorporated, interiorised, constitutive of subjectivity itself. Here, as in the collages of the 1960s, there is material evidence of an intense physicality – the traces of the artist's hand – in the visible pressure of the pastel marks. Most of these works depict the isolated body of a woman. She hunkers and snarls, waiting for food, baying at the moon, sitting on command, faithfully lying on her master's jacket or – in a swift reversal of gender positions that prefigures later inversions – insolently lifting a leg to piss on a bed. An animal presence lurks within the human as a reminder of 'all that is most vulnerable and all that is most alive' (Rego: in coversation).

The tender and raw physicality of these bodies evokes the canine loyalty of women watching and waiting, a poignant blend of eroticism and abjection occurring within conditions of intimacy. Expectancy, a sadomasochistic vertigo of pain and desire, the abdication of self that lies at the heart of the lover's affliction: these are not so much given physical form as located in the gestures and placement of a body. Rego's work literalises, then, the Freudian conception of the ego as a *bodily* ego. 'The experience of the spiritual and the psychic is right there in the body', she has affirmed (Rego: in conversation). Indeed, like that frontier creature, the ego itself, this is a body that is at once acting and acted upon. Here, perhaps in more distilled form than in any of Rego's works, we see the body as a critical site of 'oppressions and exploitations, the locus of social disciplines and violations, the field of pleasure and desire as all are traversed and differentially lived' (Pollock, 2001: 76).

However, if these bodies stage dramas that bind the political to the psychic, they do so without establishing suffering as a measure of virtue. But if, in refusing to take on the persona of the victim, these figures acknowledge what many of Rego's other figures cannot – that revenge itself locks a subject to the history that produced it – they do also run the danger of appearing to be complicit with such 'oppressions and exploitations'.[3] Indeed, their lack of manifest anger, their compliance and dogged staying power, might, for some, appear to vex Rego's relation to feminism. Yet, crucially, Rego does not picture such subjection as reactive to the slights and injuries dealt by men. Rather, as we shall see again in Chapter 4, the abjection of these bodies points to an oppression and exploitation of the ego itself – the ego's loss of its boundaries, its shedding of its instinct for self-preservation – when the subject finds itself in thrall to another. For these are, first and foremost, representations of the state of being in love.

The *Dog Women* and other single-figure works of the 1990s – such as those dealing with schoolgirl abortions (*Untitled* of 1998–99), and, I would argue, *The Interrogator's Garden* (where the half-undressed woman in the background acts more as theatrical or symbolic prop than as a character in a narrative) – occupy a privileged place in the artist's work. Operating on the site where the psychic and political intersect, it is these bodies themselves that bear the burden of narration. In the context of an oeuvre that has privileged the point of view of the female subject, what, we might ask, are the politics of *The Interrogator's Garden*, a work where the subject and object of violence seem to have been conflated and confounded? Why is the interrogator a woman? Why is she in drag? What is being mocked – and who is laughing last?

Engendering roles

In a series of drawings made around *The Interrogator's Garden*, a concern with cross-dressing as the disturbance of social norms is fleshed out. Here, transvestism underlines the identificatory impulses underlying subject formation, the ways in which being is also being *like*. Executed in conté on paper, these drawings are less compactly worked than the more finished *Interrogator's Garden*. In all of them, what the characters are engaged in looking: narrative is honed to the gaze. In the context of crossed identifications, the play of gazes and glances across the visual field highlights the extent to which spectatorship is both implicated in desire and engaged in teasing out signs of difference.

Again, in *Study after 'The Interrogator's Garden'* (2000), the interrogator looks out imperiously, soliciting or challenging the viewer's gaze, while now the naked woman who has stepped out of the bin-liner in *The Interrogator's Garden* covers herself modestly and lowers her eyes, fending off our intrusive spectatorship. The drawing *Chéri I* (2000; Figure 15) again includes this figure of the cross-dressed interrogator, now standing awkwardly in the embrace of a partially undressed young woman, similar to the woman in underwear in *The Interrogator's Garden*. The interrogator's moustache and red gardening gloves stress the link between the two works. But in *Chéri I* the young woman clings possessively to the interrogator, as if for protection or consolation.

In two other drawings made at around the same time, *The Recruit* and *The Inspection* (Figure 16) (both 2000), elements of the interrogator's military costume (the jacket and the peaked cap) are pluckily worn by a little old woman who addresses a cringing younger man, dressed in the first drawing, partially undressed in the second.

The same two characters reappear in another, larger drawing, *Chéri II* (2000; Plate 9). The man, wearing an open shirt, boxer shorts, and socks and shoes, lies sleeping on the floor, his head thrown back on a pillow, his lips loosely parted. As in the earlier *Joseph's Dream* (Figure 17), a work that also pictures the mastery

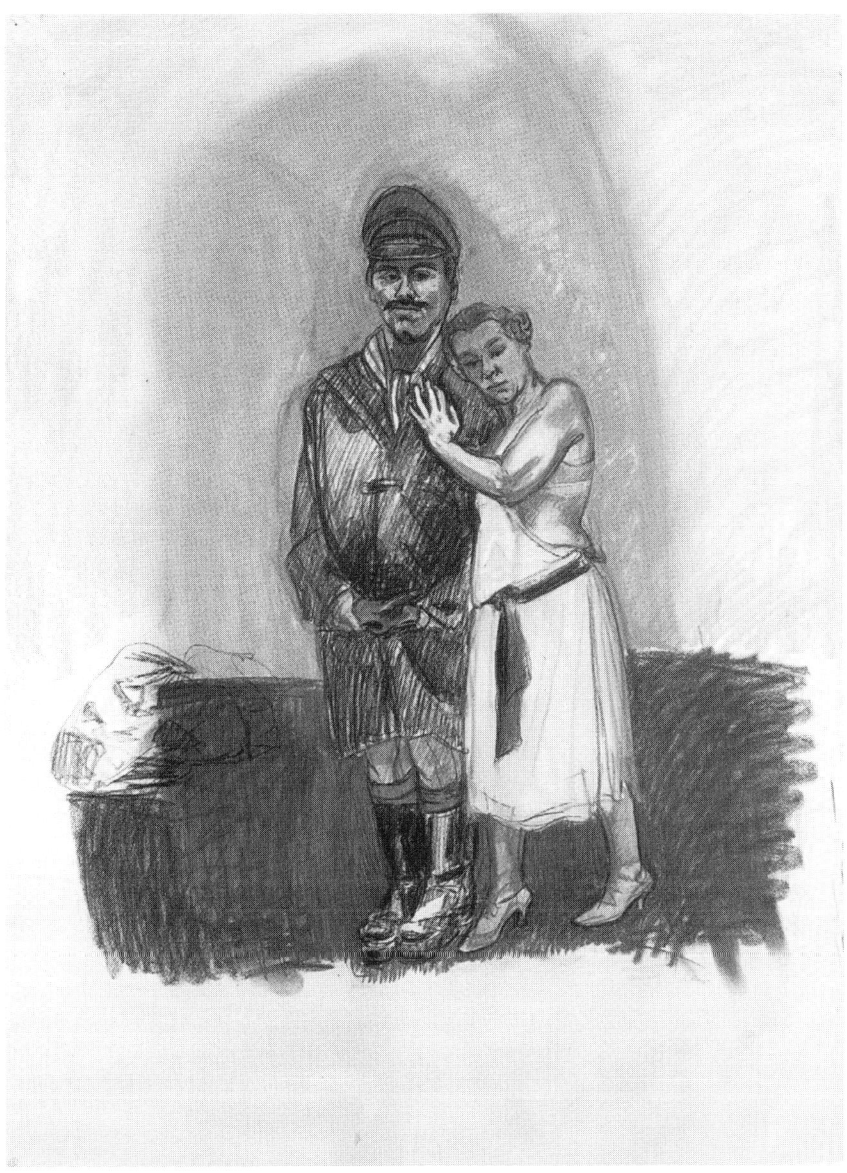

Paula Rego, *Chéri I*, 2000   Figure 15

of an insentient male body by a female gaze, the sleeper is being
watched by the diminutive old woman. This arrangement of bodies
clearly inverts the gendering and age-ing of that paradigmatic motif
that so overwhelmingly represents spectatorship in the history of
Western art: that of the male artist painting a female model. But the

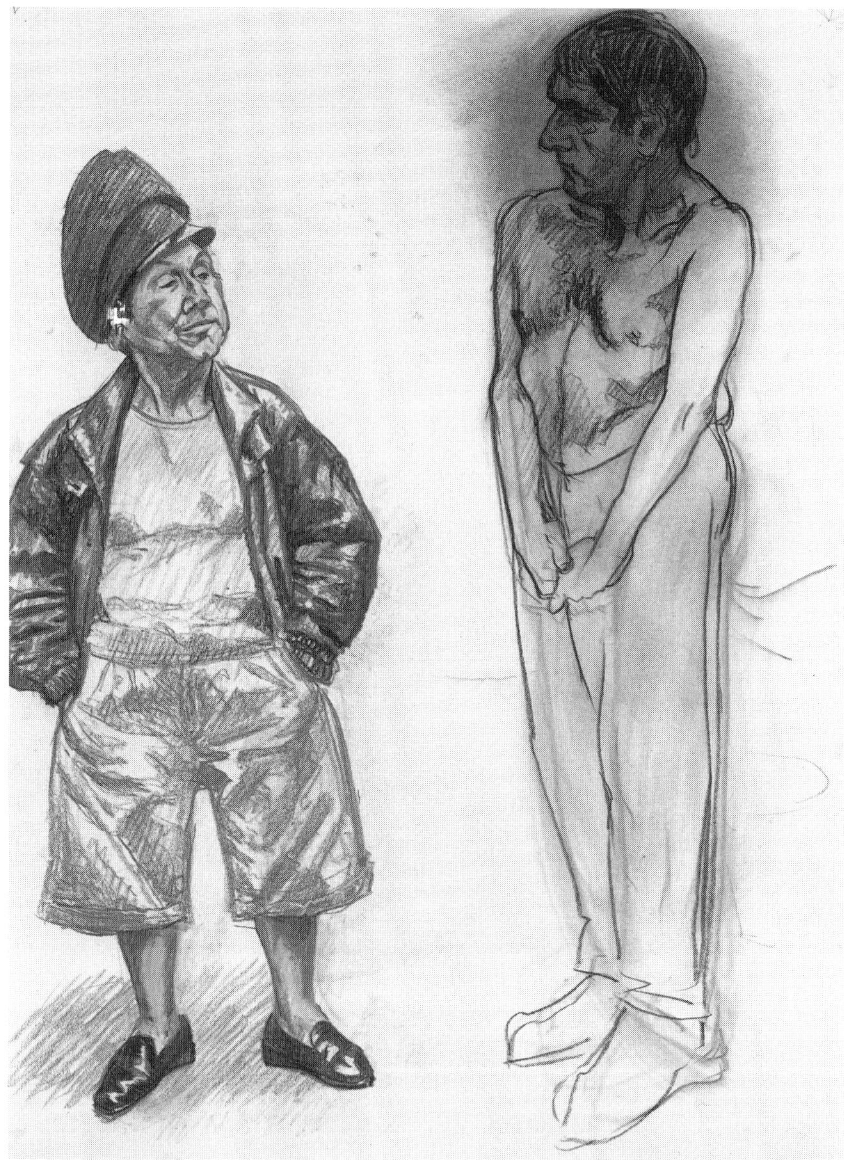

Figure 16   Paula Rego, *The Inspection*, 2000

old woman's look is not one of power; rather, it is at once bemused, solicitous and melancholy. Perched as she is between the man's relaxed, parted knees, in effect it is his crotch that is in her direct line of sight. As a meditation on desire as an impossible project, and, more specifically, on the closing in of erotic possibility for

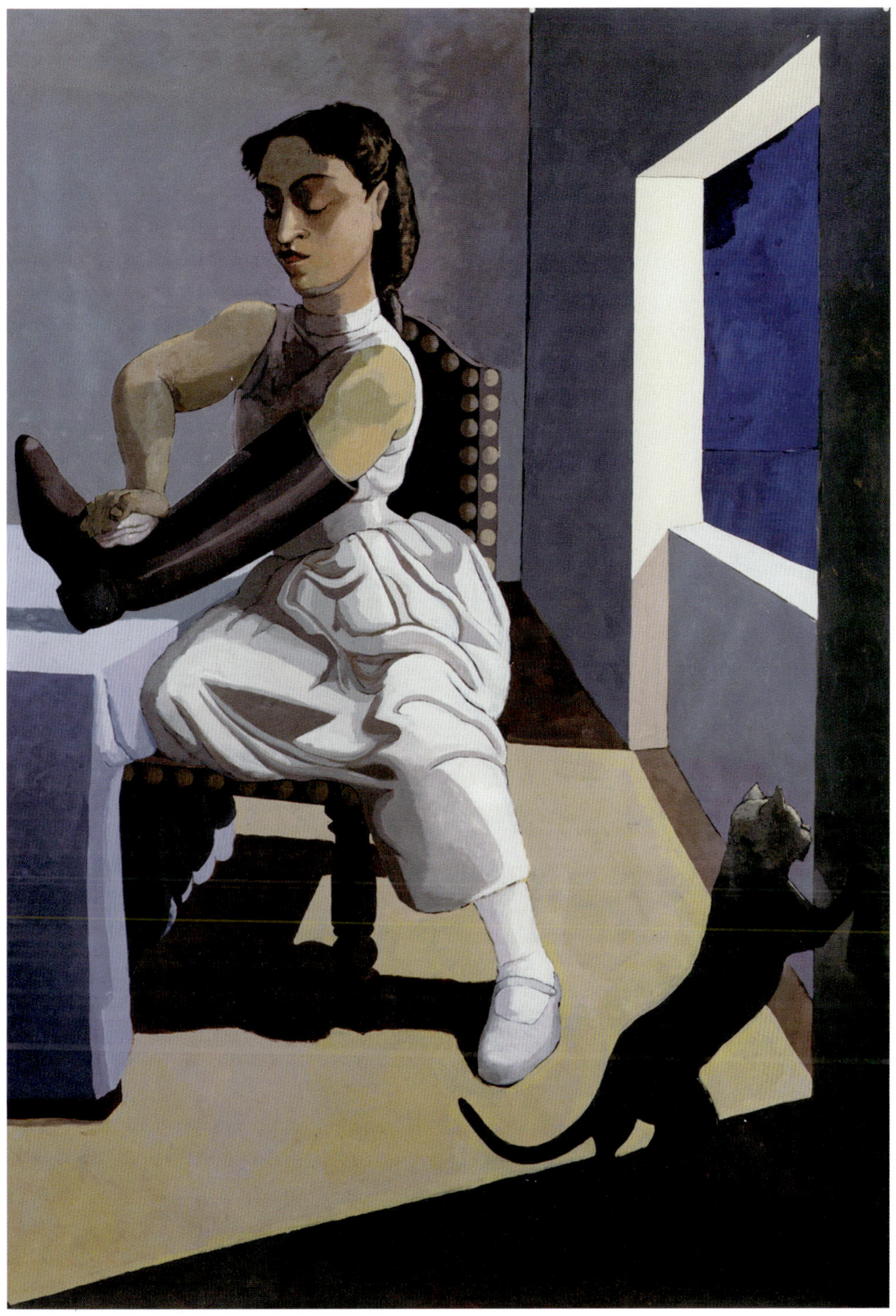

Paula Rego, *The Policeman's Daughter*   Plate 1

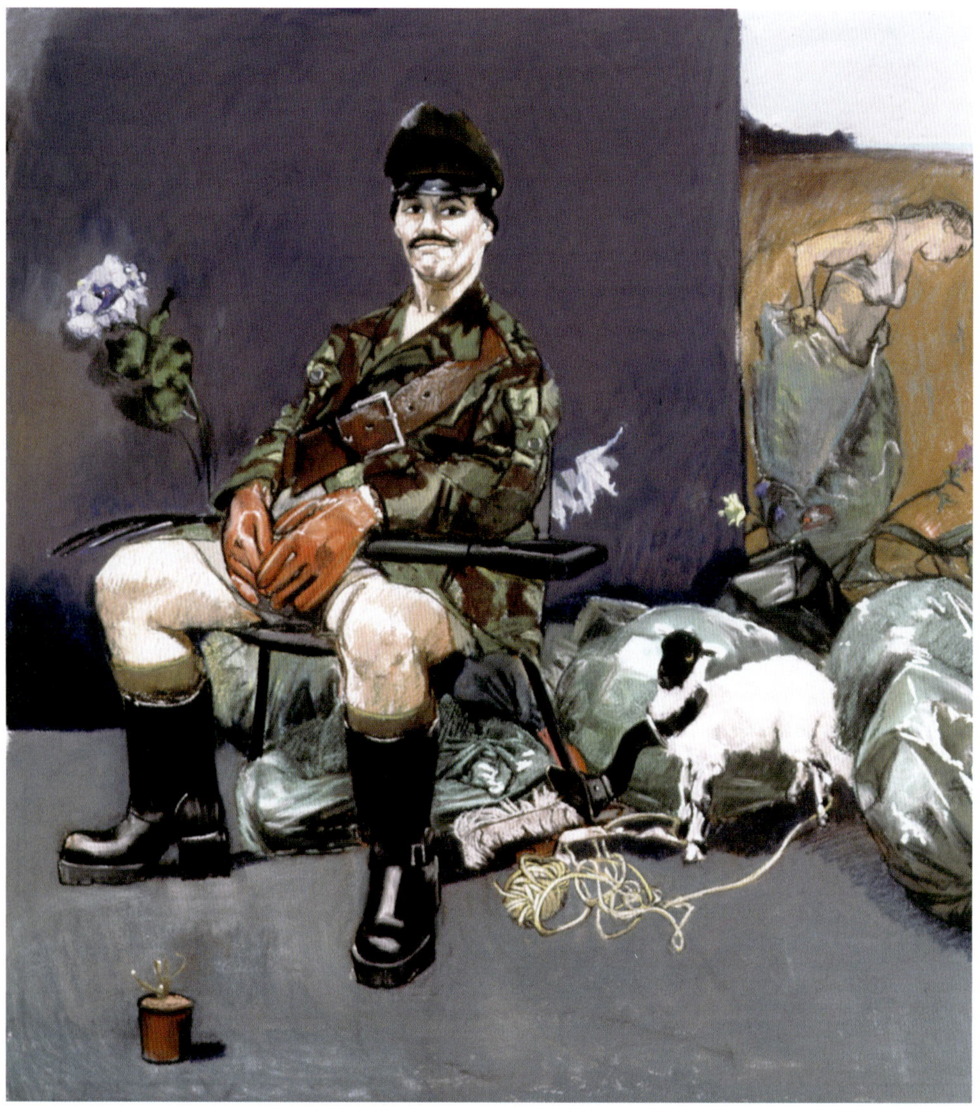

Plate 2   Paula Rego, *The Interrogator's Garden*

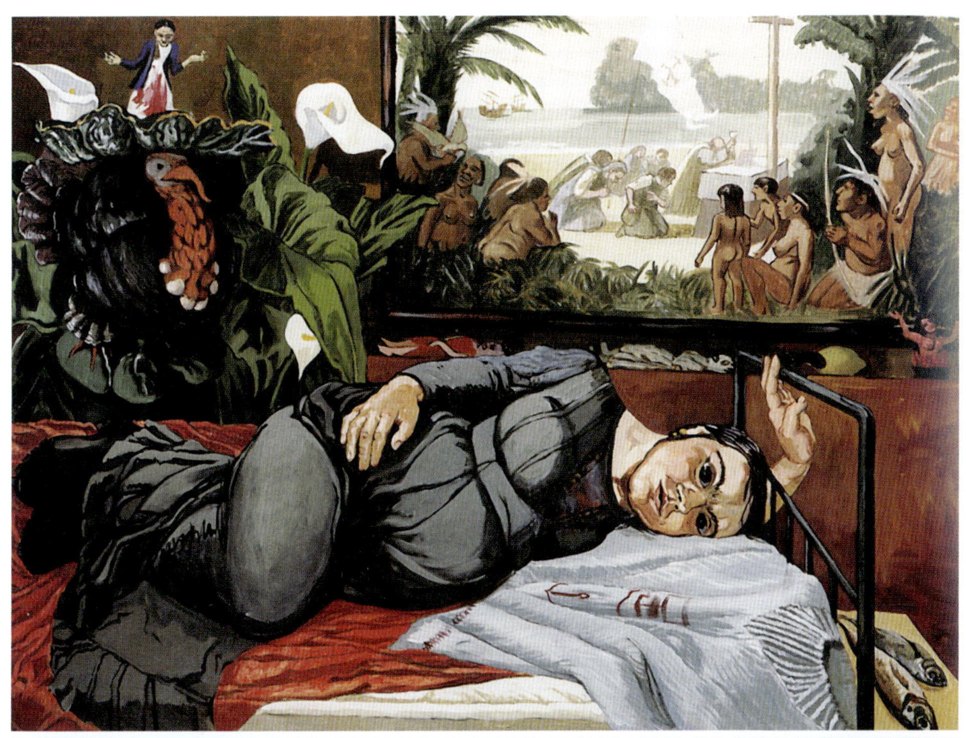

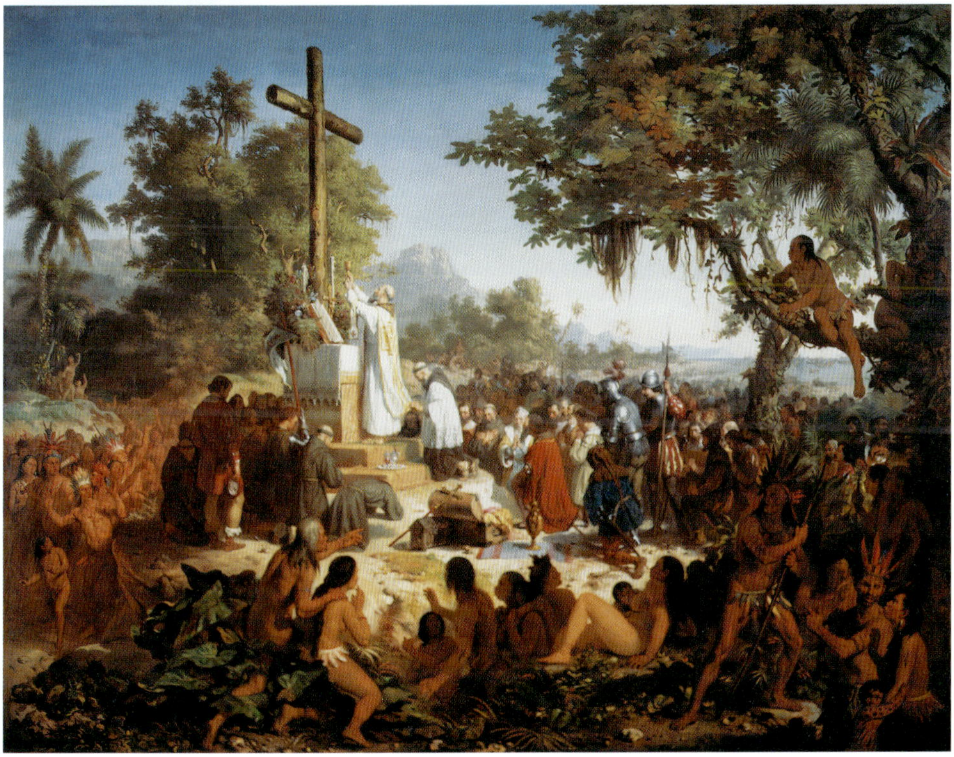

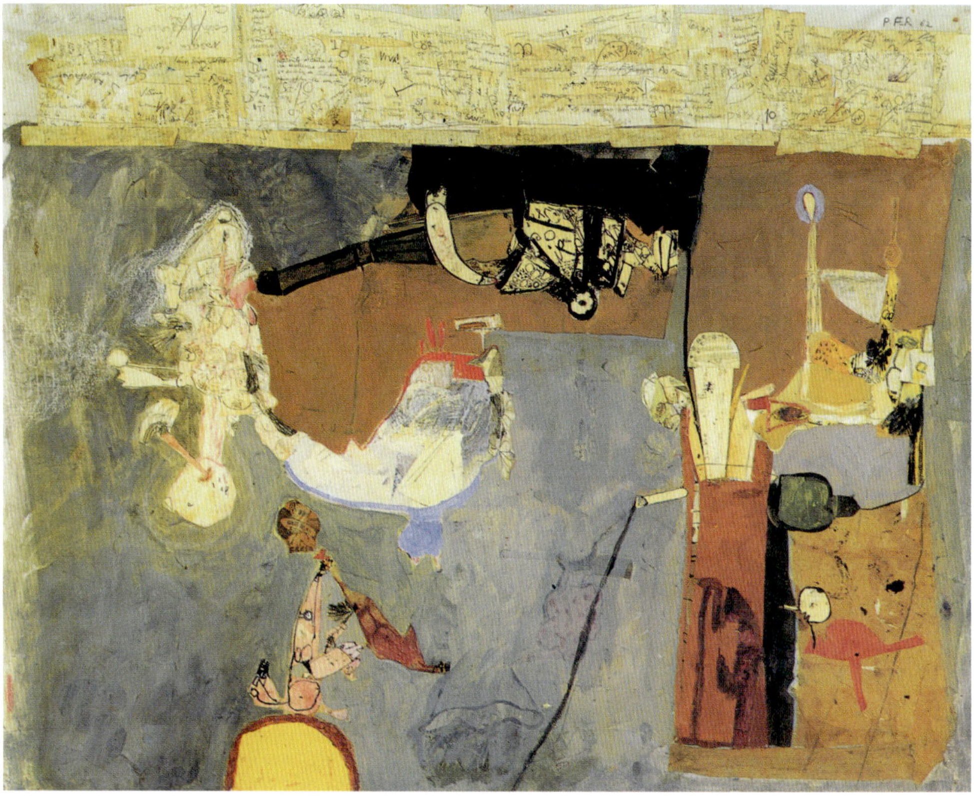

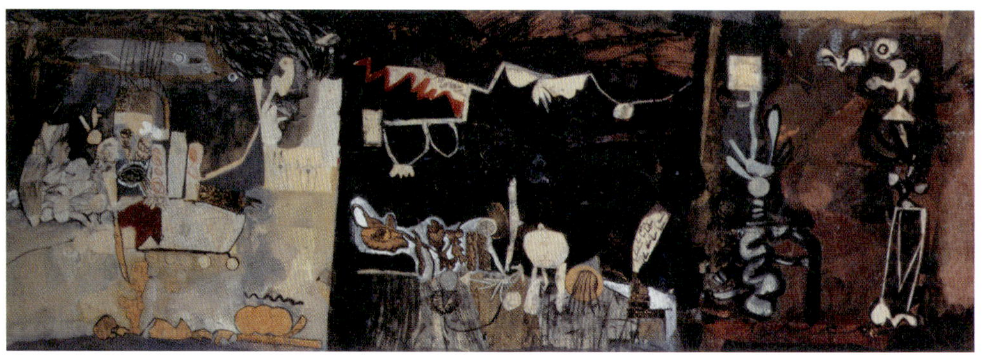

Plate 5   Paula Rego, *Iberian Dawn*

Plate 6   Paula Rego, *When We Had a House in the Country*

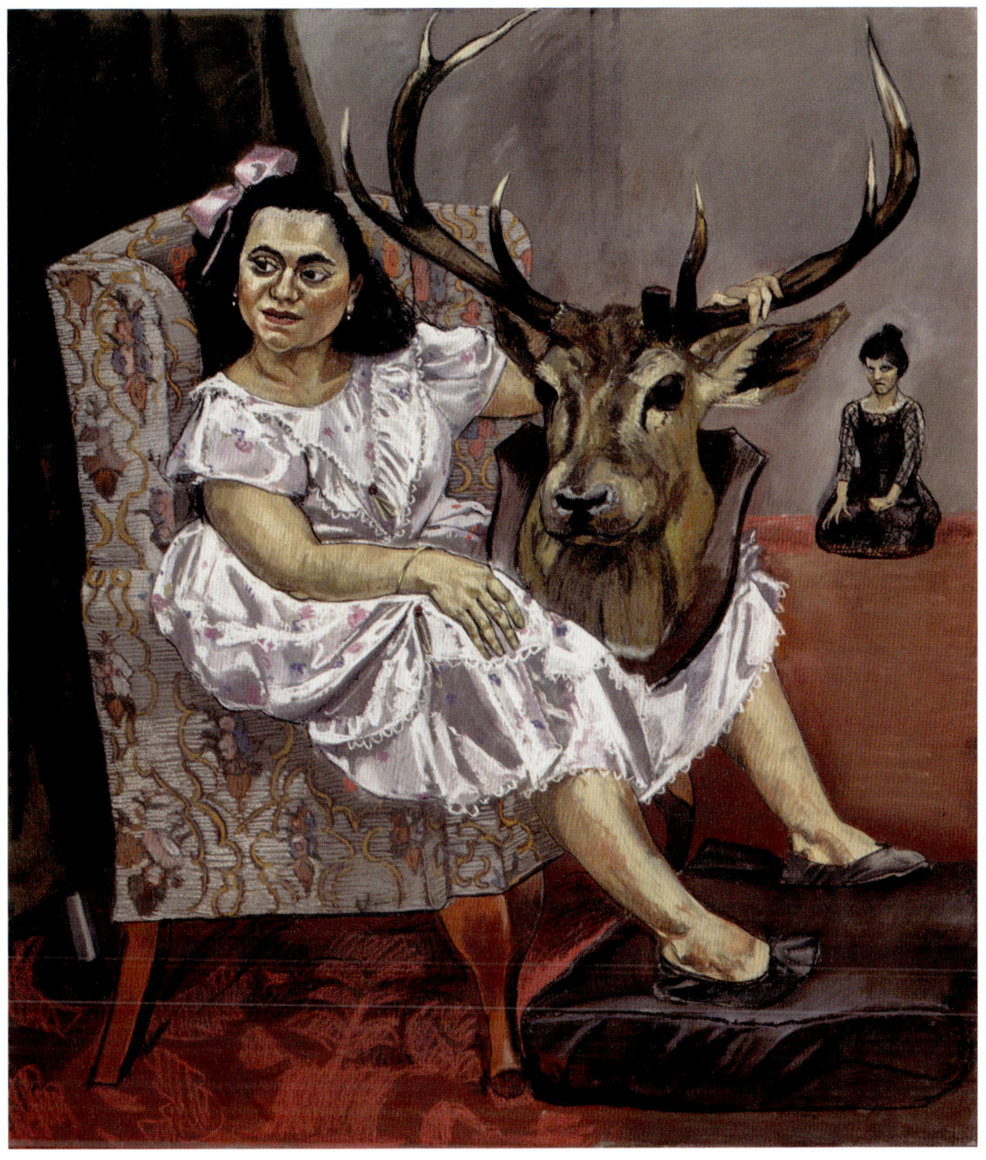

Paula Rego, *Snow White Playing with her Father's Trophies*   Plate 7

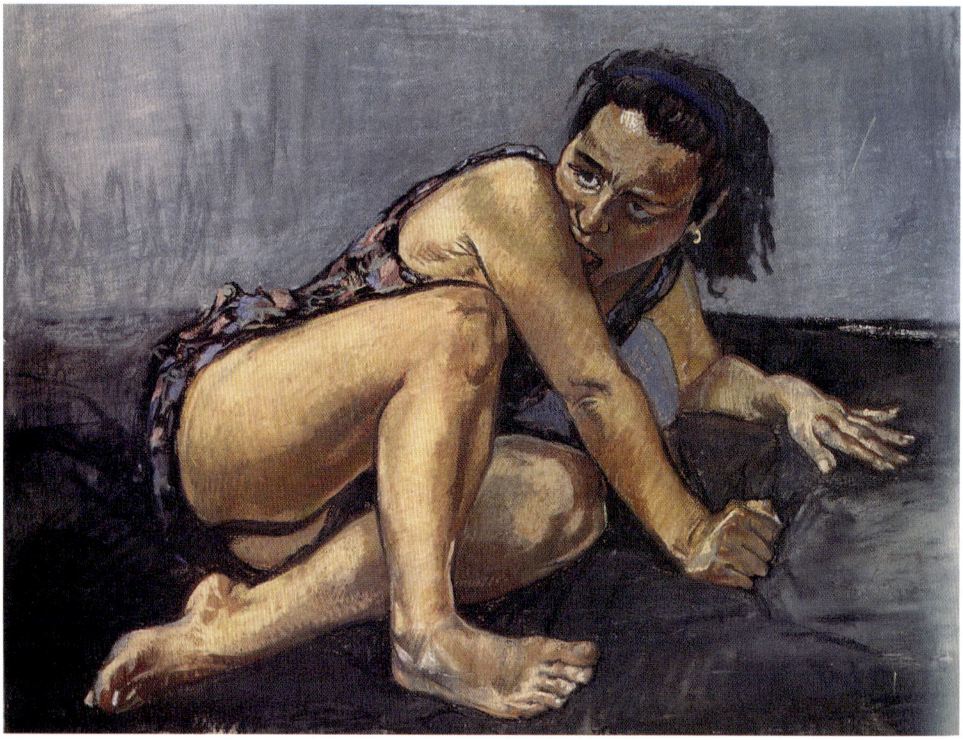

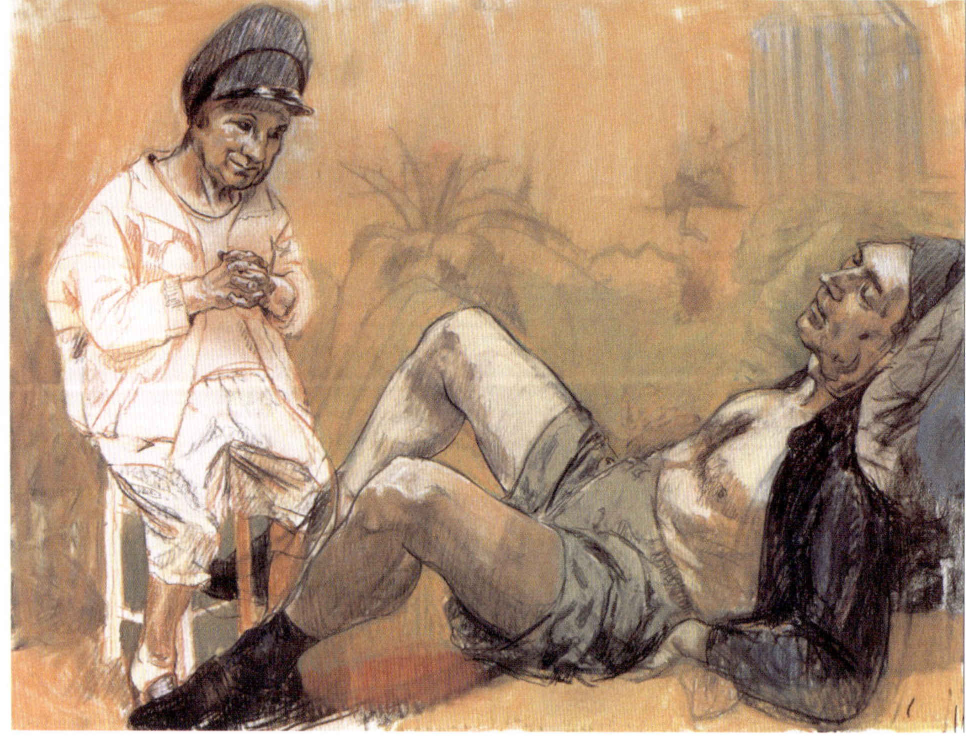

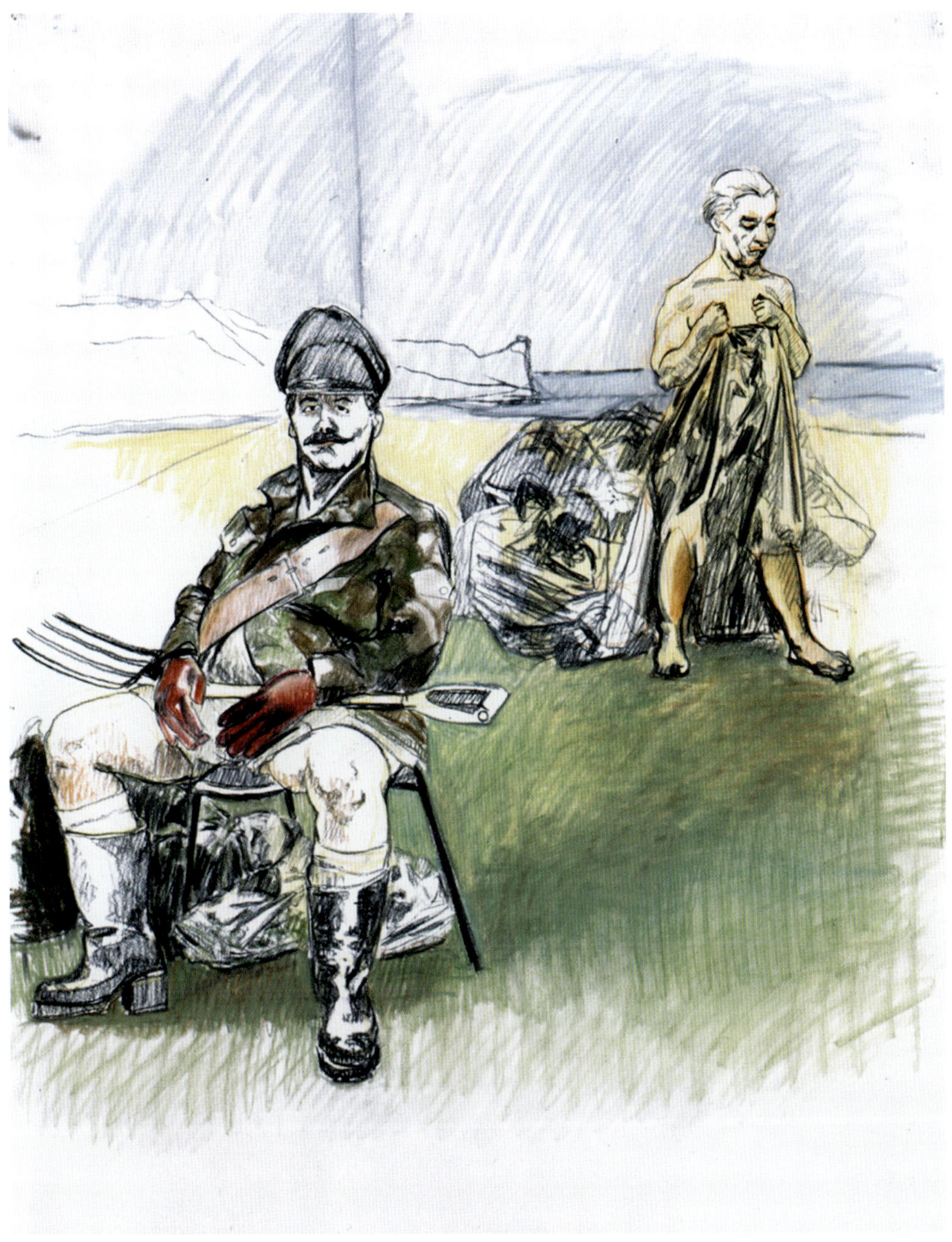

Paula Rego, *Study after 'The Interrogator's Garden'*   Plate 10

Opposite; above and below
Paula Rego, *Grooming*, from the series *Dog Woman*   Plate 8
Paula Rego, *Cheri II*   Plate 9

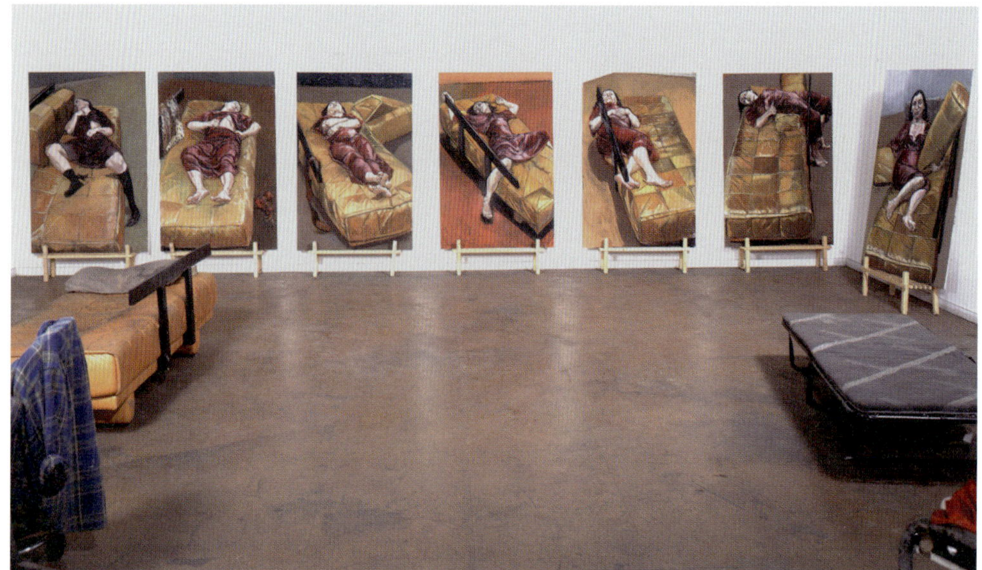

Plate 11   Paula Rego, *Possession*

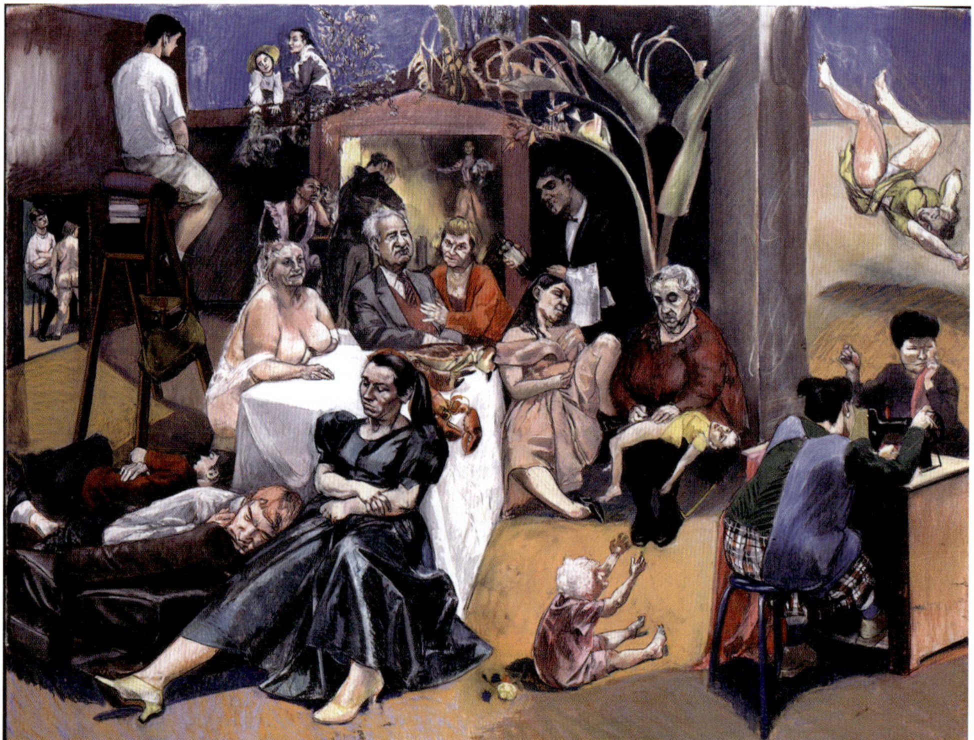

Plate 12   Paula Rego, *Celestina's House*

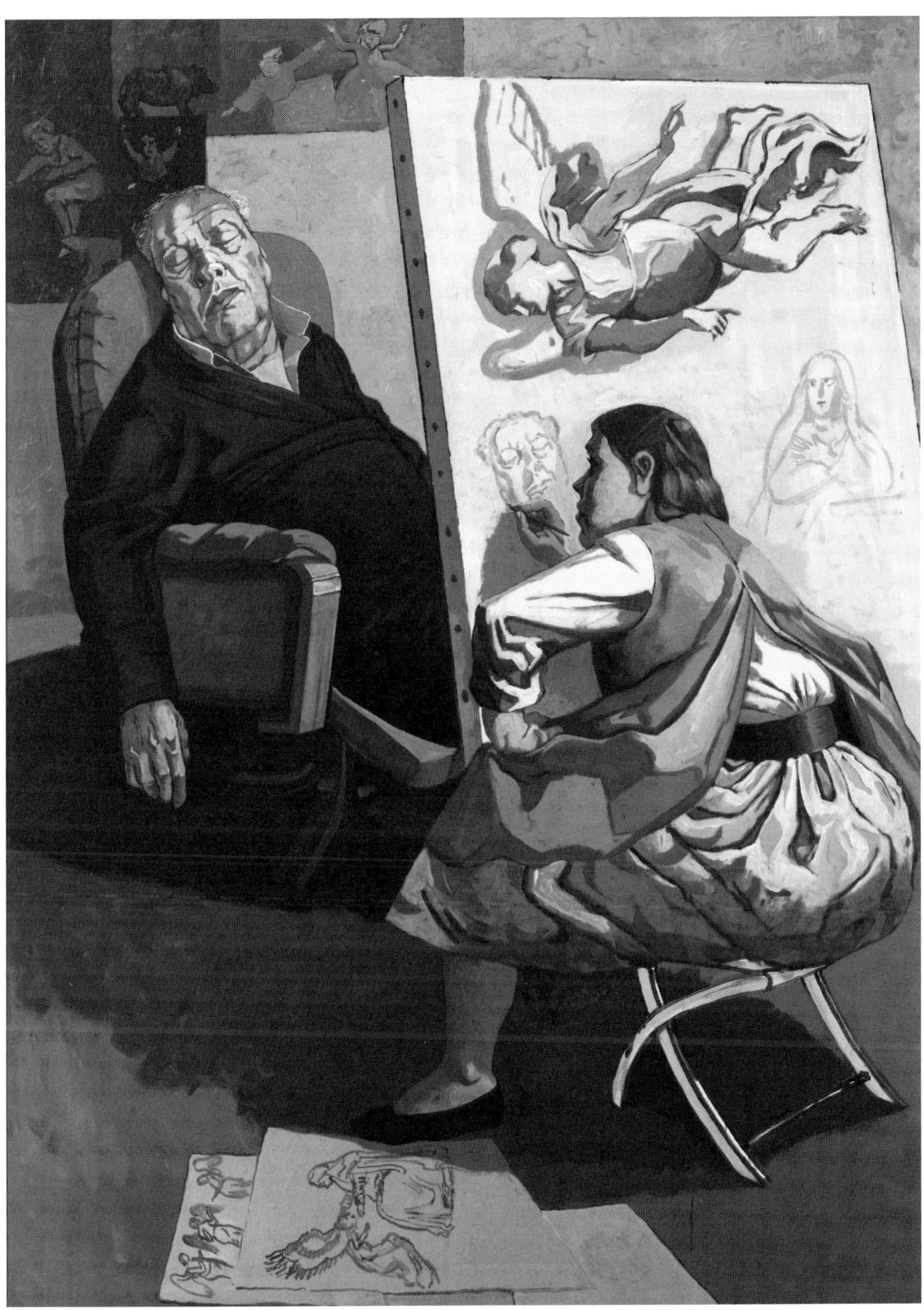

Paula Rego, *Joseph's Dream*, 1990   Figure 17

the non-reproductive woman, the drawing poignantly exposes the vulnerability of both the woman and the man. The work seems more like a wistful homage to paintings such as Piero di Cosimo's *Nymph and Satyr* (*Death of Procris*, ca. 1500) or Botticelli's *Venus Watching Mars Asleep* (ca. 1483) than a parody of them.[4]

There are other instances of cross dressing and ambiguous gender identity in Rego's work. In *The Artist in her Studio* (1993; Figure 18), the body of the artist is the site of intersection of divergent signs: the boots seem manly, the flowing shirt evokes the attire of nineteenth-century romantic male *auteurs*, while the skirt is a typical regional female costume from the Minho province of northern Portugal.

Occupying her place at the centre of the canvas, the artist sits confidently, knees splayed, offering the viewer her haughty profile. There is an overt allusion to Courbet in the placement of the artist in a studio surrounded by the accoutrements of her trade, reinforced by the artist smoking a phallic pipe as Courbet had done. Manifestly, such an allusion challenges the traditional male gendering of 'the artist', whose studio serves not merely the site of an exercise of self expression, but also the locus of the artist's discursive and institutional insertion. Would it be correct to speculate that the refusal to take on the full masquerade of femininity is evidence that the woman's agency within the Symbolic Order is bound by phallic signification? Put otherwise, if this is an assertion of female agency in the cultural field, it nevertheless casts that autonomy in phallic terms. This, then, is a visualisation of the difficulty female subjects experience, in departing from the Oedipus complex, in finding a resolution to the identification with masculinity.

The Maids (1987) is a scene directly related to Jean Genet's eponymous play. Within a proscenium setting, the lady of the house is about to be murdered by her maid. She wears a boxy tweed jacket, has distinctly masculine features and a dark shadow on her upper lip. 'She is almost male', Rego has commented (Rego: in conversation). *Good Morning* (Rosenthal, 2003: no. 28), an etching made a year later, shows three Lilas, one of them dressed as a man, 'but you're meant to see that it's Lila at the same time' (Rego: in conversation). There is in both of these works then, as in the later *Interrogator's Garden*, the desire not to pass so smoothly that the masquerade goes unnoticed, but, rather, to acknowledge in the transvestism the simultaneous co-existence of both genders as variable options within a single body. A similar logic operates in *Olga* (2003; Figure 19).

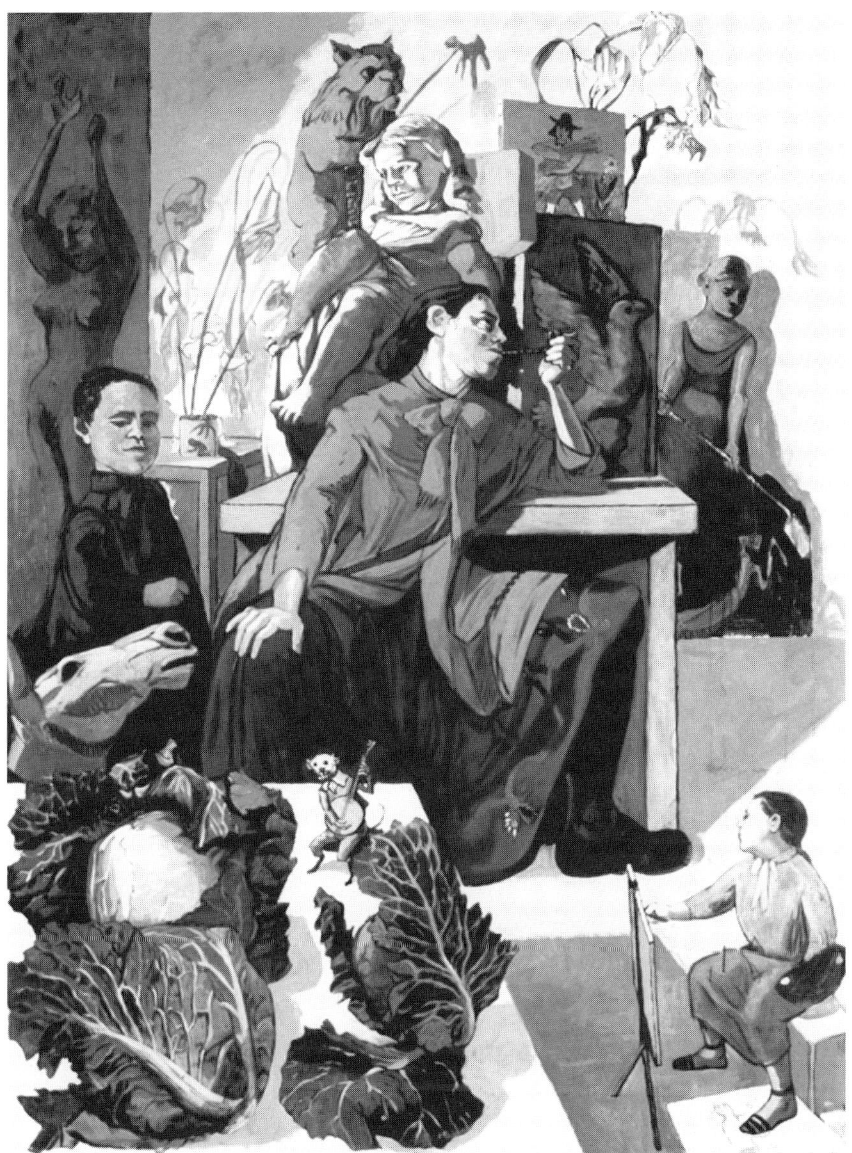

Paula Rego, *The Artist in her Studio*, 1993   Figure 18

Through the awkward body of a blonde-wigged male model
(Rego's friend Anthony Rudolf), *Olga* reconstructs a generic figure
that Rego recollects from her youth. 'There were these women
who came to Portugal from Germany in the late 1940s and 1950s
to be nannies,' she recounts, 'and they were either running away

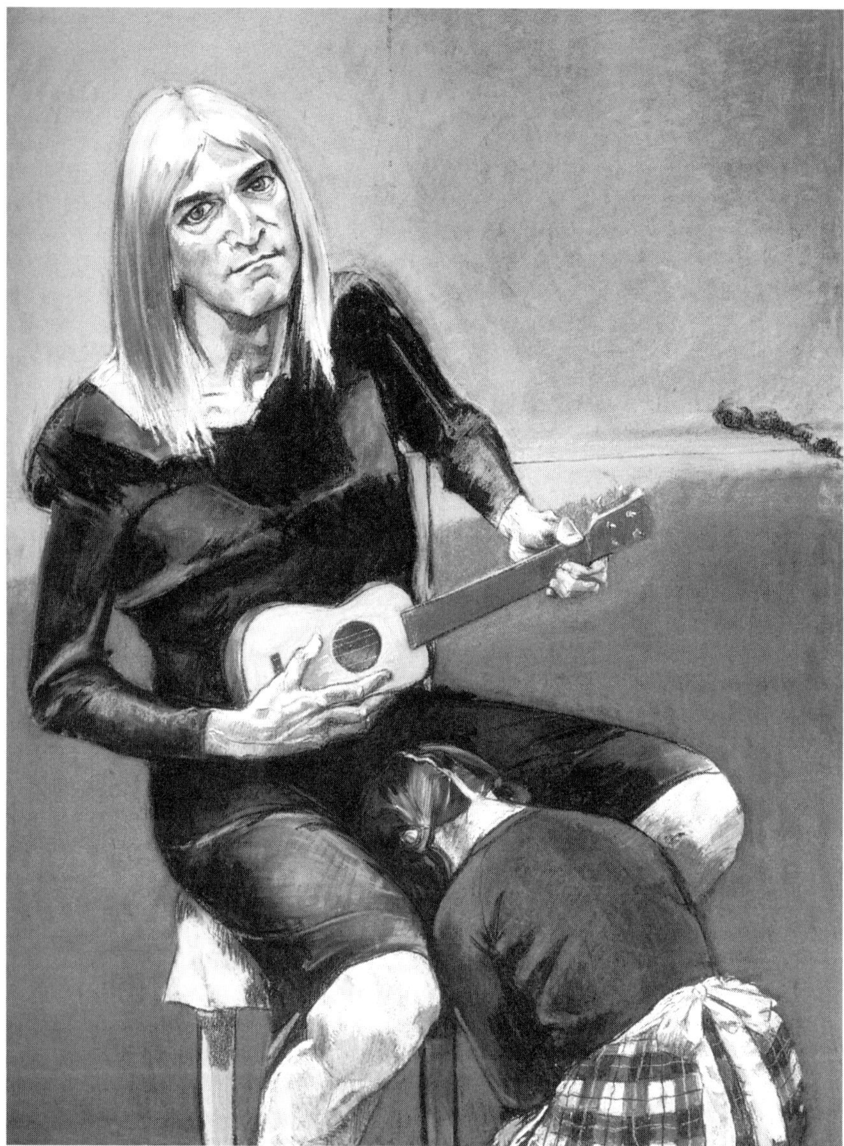

Figure 19   Paula Rego, *Olga*, 2003

or had some dark past, a dark secret, like Schlink's *The Reader*. Someone like Olga is an evil victim, like those women who worked in the concentration camps, who were really quite ordinary' (Rego: in conversation). The 'evil victim' is, like the abused child turned child abuser, both an unwitting casualty of evil and its perpetrator.

Olga, with her broad shoulders and baggy dress, in her lank blonde wig and strumming a small Portuguese *guitarra*, gazes out blankly, ignoring the little girl kneeling at her feet. The girl's supplication, tinged with disturbing overtones of barred eroticism, literalises the distribution of power between the two characters.

The discomfort generated by the work's gender bending raises, of course, the spectre of paedophilia. But, more blandly, such discomfort is also the outcome of a strategy frequently operative in transvestite enactment: not the erasure of one sex by another, but rather the provocation of a sustained consciousness of their co-existence. This is a bodily performance of the logic of the fetish. For it is commonly noted that male-to-female cross dressers extend the disavowal of castration by requiring the reassurance afforded by *being* a phallic woman: the reassurance, in other words, of dressing in women's clothes *and* having the penis, and in that way converting humiliation to mastery. In this performance, s/he attempts to eradicate the dramatic dilemma between *having* (the penis) and *being* (the Phallus) as mutually exclusive gender positions, by introducing a third term, that of *seeming*. Olga as cross-dressed man, blonde among Rego's almost ubiquitously dark-haired characters, becomes a self-conscious figure of Teutonic camp, passing in both gender and ethnicity.

Here is a crystallisation not of an Oedipal struggle gone awry, but, for the Freudian female subject that Rego's work proposes, of Oedipalisation *per se*. For, as we have seen, it is Oedipalisation that sets in motion the economy of sexual difference through the tribulations of gender identification, and that situates women forever uneasily in femininity. Put otherwise: Freud suggests that in taking up a position as a desiring subject, the male has simply to substitute his mother for another woman, but for the female subject, the operation is more convoluted and involves a disinvestment of her first attachment and a possible identification with the opposite sex. If Freud remains always evasive about female sexuality, and if, for Lacan, 'Woman' does not exist, this is because, in Parveen Adams' words, 'in the girl's case the Oedipus complex admits of no solution; everything that looks like a solution is secretly wrecked by the havoc of *Penisneid* [penis envy]' (Adams, 1989: 248). As a representation of a woman who is 'really' a man, it is just such an impossible female subjectivity that Olga performs. And as a representation of a man passing as a woman, Olga exposes an anxiety at the heart of male subjectivity.

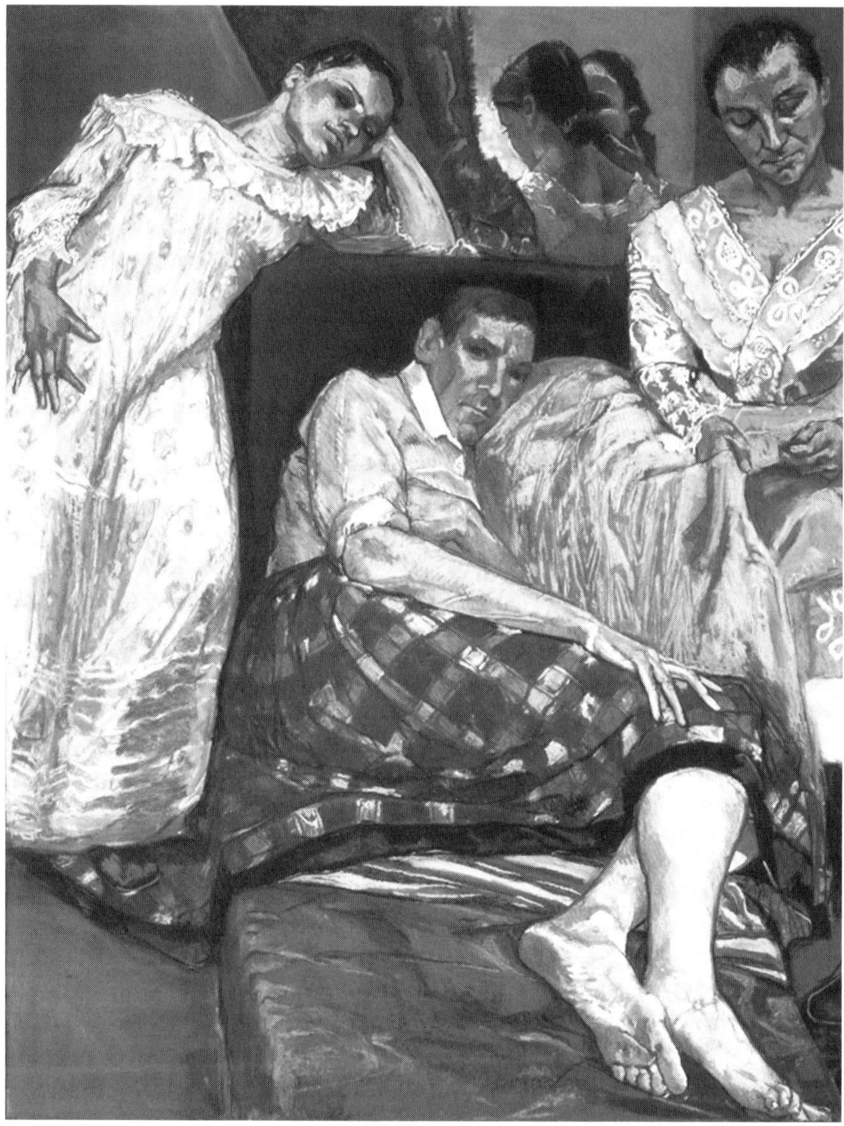

Figure 20   Paula Rego, *The Company of Women*, from the series *The Crime of Father Amaro*, 1997

In two earlier works, *The Company of Women* (Figure 20) and *Mother* (both of 1997), both from the body of work based on the nineteenth-century anti-clerical novel *The Crime of Father Amaro* by Eça de Queirós, Rego dresses her model, again Anthony Rudolf, in a skirt. In this series, Rudolf is cast in the role of the unctuous protagonist of the novel, a priest in the provincial Portuguese town of Leiria. In another work of the same series, *The Ambassador of Jesus* (1997), Rego had Rudolf pose in priest's garb, underlining a quality of camp artifice and revealing that dressing is also *dressing-up*, that wearing even the most appropriate costume is a form of interpellated mimicry, and therefore not only a performance of identity, but also a display of identity *as* performance. Marjorie Garber notes how one of the most significant symbolic aspects of the cassock is its disturbance of conventional gender categories: its resemblance, in other words, to women's clothing (Garber, 1992: 210). Male vows of chastity are accompanied by a wilful symbolic de-sexing, or, indeed, re-sexing. In Eça de Queiros' *The Crime of Father Amaro*, the priest's insecurity about his masculinity is frequently expressed in terms of his clothes: 'a man who couldn't satisfy the vanities and tastes of a woman and who always dressed in a black cassock' (Eça de Queirós, 1962: 227). Similarly, his clean-shaven face provokes anxiety, especially in relation to his hirsute sexual rival for the affections of the novel's heroine, Amélia: this rival 'was a man, and had his liberty and all his hair, his moustache, and his arm free to offer her in the street!' Clean-shaven and cassocked, Amaro experiences his gender identity as precarious.

Amaro's gender anxiety in Eça's novel is central to Rego's reading of the book. In *The Company of Women*, she places her Amaro not in the adult world of male professional and social camaraderie in which he circulates in most of the novel. Such a world is described in Freud's *Group Psychology and the Analysis of the Ego* (Freud, 1921) as bound by homosocial ties. Citing as examples the institutions of church and army, Freud notes that a simple collectivity does not constitute a group. What distinguishes a group is a libidinal linking of its members, and a leader who acts as a substitute for a father, distributing his love equally among his followers. Fervently anti clerical, Eça's view of such institutions is corrosive and bleak: for him, the libidinal ties of the group are non-existent and each member is motivated by a profound and corrupting self-interest.

Rego dismisses the professional and social world of male liaisons in Eça de Queirós' novel, preferring to focus instead on the domestic, a field traditionally identified with women. She situates Amaro's adult body back in the homely, feminine enclave of his childhood, leaving him mired in ambiguity: between adult and child, male and female, living body and corpse. A sense of Oedipal arrest is invoked not only by the man's feminisation, but also by his infantilisation.

This is underlined by the detail of the towel placed under his body, a prop that brings to mind the word 'soiling': a woman, a child, an invalid – anything but a 'real man' might need to lie on a towel. The inclusion of this detail is as biting as Eça's own irony: it speaks of the destabilisation of the normative categories of both 'man' and 'adult'.

Surrounded by suffocating women, the boy Amaro in Eça's novel is not only disempowered, he is damaged. Eça paints a picture of a sycophantic sissy who quickly learns the advantages to be gained by manipulating others. Rego places the adult male Amaro in 'the company of women' – the servants with whom he associated in his childhood and who used him as a pathetic mascot. But the potential humiliation of dressing the adult male in skirts is tempered, in Rego's works, by poignancy and empathy entirely absent from Eça's mordant text. What is most striking about both *The Company of Women* and *Mother* is the way in which the man's long, bare feet, his delicate hands, the contrast between his flesh and the fabric of the skirt, and his passive resignation make him an object of empathy rather than derision. Rego compares her Amaro to medieval Spanish effigies of Christ wearing a skirt (Rego: in conversation), suggesting a sacrificial metaphor: a man in a skirt as an object of exchange and propitiation among women.

The ambiguously titled *Mother* has no equivalent in the literary source. While for Rego, it is the spiky conch at the centre of the painting that is a metaphor for motherliness (Rego: in conversation), Amaro's identification with a mother figure is visualised in the soft, naked flesh of his torso and the full skirt. As in *The Fitting* (1990), a maid bends down to touch the fabric of the skirt, and in the pictorial structure of a person bending while another stands, a class structure is figured. There is tenderness in the pastel rendering of Amaro's exposed flesh, casting the character as more complex and more vulnerable than the literary protagonist on whom he is based. It is as if Rego has removed him from the corrupt context of the book in order to install him in her own moral universe. Unlike *Olga*, there is no display of fetishistic substitution. Rather, dressing the man as a woman exposes an intimate spectacle of subjective and domestic crisis.

A careful reading of Eça de Queiros' acerbic novel might prompt us to ask what a woman *is* in a context where maternity is figured not as the nurturing Christian ideal, but as resentfully or expediently appropriated, or altogether eschewed. In response,

Rego's two paintings seem to ask a counter-balancing question: what, after all, is a man? Speaking of her representation of Amaro, Rego notes that 'dressed as a woman' – performing femininity, in other words – he 'becomes more man' (Rego: in conversation). Indeed, it is not too far fetched to assert that a male in female drag is the paradoxical embodiment of *male* subjectivity, for it is the male's anxiety about his identity that engenders the masquerade. The paradoxical function of such cross dressing is, then, not so much to undermine the difference between men and women as to emphasise it.

Whether disavowing castration, performing ambiguity or confirming gendered identification, such cross dressed representations give body to a category crisis that readily opens the way to others: frequently, where there is 'gender trouble', there also occurs a disturbance in other classificatory categories (such as class, race or age). The vexing of category boundaries becomes a way of uncannily invoking the return of the psychically repressed: the return of all that we have had to repudiate in becoming who we are. It could thus be argued that cross dressing is a way of corporeally figuring the disavowed parts of the self that categorically belong to the 'other'; a form of projection, a way of 'locating whatever we imagine, or wish, ourselves to be lacking' (Phillips, 1994: 126).

The integration of otherness that characterises the performance of transvestism invokes Lacan's oxymoronic neologism 'extimacy', vexing the relation between the intimate and the social (Lacan, 1957: 172). Extimacy describes the condition of the interpellated subject, for it exposes the unconscious as an intersubjective structure, ex-centrically constituted by the discourse – indeed, the call – of the Other. Like a Möbius strip, extimacy is an interiorised exterior. Elisabeth Bronfen notes that to speak of cross dressing as the performance of extimacy means

> highlighting precisely the manner in which an external and to a degree injurious law, having been internalized by virtue of intepellation (with the repetition of the symbolic call ensuring the survival of this constitutive intimate foreign kernel), is materially re-enacted at the body by virtue of a gesture that clearly says of itself, 'I am assuming clothes, and with these a symbolic dress not legally ascribed to me'. (Bronfen, 2001: 219)

Bronfen's observation is an important one, for it addresses the relationship between our lack of autonomy as interpellated subjects, and the pleasures of self fashioning that we enjoy when we think we choose what to be by choosing what to wear.

The clearest marker of transvestism in *The Interrogator's Garden* and its related drawings – the one that confirms all others – is the moustache. The moustache is also the most shorthand allusion to tyrants and dictators,[5] serving, in the ironic manner of Chaplin's *Great Dictator*, both to metaphorise and to satirise authoritarian power. But the other signs – the positioning of the body, the clothes and accessories – are set in place for a troubling of gender performance.

Rego takes extreme care – and manifests extreme relish – in the way her protagonists are attired: 'the clothes are never masquerade', she has said, 'nor make-believe nor fantasy. The choice of clothes is practical. It sets the character and helps the specificity of the stories' (Rego: in conversation). Clothes, in other words, place the body in narrative and in history, rendering them culturally visible and endowing them with meaning. Today, Rego's studio is a theatre filled with costumes, mannequins and props, some old and belonging to her mother or herself, others, both period and modern, bought with a specific narrative purpose in view. Speaking of *The Interrogator's Garden*, she remarks 'I bought the clothes at Laurence Corner and improvised. She's dressed up to the nines. A mockery of what a soldier should look like in Africa' (Rego: in conversation).

A soldier in Africa

Rego frequently asks friends and relatives for ideas for 'stories', narratives that prompt the genesis of a work. So the narrative impulse behind *The Interrogator's Garden* lay in such a story, told when she was asked to donate a work to the Medical Foundation for the Victims of Torture. The work she finally donated to the Foundation was an untitled drawing, similar to *Obedience* (2002; Figure 21) made at around the same time. The story, set in Africa and involving a woman saved by being thrown onto a rubbish heap, invoked more personal associations with soldiers in Africa, linked to the Portuguese colonial presence there and the ensuing wars of independence. Allusions to the Africa of Portuguese colonialism are not new to Rego's work.[6] *When We Had a House in the Country. . .* (1961) (Plate 6) is directly linked to the violence of the wars of independence, also known as the Colonial War, that erupted in the year the painting was made, and that lasted for over a decade. The absent second clause of the title ironically alludes to the crass simultaneities and consequences of empire: *When We Had a House in the Country, We Used to Give Big Parties and then Go Out and Shoot the Negroes.* 'I used "negroes" purposefully, rather than blacks, because it was ruder', Rego has stated. 'This picture was done at the beginning of the Colonial War . . . I did others with the same subject. Even the picture called *Julieta* [1964] has a frieze of her children, her sons, fighting in the war' (Rego: in conversation). Like other works of this period, the figuration in *When We Had a House in the Country* evokes not only the visceral surrealism of Arshile Gorky, but also the fierce political critique of Picasso's *Dream and Lie of General Franco* of 1937, the eighteen-part series of cartoonish, small etchings in which the Ubu-like dictator is portrayed as a massive phallic tuber slaying women and horses.

With its bruised tonalities and dilacerated forms, this collage-painting points an accusing finger at the wealthy upper echelons of the metropolitan bourgeoisie, glamorously entertaining in their holiday homes sustained by labour in the African colonies, gesturing not only to a culpability for distant atrocities, but also to what Sara Suleri calls the 'unsettling economy of complicity and guilt' (1992: 3) of the colonial encounter. Through the vertical divisions structuring the panoramic sweep of the work into narrative sections, Rego evokes the simultaneity of the destinies of coloniser and colonised (light on the one side, dark on the other), and traumas suffered by the yoking together of heterogeneous cultures by violence.

The prolonged and bloody Colonial War in Africa (1961–75) fractured Salazar's regime, sapping the *Estado Novo* both economically and morally, finally contributing to its demise. In effect, as it is impossible to understand the longevity of the *Estado Novo* without taking colonialism into account, the dismantling of colonialism powerfully contributed to the unravelling of the regime.

In Portugal, the Colonial Act of 1930 established the possession of the colonies as the bedrock of the *Estado Novo*. Absorbed into the Constitution of 1933, this act legitimised the policy of centralisation, putting paid to the economic autonomy of the 'overseas territories'. The Colonial Act claimed for Portugal an 'essential and historic function' to 'civilise the indigenous populations' living in the 'Colonial Empire', while exerting a 'moral influence' (*Constituição Política da República Portuguesa e Colonial,* art. 2) upon them.[7] Integrating the colonies into the concept of nation itself, while differentiating legally and administratively between colonies and metropolis, the Colonial Act aimed at instating administrative stability. In this, the idea of an imperial-colonial possession, legitimised by historical tradition and purportedly based on a Christianising ethic rather than on the logic of expansionism, received an official imprimatur. The Act spelled out aspects of legislation and administration that were to apply to the territorial possessions, distinguishing between 'indigenous subjects' and 'Portuguese citizens' – the 'we' and 'them' of *When We Had a House in the Country*. As late as 1954, in what was known as the 'Native Statute' (*Estatuto do Indigenato*), the indigenous people of the colonies were defined as 'individuals of the black race or their descendants, either born or resident there, who do not as yet possess either the instruction or the individual and social habits necessary for the exercising of public and private law of the Portuguese citizens' (*Estatuto do Indigenato, Dec. Lei n° 39 666*, art. 2, 20 May 1954, cited in Braga da Cruz, 1988: 66).

In the wake of the democratisation of Europe after World War Two and the signing of the Universal Declaration of Human Rights in December 1948, both Portugal and Spain felt pressed to shed the symbols and slogans that smacked overtly of Fascism. In Portugal, these changes were officially sealed in the constitutional revision of 1951. Although some details of the Colonial Act were revised, these alterations were basically nominal and cosmetic. The most overt of these was the change of designation of 'Colonial Empire' to 'Portuguese Nation' and 'colonial dominions' to 'overseas provinces', together constituting what Salazar euphemistically termed 'a composite nation' (Salazar, 1959: 374). Salazar himself later confirmed that 'the change in name won't alter the nature of the thing' (Salazar, 1967: 38). While, in the early 1950s, the polemic around terminology reflected the antithetical pulls of assimilation and autonomy, in all essential details, the constitutional revision maintained the earlier centralising tenets. It held on to a notion of empire, now anachronistically and contentiously validating the historical significance of the colonies by calling them the *Terras dos Descobrimentos* – the Lands of the Discoveries.

In the heyday of the *Estado Novo*, the heroic period of ocean travel and Atlantic expansionism of the sixteenth century, together with the medieval Christian re-conquest of Portugal from the Moors played a foundational role. Today, some decades after Portugal became a democracy, there remains a popular, unreconstructed notion of these two historical moments. For Salazar, Portugal's imperial pretensions were at the very core of national identity, rooted 'in the soul of the Nation' (Salazar, 1934: 339). Such mythical speech was turned into spectacle at the paean to the reigning symbology of nation, the Great Exhibition of the Portuguese World in Lisbon in 1940, which, together with a string of conferences and public lectures through the 1930s, highlighted the extent to which the notion of empire lay at the ideological heart of the *Estado Novo*. The survival of the colonies remained a key factor in Portuguese foreign policy. Assisted by South Africa, for whom Mozambique and Angola served as buffer zones from the rest of the 'dark continent', Portugal clung onto its colonies for economic as well as ideological reasons: Salazar's anachronistic political survival into the post-war period was made possible by revenue from Portugal's territorial possessions.

However, finally, the colonies as mainstay of the regime became an economic and moral liability. The Colonial War consumed more than a third of public spending. It had also erupted at a time of acute national crisis: Salazar's authority had been seriously challenged by reformist factions in the government and in the Armed Forces, and there had been an aborted military coup in April 1961. Salazar appointed himself Secretary of Defence for the duration of the emergency in an attempt to prolong his political life, which was to last until ill health forced him to retire from office in 1968 – two years before his death – when Marcelo Caetano succeeded him.

But already, at the beginning of the 1960s, the logic of empire was radically challenged. The attack by Indian troops on Goa, the so-called Portuguese State in India, and the almost immediate surrender by the Portuguese in December 1961, signalled the beginning of the unravelling. The lack of reaction to pressure for a peaceful transition to independence ('progressive autonomy', which in effect meant simply administrative decentralisation) in the African colonies led to the armed struggle. Sending troops to Angola in response to two attacks in early 1961 – first an attack on Luanda Jail by members of the MPLA (the Popular Movement for the Liberation of Angola) followed by an attack by the rival UPA (Union of Angolan Peoples) on white settlers – Salazar began a war that finally, thirteen years later, extinguished the Portuguese dream of empire. The outbreak of war in Angola in 1961 was followed by that in Guiné Bissau (1963) and then Mozambique (1964). The expense of the military campaigns in Africa and the consequent loss of trade drained the *Estado Novo* economy. With the weakening of the balance of payments, the loss of lives, the undermining of national morale, and the incremental politicisation of both the working classes (who now suffered the consequences of war in low wages and unemployment) and the middle classes (whose sons were liable for conscription), by the mid–late 1960s, the system had fractured from within.

Although the independence of the African territories was considered to be inevitable, its realisation was delayed by the ideology of 'progressive autonomy'. A new constitutional revision in 1971 introduced alterations in the political and administrative governance of the 'overseas provinces', endowing them with special status as quasi-autonomous regions under the banner of a 'unitary decentralised state'. The changes introduced by Salazar's successor did not significantly alter the values of Salazarism but simply redesigned them to fit in with the times. As Fernando Rosas points out, the normative values of 'Fatherland', 'family', 'property', 'work' and 'authority' promulgated in Salazar's famous speech in Braga in 1936 were simply refashioned in Caetano's 'Setúbal Speech' in 1972 (Rosas, 1994: 547). While ostensibly grasping that change was inevitable, Caetano also claimed he considered it wrong to abandon the white populations in the African territories. The resolution of the long, destructive campaigns was further delayed by factionalism in the African freedom movements themselves. The colonies finally gained independence in 1975, after the 'Carnation' revolution that brought democracy to Portugal, but the process left both the metropolis and what had been the 'overseas provinces' in a shambles.

Dressing and passing

The interrogator, then, is 'dressed to the nines' like a 'soldier from Africa'. The precision of sartorial purpose in Rego's work is aimed not only at historical positioning, but also at honing and particularising the narrative. An important aspect of such attention to dress must be related to what might be called the theatre of gender (Laqueur, 1990: 102), its performativity and staging. Clothes reify the part played by culture in the making of bodies, not only in the attribution of social roles, but also in the very constitution of subjectivity, the concomitant construction of gender identity, and, in the case of women's clothes in particular, in the production of (hetero)sexual excitement. Clothes, in other words, are fashioned in response to an interpellative demand, and it is as such that they act as indices of identity, station or status. It is for these reasons that the social roles signified by dress codes must themselves be seen as modes of appro-priational dressing. But of course sartorial style is unstable: it can be imitated, socially promoted or it can become demotic. As expres-sions of identity, then, clothes are prone to symbolic theft. It is such symbolic theft that the gender mimicry of cross-dressing performs.

If, historically, male and female clothes play different roles as cul-turally freighted envelopes of the human body, there is a concomi-tant asymmetry between male and female transvestism. Arguably, in contemporary Western society, the adoption of female dress by men tends to operate according to the 'and–and' logic of the fetish, which simultaneously acknowledges and disavows sexual difference. Contrariwise, male dress has traditionally provided women with an escape from gendered disadvantage, enabling both greater physical freedom and greater social and cultural mobility by making women, to all intents and purposes, invisible.

Marjorie Garber has lucidly challenged the progress narrative that presupposes a real or essential identity behind the transvestite mask, a separation between person and his or her social wrapping. Both she and Adam Phillips, writing about her work, urge that trans-vestites disrupt the reassuring binarism of gender assignment in such a way as to show up 'how precarious our categories are, . . . how uncertain we are as the makers of categories . . . and how a world of entitlement – of privileged positions and secure identities – conceals an underworld of (sometimes desperate) improvisation' (Phillips, 1994: 127). From the oldest traditions of carnivalesque cross-dress-ing to present-day passing and voguing, transvestism also heralds a destabilisation or crisis in other representational fields.

Yet, in considering transvestism, we should also bear in mind the important point made by both Judith Butler and Elisabeth Bronfen, that the disruption of social norms is not itself necessarily subversive. Butler discusses the ways in which reversal might in effect serve to reinforce and buttress the status quo in the relation between het-erosexual and homosexual desire. In turn, Bronfen comments on Butler's refusal to declare every performance of drag subversive by focusing on such instances of culturally sanctioned transvestism and recognising their interpellative function:

> [C]ross-dressing emerges as such a vexed issue precisely because it explores the murky interface between the resilience of individual pleasure and the constraint of public law, pitting imaginary fantasies of self-fashioning against the recognition that we are always already

> positioned within the parameters of behaviour dictated to us by the symbolic codes of our culture. (Bronfen, 2001: 216)

In exposing the limits set upon the always-already interpellated subject, cross-dressing also highlights the limitations of resistance or subversion. Such a view works in tandem with that voiced by many historians and social anthropologists, that rituals of hierarchy or gender reversal symbolically perform instability, only to restore a sense of order in hierarchical societies: they express misrule in a way that does not, in the last analysis, transform the given order. As such, they act as safety valves for conflicts *within* the system, reiterating the dominant values of patrilineal societies. They can, it is argued, 'correct and relieve the system when it has become authoritarian', but 'they do not question the basic order of the society itself' (Zemon Davis, 1975: 130).

Reversals like these – comparable to what Freud calls negation, an affirmation of what is ostensibly disavowed – are thus simultaneously sites of insurgency and the location of a reinforcement of that norm itself, and, as such, they serve as measuring rods for a cultural ideal. The relationship between subversiveness and the reinforcement of social cohesion is a lively one. For cultural anthropologist Victor Turner, carnivalesque strategies are deployed in order to realise a symbolic renewal of social and cultural cohesion and communality (Turner, 1977). Commenting on this, Mary Russo notes that the difficulty of producing lasting social change does not diminish the 'usefulness of these symbolic models of transgression, and the histories of subaltern and counter productive cultural activity are never as neatly closed as structural models might suggest' (Russo, 1986: 215). Discussing the concept of the disorderliness of the female sex in early modern Europe, Natalie Zemon Davis analyses festive rituals of reversal and disruption not in the traditional sense as a 'temporary means of release from the traditional and stable hierarchy', but also as agents that, as Russo suggests, *do* undermine that hierarchy, rehearsing the possibility of true subversion and serving the effort 'to change the basic distribution of power within society' (Zemon Davis, 1975: 131).

Whether disruptive, or paradoxically conservative, what these divergent views of the power of reversal through cross-dressing reveal is the range and nuance present in gender performance, and the fact that there is no taken-for-granted *political* position that can be assigned to cross-dressing. In other words, if passing is to produce a narrative that counters the Oedipalised version of heterosexual gender identification and assigned gender identities, subversion has to declare itself in combination with other signifying elements.

Acknowledging a profound ambiguity at the heart of gender identities, Judith Butler's landmark publication, *Gender Trouble* (1990), a critique of the naturalisation of gender identity and identification, opened the way to new readings of gender mimicry. Examining historical constructions of anatomical difference, Thomas Laqueur was making a similar point at the same time (Laqueur, 1990). In *The Psychic Life of Power*, published some years later, Butler took this argument further, linking gender to melancholia and proposing that 'gender' itself might be understood as an acting out of an unresolved grief for a disavowed object of homosexual attachment: an object that was never loved, and consequently never mourned. Butler summarises the observations she had made on cross-dressing in *Gender Trouble*: 'there I argued that gender is performative, by which I meant that no gender is "expressed" by actions, gestures, or speech, but that the performance of gender produces retroactively the illusion that there is an inner gender core' (Butler, 1997: 144).

This anti-expressive, anti-essentialist theory of gender is doubly vexed in the case of cross-dressing, which exposes the 'normal' constitution of gender presentation to be not essential, but rather, already mimetic:

> [If] one considers that gender is acquired, that it is assumed in relation to ideals which are never quite inhabited by anyone, then femininity is an ideal which everyone always and only truly 'imitates.' Thus, drag imitates the imitative structure of gender revealing gender itself to be an imitation. (Butler, 1997: 65)

The mimetic structure of gender performance was first theorised in that now iconic text by Joan Riviere, *Womanliness as Masquerade* (Riviere, 1986), published in 1929. Like Freud's essay 'Fetishism', published two years earlier, it is embedded in a broader discursive context on the production of sexual difference. Freud examines this production of difference in relation to the categories of pathology and normality. Riviere addresses her paper specifically to questions of female sexuality using a model she derives from Ferenczi, and employing a typology set forth by Ernest Jones' paper 'The Early Development of Female Sexuality'. Two key questions are interwoven in the relation between fetishism and masquerade: the first concerns the relationship between pathology and normality and their gendering; the second concerns the nature of femininity in the context of a normative heterosexuality and a naturalised masculine subjectivity.

Riviere famously theorises 'femininity' – or 'womanliness' as she calls it – as a mask, proposing aporetically that it might be worn as a disguise to cover up an over-identification with a male subject position and with the authority that accrues to it. In this reading, femininity itself is a kind of transvestism. Where, some four decades later, writers like Betty Friedan or Linda Nochlin were discussing the 'frilly blouse syndrome' as 'that innocuous version of the feminine protest which . . . compels successful women psychiatrists or professors to adopt some ultra-feminine items of clothing' (Nochlin, 1991: 173), the conclusions of Riviere's seminal essay are more far reaching. For her, there is no authentic femininity prior to the mimicry that performs it: in effect, such dressing up *produces* womanliness. Riviere discusses the manipulation of the image of femininity by women wishing to participate as agents and equals in a 'man's world'. She makes explicit an analogy between an aggressive and competitive professional world and masculinity, so that 'women who wish for masculinity may put on a mask of womanliness to avert anxiety and the retribution feared from men' (Riviere, 1986: 35). The fear of reprisal results from women's fantasy of replacing men in the public sphere, or, more specifically, of rivalry with the father, especially with the professional role he plays. It is, in other words, an anxiety with regard to woman's place of entry in the Symbolic Order. This rivalry, then, has no sexual object: it is not over the desire of the mother but over the place of the father in public discourse, or, as Judith Butler puts it, 'as a user of signs rather than a sign-object, an item of exchange' (Butler, 1990: 51).

So if, for a woman, dressing hyperbolically in female finery is a kind of transvestite performance concealing an anxiety about gendered emplacement, how would we read the female-to-male cross-dressed performance? In Europe, from the nineteenth century, cross-dressing was a practice with asymmetrical implications for the two biological sexes, and as fetishism was masculinised, the female-to-male cross-dresser came to embody women's sexual perversion par excellence (see Matlock, 1993: 36). It was, however, also practical: a tool for the acquisition of mobility, privileges and freedoms – women travellers and writers alike took on male disguise – as well as social transformation and professional empowerment, from which the female subject was otherwise barred. Despite the pathologisation of transvestism, for a woman to want to dress as a man was regarded by many as understandable: as a popular French proverb has it, *qui culottes a, liberté a* (quoted in Matlock, 1993: 52). 'The idea', Mary Ann Doane notes, 'seems to be this: it is understandable that women would want to be men, for everyone wants to be elsewhere than in the feminine position' (Doane, 1997: 184).[8]

Clearly, the meanings of parodic gender posturings vary according to context, and clearly, too, the disturbance produced by gender bending shifts in relation to the amount of cultural anxiety invested, at particular historical moments and in different ideological contexts, in a heterosexual economy, in reproductive sexuality, in sexual and social hierarchies and in maintaining the two sexes categorically apart.

In situating her cross-dressed interrogator in a hypothetical 'Africa' and in alluding to the *Estado Novo*, Rego is mobilising a set of psychic and ideological expectations. The interrogator clearly disturbs not only the certainty and fixity of naturalised gender positions, but also an ideological investment (at once imperialist and patriarchal) in that distinction. But she also disturbs other expectations in the refusal to submit to a Manichaean binarism that allows good and bad to settle into two neatly opposing camps: us versus them, women versus men. Interrogation cannot be separated from physical brutality or torture: the word and the deed are interlinked, and the threatened outcome of every scene of intimidating interrogation is physical pain. What *The Interrogator's Garden* shows us is difficult to assimilate into an optimistic feminism: a woman passing as a man not for personal transformation or professional empowerment, but in order to exercise the most dehumanising of all practices.

The lingering spectre in Portuguese collective memory of the PIDE (*Polícia Internacional de Defesa do Estado* – International Police for the Defence of the State) as both a symbol and a pillar of the dictatorship delayed the establishment of a civilian intelligence agency in Portugal for ten years after the regime was toppled in 1974. But a spate of independent publications and reports in the free press appeared shortly after that date, denouncing the PIDE's abuses. Over the years, documentary evidence and personal testimonials came to light, and the PIDE archive was opened to the public in the 1990s.

After the signing of the Constitution in 1933, Salazar reinforced the power of the Repressive State Apparatus by joining two existing police forces to form the PVDE (*Polícia de Vigilância e Defesa do Estado* – Police for the Vigilance and Defence of the State), the PIDE's immediate predecessor, which, together with official state propaganda and institutionalised censorship, ensured the advance of Salazarism. The PVDE oversaw a vast network of articulated agencies: the political police, the penal system, special courts for the trial and punishment of political insurrection and crimes against state security, and a programme of political purges in the labour force. It was a hierarchically structured, centralised organisation to which all other police forces, as well as the administration of diverse councils and public offices, were answerable. Its methods of interrogation and torture were, between 1937 and 1939, refined through direct contact with Mussolini's OVRA and Hitler's Gestapo. In January 1934, the first of the regime's penal colonies was established in Cunene in Angola. Tarrafal, on the Cape Verde island of Santiago, was the more infamous colony – some would call it a concentration camp – receiving its first prisoners in October 1936. It came to be known as the 'camp of slow death', claiming the lives of many, some of whom had been sent there without trial. It was not closed until 1954.

With the end of World War Two, Portugal found itself under international pressure not only to renounce the colonies but also to relax its regime and shake off its isolationist image: 'now that the War is over, neutrality is over too, and Portugal is, like any other country, a member of the international community . . . [dedicated to] the reconstruction of Europe', Salazar announced (Salazar, 1951: 106–107). A phase of progressive, if reserved, opening to international markets was accompanied by a slight loosening of the regime's obsessive uni-culturalism, which was to last till 1958, when internal and external opposition (principally to the politics of empire and the Colonial Wars in Africa) inaugurated a new phase of isolation and a hardening of political positions.

The refashioning of the image of the regime in 1945 included alterations in the public image of the political police. Now renamed PIDE, it was responsible for intelligence and for the vigilance of those suspected of oppositional activities, as well as for the criminalisation of acts against state security. The designation 'secret police' was altered to the euphemism 'autonomous organ of the Judiciary Police' (*Organismo Autónomo da Polícia Judiciária*). This change was merely cosmetic, as was the shift from the cursory trial of political prisoners at a military tribunal to trial in special criminal courts after 1945. All aspects of so-called 'political justice' remained in the hands of the PIDE, and the judicial system was organised in such a way as to cover up illegal acts of violence committed by this organ. Frequently, in the 1950s and 1960s, judges at the special courts would permit beatings and enforced silencing of witnesses by PIDE agents during the hearings, when witnesses reported on maltreatment or simply attempted to defend their political convictions.

The PIDE ran undercover intelligence operations in communist organisations, universities, the armed forces, the Portuguese emigrant communities and the government-run labour unions – the only unions permitted. From 1954, detention without trial could be enforced for up to 180 days, and later 360 days. With no form of external monitoring, the detained were subject to secret interrogations, intimidation and torture. Measures were tightened yet again in 1956, making it possible to hold prisoners indefinitely without trial, even if this meant overriding the decision of the Supreme Court. Disappearance and secret detention were commonplace, making it more difficult to apportion blame and '[increasing] the latitude of security agents over the lives and wellbeing of people in custody' (Amnesty International, 1984: 11).

From the mid-1960s, with the Colonial War showing no sign of resolution and the sustained resistance of militant anti-fascists in the metropolis, the regime's anxiety about loss of control became manifest in the tightening of its intelligence and methods of intimidation. The PIDE's repressive and coercive actions became more pervasive; agents from the metropolis were also sent to the African colonies in order to suppress opposition to the war effort. In 1966, an intelligence agency, the CDI (*Centro de Documentação Internacional* – Centre of International Documentation), directly subsidised by the PIDE, was set up as a means of infiltrating the student milieu (which, in Portugal as elsewhere in the 1960s, was agitated) and gaining intelligence on political movements against the regime, which were gathering momentum in the 1960s.

After Salazar's resignation in 1968, Marcel Caetano's project of ostensible liberalisation in the name of 'change in continuity' led to a slight relaxation of repressive state control, a return of some high-profile political exiles and a loosening-up of censorship and of the functions of the political police. Under his aegis, the PIDE, with its sinister connotations, was yet again renamed, now becoming the DGS (*Direcção Geral de Segurança* – General Security Directorate). But the DGS remained linked to the Ministry of the Interior, and, to all intents and purposes, its functions perpetuated that of its predecessor. It was abolished on 26 April 1974, a day after the Carnation Revolution that toppled the *Estado Novo*.

Dark twins: torture and confession

In his darkly allegorical story *In the Penal Colony*, Franz Kafka ironically twists the well-worn belief in pain as the condition for the emergence of truth. The story centres on 'the Harrow', an elaborate mechanism devised to execute a prisoner slowly, while literally writing his sentence upon his body. Through this contraption, truth is spectacularly published in a way that reproduces the logic of the theatrical spectacle of judicial torture and execution.

In Kafka's nightmarish vision, the prisoner does not previously know the nature of his crime, learning it in the excruciating momentum of his own pain, which also acts as a textual caution to others. Text here acts analogously to earlier penal customs such as flogging or branding, where, through their social visibility, traces of corporal punishment served as public warning. The instrument for the execution of a dark and irrational justice is also, then, as an epistemological tool. However, what Kafka really shows us is 'the implacable power of an inaccessible, unaccountable apparatus of bureaucratic reason' (Morris, 1991: 184). When the Harrow is used on the authority that commands its use, it breaks down and instead of issuing its rational decree, pierces the body repeatedly in a berserk gibberish of broken phonemes and blood. The breakdown of language is inextricable from the breakdown of coherent bodiliness.

If Kafka's story allegorises the bureaucratisation of a faceless authority that is empowered through the control and administration of technologies of pain, it also exposes the relationship between pain, power and language. The decomposition of sentence into senselessness accompanies the transformation of a body into a corpse, while performing the ultimate characteristic of pain: its inexpressibility. The obscene nature of pain taken to the limit not only resists articulation, but, Kafka suggests, shatters language itself. Pain cannot be spoken, or spoken for.

In the infliction of pain in calculated increments – a pain that ceases only in death – the torturer snatches power in the name of an ideology or a regime. As the power embodied by the torturer is not his (or her) own, essential to this procedure is the sense that, at the scene of interrogation, the interrogator controls everything. What torture purports to gain is perversely called 'intelligence', where words play a crucial role. As Elaine Scarry has importantly shown, in the intertwined structuring of interrogation and torture, words are inseparable from the context of their iteration and are intimately connected to acts (Scarry, 1985: 28 ff.). Interrogation and torture are, then, structurally linked procedures. They are distinct from other kinds of pain infliction used as sanction: 'no punishment, no matter how gruesome, should be called torture' (Langbein, 1976: 3). Indeed, the confession is aimed not so much at gaining information, as at justifying the procedure of intimidation, and therefore at acting out the intractable power relation between torturer and victim.

As implacable agents who cannot be addressed in the name of a shared humanity, interrogators are mediators in a relay of power, impersonally standing in for it. Legal historians have stressed the public dimension of torture (the power, in other words, is held in the name of a collective body), whether legitimate or not, whether enforced as part of state procedure or by state officials outside the judiciary proper. As we all now know too well, the successful abolition of torture in the eighteenth and early nineteenth centuries principally involved torture practised as part of a criminal procedure and not a political one: not, in other words, the instances of torture exercised outside of the jurisdiction of 'Bench and Bar', which by then 'had ceased to comprise the entire legal power of the state' (Peters, 1985: 6).

In the scene of interrogation, the negotiation around words is effective because into its very fabric is woven the threat of an incommensurable pain; a pain that erases the victim's entire world, whether as visible threat (in the grisly objects of the torture chamber), or as realised action. In the twinning of interrogation and torture, the destruction of affect, the dismantling of language and the obliteration of the prisoner's voice are interrelated processes. Scarry furthermore stresses the ways in which the space of torture and the torturer's repertoire of implements parody the spaces and instruments of civilisation itself, scandalously mimicking the discourses of domesticity, medicine and the law. In this process of malevolent parody, architectural space itself (walls, windows, doors) is summoned as an agent of personal and civilisational undoing.

Here both language and vision are invoked: words (threat, question) and sight (room, instruments) are convened in a bid to induce a confession. In the arrangement of signifiers it elicits, the sighting of the instrument (the syringe, the pitchfork) invites an association not with the civilisational virtues of curing or tending, but with bodily damage. The projection of pain onto these instruments transforms them into what Elaine Scarry calls the insignia of power. The power they symbolise is that over life itself, threatening it 'at least as a last resort, with absolute menace' (Foucault, 1978: 144). These insignia bring pain into the visual field and represent an authority that, at the time of interrogation, is absolute.

In torture, investigation and sanction converge, functioning, as Michel Foucault has observed, 'in that strange economy in which the ritual that produced the truth goes hand in hand with the ritual that imposed the punishment' (Foucault, 1977: 42). The purported aim of this ritual is to elicit a confession figured as truth. But because the sheer overwhelming assertiveness of pain annihilates all vestiges of the world and shatters language and voice, there is no necessarily direct relationship between a confession extracted in this way and the truth. Foucault quotes Augustin Nicolas's *Si la torture est un moyen à verifier les crimes* of 1682: 'Judicial torture is a dangerous means of arriving at the truth . . . Nothing is more equivocal. There are guilty men who have enough firmness to hide a true crime . . . and innocent victims who are made to confess crimes of which they were not guilty' (Foucault, 1977: 40). Wielded in the name of truth, the power embodied by the agent of interrogation forces one to ask what, with utterance extracted under such duress, has happened to the notion of truth itself.

Inaugurated by the Catholic church, confession became a formative technique for the production of truth in the West. The linking of confession and violence is, however, as ancient as Greek and Roman law: torture, Foucault tells us, 'has accompanied [confession] like a shadow, and supported it when it could go no further: the dark twins' (Foucault, 1978: 59). Foucault argues that the spreading of confession into the fields of 'justice, medicine, education, family relationships, and love relations, in the most ordinary affairs of everyday life, and in the most solemn rites' hides an internal ruse. That ruse consists in the reversal of power and freedom. Confession is figured as liberating, power as constraining. What the alliance of truth with a liberatory discourse in confession hides, Foucault argues, is that the production of that truth itself is 'thoroughly imbued with relations of power' (Foucault, 1978: 60). Confession, in other words, plays out the relations of power already invested in its production. In producing truth-telling as a key to freedom – and here Foucault's critique of the confession includes that undertaken in the psychoanalytic encounter – we forget the extent to which such a truth is deemed to be liberatory by those who would discipline us through it. Confession wrought from torture performs scandalously, at the level of the body, the power relations implicit even in voluntary confessional utterances.

Coming home to roost

If the physical spaces deployed in torture and the vocabulary used to designate these spaces parody the civilisational values of domesticity, the figure of the interrogator turns un-homeliness into performance. Indeed, Rego's interrogator is doubly parodic, for in being improperly uniformed (the separate items of clothing do not cohere around any formal code) and cross-dressed, s/he mocks the authority in whose name s/he exercises power. This parodic figure of (non)-hospitality, surrounded, as if they were heraldic insignia, by symbolic accoutrements (the tethered lamb, the white feather, the severed plant), is the gatekeeper of a home that is a place of pain rather than healing. The pitchfork is only the most literal objectification of such wounding intimacy. But if pain and humiliation enter the home and injuriously penetrate those most private psychic and corporeal spaces, they also, Rego's work suggests, already exist within that scene. Aggression is both native and homely.

This interrogator's performance takes place, as we have seen, in a bare room giving onto a bleak exterior space, a kind of antechamber or threshold. From this liminal space s/he guards the boundary – the limits – of domesticity itself. On the one hand, on a metaphoric level, it is tempting to identify the interrogator with the ego, that 'frontier creature' negotiating the division between self and world. But simultaneously, as a sadistic figure, the interrogator performs the role of the superego, which not only behaves cruelly towards the ego and 'confronts [it] as a strict father confronts a child' (Freud, 1926: 223), but also displays the very aggressiveness that the child would like, in turn, to direct towards the father. Indeed, in Rego's work, the performance of nurturing and domesticity is a masquerade employed to avert anxiety about its opposite, the inherence of destructiveness. In the cruelty that the interrogator metonymically embodies (the smirk, the moustache, the gloves, the pitchfork, the boots), that disguise is here baldly exposed. Cruelty comes home to roost. That which is revealed is a cornerstone of late Freudian theory: love pitches its tent in a bloody battlefield.

As I have already suggested, this is one of the conclusions that Freud reaches in his late, dark work, *Civilization and its Discontents*, an investigation into the self-defeating nature of social law and the self interest that goes by the name of love. Here Freud tortuously arrives at the conclusion that the evolution of civilisation presents the struggle between 'the instinct for life and the instinct for destruction, as it works itself out in the human species' (Freud 1930: 122). From early on, Freud had begun to theorise the links between Eros and a destructive impulse, although these changed radically with his formulation of the death drive in 1920. In *Civilization and its Discontents*, he explicitly affirms that aggression is native to the subject – 'Homo homini lupus' (man is a wolf to man; Freud, 1930: 111). Freud's state of nature, like Hobbes's, is a place where the human being is exploitative, ruthless, driven by self interest alone. There is relentless violence in his observation that man's 'neighbour' is

> not only a potential helper or sexual object, but also someone who tempts them to satisfy their aggressiveness on him, to exploit his capacity for work without compensation, to use him sexually without his consent, to seize his possessions, to humiliate him, to cause him pain, to torture and kill him. (Freud, 1930: 111)

The main objective of civilisation, then, is to domesticate 'this primary mutual hostility of human beings' (Freud, 1930: 112). Thus, the commandment 'to love one's neighbour as oneself' is a bid for an individual to commit the ultimate civilisational act, being 'really justified by the fact that nothing else runs so strongly counter to the original nature of man' (Freud, 1930: 112) as does the equation of the love of others with the love of self. But, Freud tells us, man's natural aggressive instinct, which 'opposes [the] programme of civilization', is the derivative and the principal representative of the death instinct, a pulsion that exists 'alongside Eros' (Freud, 1930: 122). The evolution of civilisation, in other words, stages a battle between the life drives and the urge to destructiveness, to death.

Freud famously arrived at the death drive through his attempt to explain the compulsion, observed in some of his patients, to repeat in dreams or fantasy a scene of trauma. This urge initially seemed to run counter to his earlier idea of the pleasure principle. Yet having identified a link between the sexual instinct and a sadistic impulse, Freud acknowledges in *Beyond the Pleasure Principle* a primary masochism, a foundational turning of the destructive instinct upon the subject's own ego. He asks how it is that

> the sadistic instinct, whose aim it is to injure the object, [can] be derived from Eros, the preserver of life? Is it not plausible to suppose that this sadism is in fact a death instinct which, under the influence of the narcissistic libido, has been forced away from the ego and has consequently only emerged in relation to the object? (Freud, 1920: 54)

In these questions, the pleasure principle is tied both to the instinct to preserve life, and to the drive towards death. This paradox is confirmed four years later in 'The Economic Problem of Masochism', where sexuality is explicitly linked to destructiveness and where 'the instinct for mastery or the will to power' is simply the projection of the organism's own drive towards death (Freud, 1924a: 163).

How does this affect our reading of *The Interrogator's Garden*?

It is through the suggestion, in several of the sketches made around this work, of the victim's masochistic complicity in psychological or sexual torment that Rego moves from a satirical exploration of power in the political domain to a reflection on the subject's psychic constitution. What is suggested by reading *The Interrogator's Garden* alongside its companion sketches, where masochism is more graphically explicit, is the binding together of the interrogator as a haunting, a memory of political repression, and the interrogator as a figure of interpellated and ethically ambiguous subjectivity. The image oscillates ceaselessly between these two registers, the one literal, the other symbolic. On an analytic level, these registers must be distinguished or separately acknowledged, if one is not to suggest (as indeed one must not) that real victims of torture are in any way complicit with their own torment and annihilation. Here it is important, in other words, to tease out the distinction between political and psychic agencies.[9]

A close link between sadism and masochism is implicit in *The Interrogator's Garden, Study after 'The Interrogator's Garden'* (Plate 10), *The Recruit, The Inspection* and *Chéri II*. Such a link becomes explicit in the clinging embrace of *Chéri I*, and is scandalously evident in the sketchy pastel drawing *Obedience* (2000; Figure 21). Here, a young woman dressed in black kneels on a cushion before a chair, head squashed flatly against the seat, lifting her skirt as if co-operatively waiting to be spanked. In two further drawings of

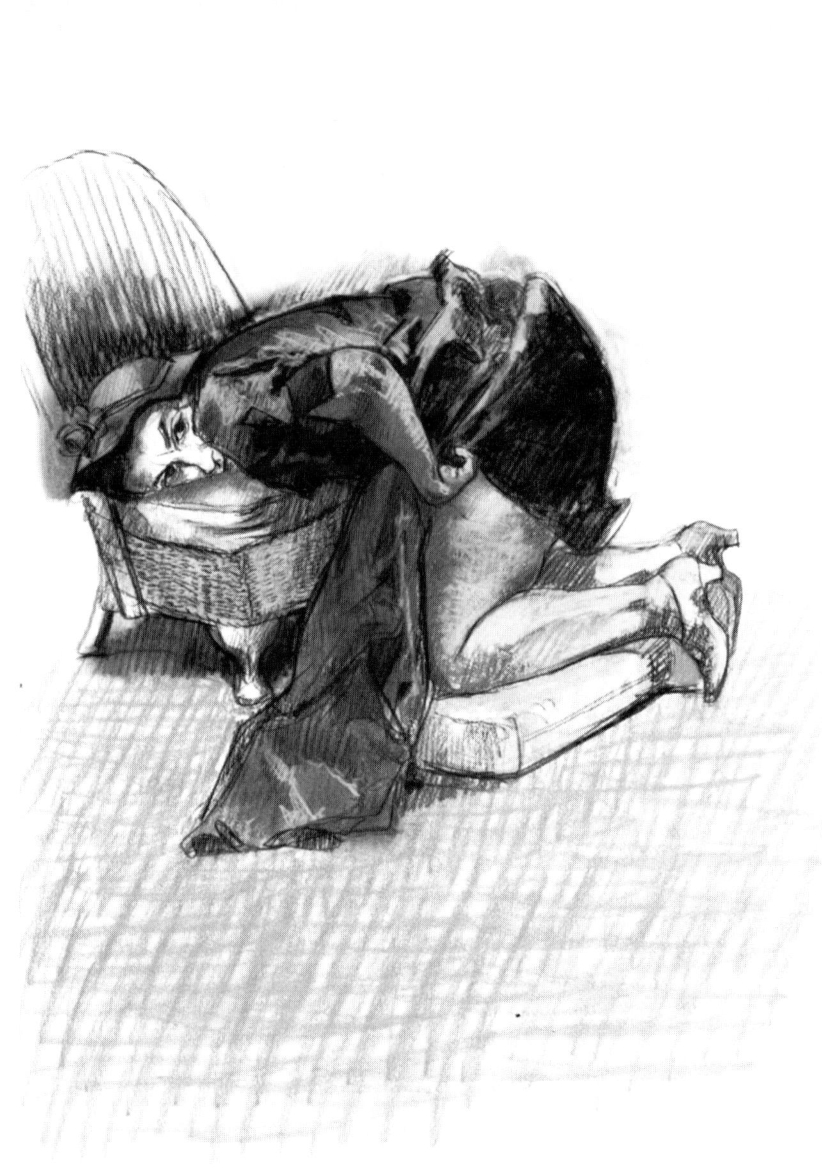

Figure 21   Paula Rego, *Obedience*, 2000

the same year – *The Frotter* and *The Frotter and his Mother* (Figure 22) – Rego places her protagonist, this time a man in a suit, in a similarly abject kneeling position, revealing that such willingness to accept punishment is not gender specific. Yet the reading of such an image differs according to gender. For, in her medieval

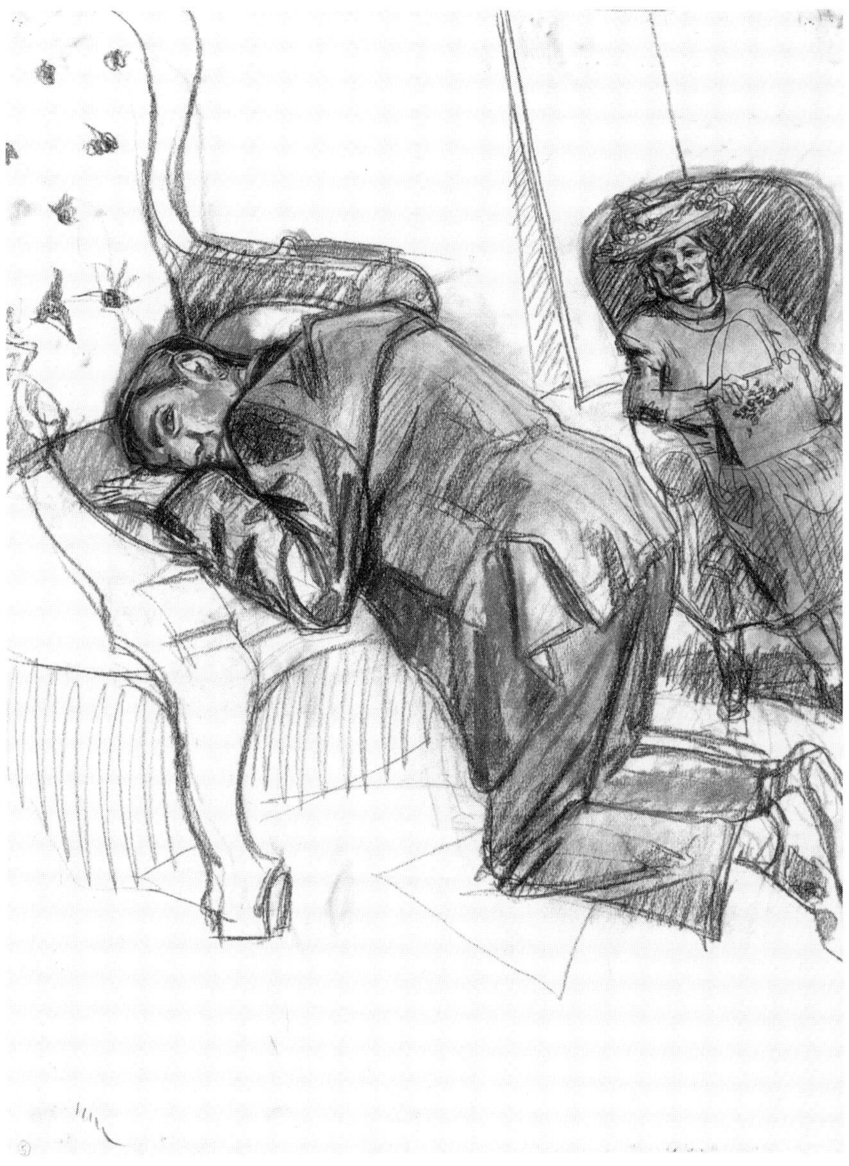

Paula Rego, *The Frotter and his Mother*, 2000　　　　　　　　　　Figure 22

compliance, the protagonist of *Obedience* embodies a Christian ideal of willing accommodation linked to the structures of an institutionalised misogyny.

Historically, obedience as a Christian virtue, reinforced by a pious Mariolatry and incubated in the heart of the Salazarist family, facilitated patriotic nation building by male subjects. Rego's treatment of such womanly aquiescence blends the wish for historic accuracy with the irony of a wilfully distanced observer. Commenting, then, on the Pieta-like configuration in her triptych *Marriage à la Mode* (1999) – a work specifically set in Portugal in the 1940s – she drolly observes that the young wife 'is doing what she feels she must do: be obedient to her husband' (Gleadell, 2000: 54). Clearly, in her compliance, the protagonist of *Obedience* is collusive with – and desirous of – her own punishment. Rego has acknowledged a connection between *Obedience* and *The Interrogator's Garden*: 'The drawing *Obedience* is like the one I gave the Foundation for the Victims of Torture. And it's the same girl as the one coming out of the bag in *The Interrogator's Garden*. There is something sadomasochistic about all this – I don't like to say it – but in the related drawings, like *Chéri* – well, she's complicit. . .' (Rego: in conversation).

In 'The Economic Problem of Masochism' (Freud, 1924a), Freud makes a distinction between three forms of masochism: 'erotogenic', 'feminine' and 'moral'. Erotogenic masochism – sexual pleasure in pain – underlies the other two, while moral masochism, as a 'norm of behaviour', is 'in some respects the most important form' that masochism takes. Feminine masochism, however, 'is the one that is most accessible to our observation', but it is not confined to the female sex. In fact the examples Freud cites are all male. Here, again, unstable gender identifications, linked to the inherent bisexuality that remains one of Freud's most radical insights, underlies the apparent investment of Freudian theory in sexual difference. In his discussion of feminine masochism, the feminine is closely intertwined with the infantile. This suggestion had been absent from 'A Child is Being Beaten' (1919), where Freud had nevertheless made it clear that spanking fantasies were related to incestuous desire, thus Oedipalising masochism, for to want to be beaten is to want to be treated like a child, a naughty child, a child that wants what he or she cannot have. In addition to this infantalisation, Freud also insists that where masochistic fantasies have been 'especially richly elaborated', one discovers that 'they place the subject in a characteristically female situation; they signify, that is, being castrated, or copulated with or giving birth to a baby' (Freud, 1924a: 161–162).

With moral masochism, which is the third form of masochism that Freud names, unerpinning the desire for punishment (and the subject's complicity with being punished) is an unconscious sense of guilt: 'the subject assumes that he has committed some crime (the nature of which is left indefinite) which is to be expiated by all these painful and tormenting procedures' (Freud, 1924a: 162). Melanie Klein was to take up this argument and elaborate upon it extensively. Arguably, it is to this sense of original guilt – a guilt that the law threatens to punish, or promises to assuage through the conferral of an identity – that interpellation is addressed. As he had already acknowledged in *The Ego and the Id*, the sense of guilt emerges from the ego's perception that it does not meet the strict demands of its ideal, the superego. It is in his discussion of moral (and purportedly desexualised) masochism that Freud returns to – and concludes with – the erotic content of all bodily excitations, whether of pleasure or un-pleasure, with the devastating conclusion that 'even the subject's destruction of himself cannot take place without libidinal satisfaction' (Freud, 1924a: 170).

The unconscious sense of guilt characterising moral masochism is not identical with morality. Freud makes a distinction between them in the following manner: in the moral being, the ego submits to the sadism of the superego, while in moral masochism, the ego 'seeks punishment, whether from the super-ego or from the parental powers outside' (Freud, 1924a: 168). As the acquisition of conscience is contemporaneous with the dissolution of the Oedipus complex, it follows that conscience – morality – coincides with a de-sexualisation of the parents. However, what Freud calls moral masochism *revives* the Oedipus complex, re-sexualising parental punishment and thus, in effect, putting paid to morality. Put more literally, where the need for punishment corresponds to a desire to be 'beaten by the father', and stands 'very close to the other wish, to have a passive (feminine) sexual relation with him', punishment is clearly eroticised and the repressive, civilising effects of Oedipalisation are undone 'to the advantage neither of morality nor of the person concerned' (Freud, 1924a: 169).

This has a direct impact on what might be termed the politics of masochism, without, however, clearly indicating the direction that such a politics might take. For to libidinise or eroticise subjection might mean to accommodate authoritarian power, but might equally mean to undermine it in the transformation of pain to pleasure, showing the subject to be, finally, invincible. Certainly, the dualism of mastery and submission is complicated with masochism. Such vexations are also played out at the level of the individual.

Around the unconscious sense of guilt underlying masochism, Freud elaborates a hypothesis for the ethical subject that inverts any intuitively held causalities linking crime or misdeed to punishment. In *Civilization and its Discontents,* Freud exposes that law to be the agency that protects us from what we really want: from our erotic and murderous drives. To enter the communal bonds of civilisation is to renounce – indeed to sacrifice – what is instinctual. As the engine of civilisation, that law also reserves the right to punish so as to 'prevent the crudest excesses' (Freud, 1930: 112) of our innate brutality. Now the relationship between instinctual renunciation and conscience is paradoxically reversed and spirals towards an entirely counter-intuitive conclusion. Having represented the sense of guilt as 'the most important problem in the development of civilization', and having shown that 'the price we pay for our advance in civilization is a loss of happiness through the heightening of the sense of guilt' (Freud, 1930: 137), Freud notes 'what a potent obstacle to civilization aggressiveness must be, if the defence against it' – conscience and morality – 'can cause as much unhappiness as aggressiveness itself' (Freud, 1930: 143). If aggression causes us unhappiness, its remedy – civilisation – Freud observes, keeps us equally locked in misery. Freud thus arrives at the astonishing contention that 'whatever way we may define the concept of civilization, it is a certain fact that all the things with which we seek to protect ourselves against the threats that emanate from the sources of suffering are part of that very civilization' (Freud, 1930: 86). Social law, then, is as destructive as the desires it asks us to renounce. Moreover, Freud makes it clear that the force of the internalised injunctions occurs in direct proportion to the violence it restrains: 'every piece of aggression whose satisfaction the subject gives up is taken over by the super-ego and increases the latter's aggressiveness (against the ego)' (Freud, 1930: 129).

We have now come full circle to the opening lines of this chapter. Through an identification with the parental agency – now specifically *paternal* – Freud envisages the childish ego as not only masochistically accepting its punishment, but also in fantasy repeating it, as if to say: 'If I were the father and you were the child, I should treat you badly' (Freud, 1930: 129). The reversal and repetition by the subject of this introjected paternal violence exposes the model for the superego to be a drama of authority taking place between father and child, where the child, resentful of the father's sadism, nevertheless identifies with his unassailable authority. The superego is both the child's appropriation of the father's authority, and the child's aggression towards the authority of an inner father, who is 'degraded to the status of a punished ego' (Bersani, 1986: 22).

In the bleak, symphonic overview of *Civilization and its Discontents*, we see the overlapping and interweaving strains connecting the life and death instincts, pleasure and un-pleasure, sadism and masochism. Freud now has it that, where conscience was initially the cause of instinctual renunciation, 'every renunciation of instinct now becomes a dynamic source of conscience and every fresh renunciation increases the latter's severity and intolerance' (Freud, 1930: 128). The convoluted and far-reaching logic of such theorising suggests that the positions of subject and object of violence are unstable, interchangeable. The contradictions multiply: guilt is the outcome of the renunciation meant to assuage it; restraint magnifies aggression; renunciation reasserts and thus preserves the desire it bars; and love and violence are locked in an ineluctable and intimate embrace.

But to suggest that Paula Rego's interrogator fully embodies the vexed position of that ambiguous superego of *Civilization and its Discontents* is also to miss the other point of the painting. On a purely narrative register, looking at the supercilious smirk, the absurd costume, the fudged masquerade, we are reminded of Rego's confessed desire 'to take the piss'. 'I made him a woman so as to undermine him', she has remarked (Rego: in conversation). The logic of this is surprising: to feminise is to mock. This is, in the tradition of old cultural practices, a man undermined in such a way as ultimately to accept and condone the restorative, conservative logic of carnivalesque status reversal. What this amounts to is a shaking, but not destruction, of the social frame: disruption in the name of renewal and continuation. But is this the case? What is the effect here of mocking laughter?

Let us turn, one last time in this chapter, to Freud. Freud addresses laughter in his short essay on humour written in 1927. The effects of laughter are not dissimilar to those of mania, which, he tells us in *The Ego and the Id*, is the reverse side of that 'extraordinary harshness and severity' towards the ego exercised by 'its tyrant', the superego, holding sway as 'a pure culture of the death instinct' (Freud, 1923: 53). In mania, the loss – which in melancholia paralyses the subject – is mastered, and the ego is suddenly left free again (euphorically so) to pursue new objects. If the melancholy subject is oppressed by the superego, the manic subject has turned this relationship around: there is triumph as the ego meets the ego ideal. Freud recognises this as one strategy among several possible tactics to overcome suffering (Freud, 1930: 78–82).

Humour, then, is a form of inoculation, controlling pain by economising on emotional expenditure: 'one spares oneself the affects to which the situation would naturally give rise' (Freud, 1927b: 162). Humour acts, in other words, upon a potentially painful situation in effigy, turning aggression into pleasure. With humour, as with mania, the ego sublates its losses and swaggers over both the 'provocations of reality' and the cruelty of its tormentor, the superego, asserting its invulnerability in the triumph of narcissism. It is this that accounts for what Freud calls the 'grandeur' of humour, its haughty self-concern. The object's self-love simultaneously asserts itself over the destructive rampages of the death instinct, and shows that the damage that the external world has wrought is no more than an occasion for the ego to gain pleasure. Narcissism, then, plays a part in keeping the tyranny of the death instinct in check by asserting the resilience of the ego in the face of both reality and of its own self-destructiveness. Is it in this light that we are to read the cropped pot-plant in *The Interrogator's Garden* – as a death-like pruning that in fact brings forth new life?

Freud states that, like the expression of humour, the triumph of narcissism allows the pleasure principle to gain the upper hand. He famously discussed the triumph of narcissism as characterising an assortment of strange bedfellows. These include children, cats and large beasts of prey, great criminals, humorists, and women, whom Freud describes as unable – owing to their narcissism – to form a true attachment to objects as men do (Freud, 1914b: 88–89). Not surprisingly, this section of 'On Narcissism' has long been under attack by feminist critics. But in opposition to such attacks, Jo Anna Isaak takes on board Freud's identification of women with primary narcissism, arguing, along with Mary Jacobus and Sarah Kofman, that women might positively and purposefully lay claim to narcissism as men lay claim to the Phallus (Isaak, 1996: 13; Jacobus, 1995b: 272–273; Kofman, 1985: 52). As an 'unassailable libidinal position' (Freud, 1914b: 89), narcissism might grant women themselves an empowering unassailability, protecting them from their own desire, whether it is 'to have' or 'to be' something else.

Freud's list of beings possessed of a narcissistic libidinal position is less random than it appears. Women and children both stand outside the phallic regime; Freud himself yokes them together in his analysis of 'feminine' masochism. Sarah Kofman reads Freud's comparison of women to cats, beasts of prey, and criminals alongside Nietzsche. Of particular interest is the notion of 'woman as the great criminal' in *The Gay Science*. One might profitably compare Freud's definition of a criminal as one who manages 'to keep away from their ego anything that would diminish it' (Freud, 1914b: 89) with Nietzsche's 'behold, the pale criminal has bowed his neck: from his eye speaks the great contempt. My ego is something that should be overcome; my Ego is to me the great contempt of man' (Nietzsche, 1974: 65). In Freud's notion of the criminal ego, it is narcissism that manages to thwart the work of the superego.[10] Kofman suggests that Freud's text 'On Narcissism' opened up numerous possibilities that other Freudian texts neglected: 'that of conceptualizing the enigma of woman along the lines of the great criminal rather than the hysteric' (Kofman, 1985: 65). For Kofman, the criminal shares with the humorist – that other great narcissist – the fact 'that he has succeeded in conquering his ego and holding it in contempt, thanks to his superego, and has thus been able to fend off everything that might debase him' (Kofman, 1985: 55). Such readings re-configure Freud's anti-feminist notion of women's narcissism, casting it in affirmative terms so as to compensate for the apparently weaker superego.

But Freud's point, in his later essay 'Humour', is not simply that in humour the ego shows itself to be narcissistically invincible. It is that it does so with the permission – indeed *as an indulgence* – of the superego, thus reinstating the authority of the superego, and, with it, affirming the Oedipal model. In the first place, Freud notes that in adopting a humorous attitude towards others – and what he describes is more akin to satire or mockery, a humour which assumes a moral high ground – the subject behaves to the objects of its mirth as an adult behaves towards a child, acquiring superiority 'by assuming the role of the grown-up and identifying himself to some extent with his father, and reducing the other people to being children' (Freud, 1927b: 163). The position of the humorist seems to be the obverse of that of the masochist who 'wants to be treated like a small and helpless child' (Freud, 1924a: 162). But Freud vexes the question when he passes from humour at the expense of another to the question of laughing at oneself. 'Is there any sense', he asks, 'in saying that someone is treating himself like a child and is at the same time playing the part of a superior adult towards that child?' (Freud, 1927b: 164).

The answer to this rhetorical question resides in the superego, which 'often keeps the ego in strict dependence and still really treats it as the parents, or the father, once treated the child, in its early years' (Freud, 1927b: 164). Humour, he tells us, '*would be the contribution made to the comic through the agency of the super-ego*' (Freud, 1927b: 165, emphasis in the original). His formulation of this is characteristically curious and paradoxical. First, he had reiterated the Rabelaisian notion of laughter as misrule, telling us that humour is 'not resigned, it is rebellious'. Now he tells us that the dangers of reality are defanged through humour ('Look! Here is the world, which seems so dangerous! It is nothing but a game for children – just worth making a jest about!'). The rebellion is, after all, contained: a storm in a teacup. What occurs is not the inflation or victory of the ego, but that of the superego, for whom it's business as usual. The analysis that had begun with the narcissistic triumph of the ego ends with the affirmation once again of the dominion of the superego, condescending to encourage the intimidated ego, in order to 'obtain a small yield of pleasure' by speaking 'kindly words of comfort' to it (Freud, 1927b: 163–166). Another way of saying this might be that, if humour is a political strategy, it is an efficacious one . . . for the powerless.

Freud ends his essay 'Humour' with the following observation: 'And finally, if the super-ego tries, by means of humour, to console the ego and protect it from suffering, this does not contradict its origin in the parental agency' (Freud, 1927b: 166). Here, then, the satirical stance leads us straight back into the familial position. While Freud's customary mapping of the family plot through Oedipalisation sees punishment and consolation structurally performed by different agents – paternal and maternal respectively – each playing a distinct role in triangulation, here, Freud suggests, there is a conflation of these roles. For what Freud represents, in his essay 'Humour', is a cross-dressed superego humouring the vulnerable ego: tyrant passing as comforting guardian, interrogator passing as homely gardener.

To see Paula Rego's work *The Interrogator's Garden* in the light of the superego in Freud's 'Humour' is to recognise not only the undermining of an authority simultaneously domestic and political: it is also to acknowledge violence as simultaneously and dialectically social and psychic. But, above all, it is to regard as relative the roles of those who punish and those who console. On such shifting ground, we are invited to speculate on the mobile and interchangeable places of those who occupy the position of power and those who are humiliated as its objects.

Notes

1 The shifts occurring in Freud's own conceptualisation of the two terms – the superego and the ego ideal – have led to some critical discord. Kaja Silverman, for instance, accepts the definition of the Freud of *The Ego and the Id*, speaking of the ego ideal as 'the psychic construct which stands to one side of the ego, as a kind of ideal version of it. This ego ideal or superego functions through the history of the subject as the mirror in which the ego sees what it should be, but never can be' (Silverman, 1983: 135). Janine Chasseguet-Smirgel, on the other hand, regrets the later absorption of the ego ideal into the superego (Chassegueut-Smirgel, 1985).

2 Neo-Realism emerged from socially committed artists of the oppositional left in Portugal in the 1940s and 1950s, and was more akin to the work of the Mexican muralists than to the socialist realism of the soviet bloc in the 1930s. Neo-Realism was fervently anti modernist and anti formalist, promoting the expression of the social and economic conditions of the time. Its exponents included Júlio Pomar, Manuel Filipe, Vespeira, Jorge de Oliveira and Moniz Pereira, Lima de Freitas and Augusto Gomes.

3 For a brilliant analysis of how injury forms the basis for political identity through the prism of Nietzsche's concept of *ressentiment*, see Brown, 1995.

4 Botticelli's *Venus and Mars* and Piero di Cosimo's *Nymph and Satyr* are in the National Gallery in London, a collection Rego knows well from her year as Associate Artist there (1990–91).

5 Hitler, Stalin and Saddam Hussein are all figures whose moustaches metonymically represented their regime. 'Evidently, Totalitarianism and the moustache walk hand in hand along the path of history' muse Greg and Jane Lodge, after providing a long list of moustachioed dictators. See www.hackwriters.com/moustacheconspiracy.htm (accessed on 19 April 2003).

6 Maria Manuel Lisboa (Lisboa, 2003) reads an anti-colonial critique in numerous of Rego's works where I see no such specific attack. Part of her argument hinges about a detailed iconographic exegesis and what

sometimes appears to be a misreading (or over-determination) of the ethnic identity of the protagonists of the painting in question.

7 Robert Young usefully contributes to the dispute about the differences between imperialism and colonialism. He opposes 'an empire that was bureaucratically controlled by a government from the centre, and which was developed for ideological as well as financial reasons', which he calls imperialism, to 'an empire that was developed for settlement by individual communities or for commercial purposes by a trading company, a structure that can be called colonial'. According to this definition, Portugal was an imperial power, for 'imperialism was typically driven by ideology from the metropolitan centre and concerned with the assertion and expansion of state power' (Young, 2001: 16).

8 Jann Matlock takes the opposite view, regarding female-to-male cross-dressing in the late nineteenth century as a form of protest in a context where, for a woman to refuse to adopt the more spectacular, fetishised and commodified masquerade of women's attire would be thought incomprehensible (Matlock, 1993: 57).

9 For a discussion of the vexed relation between the political and psychic implications of violence, see Rose, 1989. See my Chapter 1 for a brief discussion of this important text.

10 Melanie Klein inverted this position, arguing that criminality was born not of a thwarted or vanquished superego but of its opposite. Criminality for Klein is therefore an acting out effected in order to meet with punishment. See Klein 1927, 1933, 1934.

Possession and loss:
The First Mass in Brazil

The deceptively simple details of who is imitating whom, and under what conditions, stands as the most insistent, intricate, and indispensable questions for a politics of mimesis. (Diana Fuss, *Identification Papers*)

In being able to receive the other's words, to assimilate, repeat, and reproduce them, I become like him: One. A subject of enunciation. Through psychic osmosis/identification. Through love. (Julia Kristeva, 'Freud and Love: Treatment and its Discontents')

The painting

In landscape format, we are presented with a reclining woman. She is lying on her side on a bed; her knees are bent; her body describes a curve, one hand lightly touching the bed's metal frame above her head. Dated 1993, Paula Rego's *The First Mass in Brazil* (Plate 3) is painted in acrylic on paper laid on canvas. The painting is evenly lit, diurnal, as if presenting itself to scrutiny. Here is an image closely overseen by intertextual ghosts, from Titian through Goya to Manet and Gauguin, with their programmes of prohibition and desire. A young woman on a bed in full view of the observer: what could more readily invoke the gendered economy of the gaze in Western painting? But the woman disqualifies this economy: she is not beautiful, she is not naked; her blank gaze, fixed upon an indeterminate middle-distance, does not engage with the viewer's at all. This recumbent young woman with her disengaged look simultaneously appeals to and spurns the logic of scopic pleasure that figures woman as image, as a 'bearer of meaning' (Mulvey, 1989: 15) but not as its maker. Instead of a nubile, available body, we are presented with a body turned in upon itself and almost bursting with its own interiority; a heavily pregnant body.

The model for this painting was Rego's daughter Victoria. More widow than bride, the protagonist is swathed in a long black dress; the bed on which she lies is unmade. Her breasts and stomach are bursting with fecund promise. Feet shod in clumpy, black lace-up workaday boots are pressed closely together. This solid body reclines on a blood-red throw; her head rests on a grey-blue pullover, a sketchy sailing boat and anchor embroidered in red upon its front, a sailor's jumper. An absence, then, occupies a central place in the painting: a man metonymically invoked. Like Titian's Ariadne waving to the departing Theseus, this is a woman abandoned; but she does not share Ariadne's fate of rescue by a new love.

The young woman is surrounded by apparently unrelated objects, objects that invoke, perhaps, the 'exotic': two silvery fish on a low bedside table; a plump, extravagantly plumed turkey; lush arum lilies; a little figurine of a woman in a blood-smeared white dress; several small, voodoo-like dolls; and a lemon on the ledge behind the bed. All these props are rendered in fierce, emphatic brush-marks, which close in and tighten around the details of the protagonist's physiognomy: the particularity of her broad face, her strong hands. But most startlingly and drawing our attention as compellingly as the pregnant figure, framed on the wall behind the reclining body and slicing the painting in half is an image of remarkable vividness. What is Rego telling us through this juxtaposition of a melancholy pregnant woman and a picture?

The First Mass in Brazil: Meirelles and Caminha

As a metapicture – a picture within a picture – this is also a window onto another spatial and temporal order. As a conceit anticipated by a distinguished lineage from Vermeer and Velazquez, through Manet and Matisse, the purposes of the metapicture encompass a reflection on the conventions of representation and the activity of painting (not showing the thing, but showing the showing of that thing), but also a consideration of the scope of the iconography of the painting in which it finds itself. While Rego has made several works that deal with the classic trope of the metapicture – the artist painting pictures in the studio – as a means of reflecting on the changing models of studio production that have informed her own activity as a painter (Rosengarten, 2009), in this work, the metapainting functions not so much as a reflexive device, but more as a powerful pointer to meaning.

The upper limit of the metapicture is cut off by the framing edge of Rego's own painting, which contains it and which also crops the top of a tall cross within the represented image. In the blonde light of the middle ground, we see a group of white men, all kneeling, heads lowered in prayer. A priest raises a chalice upon an altar dazzling in the harsh light. One of the men holds a billowing white flag marked with a red cross. In the bleached background, a promontory reaches out into a calm sea. Sail-ships bob in the distance. The day is glassy and still. In the shaded foreground, amidst lush foliage, a group of naked or scantily dressed natives watches the devotional scene, apparently in perplexed silence. This is an image of sacralisation and possession, pitting civilisation – figured as Church and Monarchy – against unstructured nature envisioned as passive, primitive alterity. An implicit drama of cultural confrontation is staged by the presentation of whiteness as transcendental signifier, as invisible, un-raced norm, against brownness as ethnically marked.

The source of this image is an engraving, widely circulated during Paula Rego's youth, based on a nineteenth-century painting by Brazilian artist Victor Meirelles, titled *The First Mass in Brazil*. Such a print hung in the home of Rego's nanny, Luzia, in Ericiera and its invocation partakes of a poetics of childhood in Rego's work. (Rego's metapainting appropriates the orientation of the print and not of the original painting, of which it is a reverse image.)

In preparation for *First Mass in Brazil*, Rego made several drawings of her daughter reaching the final stages of her pregnancy. These drawings, as Memory Holloway has pointed out in her inspired reading of the painting, present pregnancy as 'a state of assured self-containment'. Holloway suggests that

> only when the artist put together the woman in black on the bed, under the heavy weight of the meaning carried by the engraving, did there emerge a reading in direct contradiction to the fullness and health and plenitude of the drawing on the theme of pregnancy. (Holloway, 2000–01: 702)

What heavy meanings were 'carried by the engraving'? As we shall see, historically it offered several possible interpretations and was thus able to be assimilated into the ideological apparatus of the *Estado Novo* in at least two different ways. In turn, the painting upon which it was based played its ideological part, almost a century earlier, in Brazil's project of self invention, its baptism as a sovereign nation under the sign of miscegenation. Like the written document upon which it is based, the nineteenth-century painting brings together Catholics and pagans, Portuguese and indigenous people. But it does so, again like its textual source, in a way that clearly establishes a line of civilisational ascent between them, the naked and the clothed.

The iconography of Victor Meirelles' large painting, dated 1860 and now housed in the Museu Nacional de Belas Artes in Rio de Janeiro (Plate 4) was drawn directly from a document that itself has mythical status as the founding narrative of the Portuguese 'discovery'[1] of Brazil: a letter written as an eyewitness account, addressed to the King of Portugal, Dom Manuel I, by Pero Vaz de Caminha, an official scribe on Pedro Álvares Cabral's expedition to India, which, on 22 April 1550, landed on the territory that was to become Brazil. It narrates the events between 21 April and the day on which it was written, 1 May 1500. Caminha's *Letter*, while observing the requisite conventions of address of its time, is considered unusual within the genres of travel literature and discovery narratives, because of its immersion in the empirical and its fresh, detailed observation. Moreover, as João Cezar de Castro Rocha notes, the scribe's language itself 'implies a visual style. It is as if Caminha writes not on paper but on a canvas' (de Castro Rocha, 2001). With its ekphrastic precision, the document is also noteworthy for the way it involves the reader in the circumstances of its own production and for the sense of immediacy it conveys in its engaging use of the present tense.[2]

But while it cannot be fully absorbed into the textual conventions of its time, in its evocation of Brazil as paradise, Caminha's letter foreshadows a trope that extends from Jean de Léry through Montaigne to Rousseau, and indeed to painterly evocations of Brazil as edenic, for instance the painting of seventeenth-century Dutch artists Frans Post and Albert Eckhout. It figures the newly found territory as an uncharted – and unredeemed – Eden, tamed and transformed into a safe harbour by the performance, before a native audience, of a devotional ritual. The place is evoked in rich detail. There are shady palm trees, other trees of 'infinite species', parrots, a river. The inhabitants described with a keen and sympathetic eye, are 'dark, naked, and with nothing covering their shame' (Caminha, 1990: 157). Their lack of 'shame' (*vergonha*) is reiterated seven times in the text, and is, finally, explicitly linked to the Judaeo-Christian site of primal innocence.

As the consecration of newly found land, a bold staging of Christian salvation ritually transforms an edenic state of nature into postlapsarian, civilised Christendom. For on 26 April, the Sunday after Easter, the members of the arriving party celebrate the Mass. They leave the ship carrying a flag bearing the cross of the Order of Christ, a Portuguese Military Order founded in 1319 by King Dinis after the Pope dissolved the Templars, and it is this flag that we see in Rego's rendition of Meirelles' painting, though Meirelles had not included it. Rego's addition of the flag serves to emphasise the links between the crown and the church – between political and ecclesiastic power. The emblem was used on the flags and sails of the fifteenth- and sixteenth-century sail-ships for their Atlantic missions and has come to be identified with 'the Portuguese Age of Discovery' and, metonymically, with Portugal itself.

In Caminha's account, the men set up an altar and their priest celebrates the Mass and preaches the Gospel of the day, which underlines the theme of sacrifice and salvation. Around them on the beach, a group of locals sit, watching and seeming to listen, though they clearly do not understand a word, their bows and arrows in repose. Two days later, Caminha describes how two carpenters make a large cross from a felled tree. In this act – at once material and symbolic – wood is transformed from nature's raw matter to an artefact of God-inspired culture. The potential of turning nature into culture is hinted at by the natives' fascination with the mastery of tools and the reproduction of skills, and is symbolically realised in the next celebration of the Mass. On Friday, 1 May – the day the letter describing the first Mass in Brazil is completed and signed 'from this, Porto Seguro, from your island, Vera Cruz' (Caminha, 1990: 174) – the captain orders his men to erect the cross. The party sets out once again with their flag, and many locals join the procession. Finally, they dig a hole in the ground and plant the cross on the southern bank of the river, 'where it may best be seen' (171) alongside 'Your Majesty's arms and emblem' (Caminha, 1990: 172). King and Church are thus united in a regime of visuality, invoked as guarantor of Christian truth (*Vera Cruz*) on a terrain now figured as a 'safe harbour' (*porto seguro*), having, by virtue of that very ritual, become the possession of the Portuguese crown ('*your* island').

Again, the men improvise an altar and the priest celebrates the Mass and preaches the Gospel. This ritual is attended by some forty or fifty locals, all kneeling 'like us', and when the Eucharist is raised, they all rise to their feet and raise their arms in devotion 'like us'

(Caminha, 1990: 172), anticipating by some centuries Darwin's observation on Tierra del Fuego of the 'odd mixture of surprise and imitation which these savages every moment exhibited' (Darwin, 1896: 218) when confronted with the British crew of the *Beagle*. This mimicry is as yet uncomprehending: it is represented by Caminha, as indeed by Darwin, as simian: the locals ape the gestures they observe without being caught in the web of cultural signification through which meaning accrues. This is, in germinal form, what Homi Bhabha calls 'colonial mimicry', striking an ironic compromise between signifiers that are 'almost the same, but not quite'. In this scheme, mimicry describes an ambivalent relation of colonised subject to colonial power, a camouflage which is not, and which cannot be, entirely convincing: 'to be Anglicized is *emphatically* not to be English', Bhabha drolly observes. The mimetic performance of the locals reveals, then, the interpellative effects of 'a double articulation ... which "appropriates" the Other as it visualises power' (Bhabha, 1987: 86–87).

At the end of the ceremony, Caminha comes to the conclusion that what distances 'these people' from Christianity is their lack of 'understanding of our language' (Caminha, 1990: 173), having already stated the case more strongly: 'there was neither conversation nor understanding with them, as their barbarity was such that they could neither be heard nor understood' (Caminha, 1990: 161). Separated from Christendom – and, with it, from civilisation itself – by the lack of the Word (in other words, by the lack of Portuguese), the local inhabitants are nevertheless figured as pliant raw material, unformed but ready to leave the maternal imaginary of their native beliefs, and awaiting the inevitable exile from Eden and the compensatory inauguration into the symbolic domain of language – the language of the colonisers – and the citizenship of the Church.

Finally, Caminha speculates on the possibility of shaping an innocent but elastic nature through instruction: 'See, your highness,' he notes, 'it is possible to live in such innocence, whether or not one is converted, if you teach them where their salvation lies' (Caminha, 1990: 173). A Rousseauian image of the savage as *tabula rasa* underlies such a view of the morally edifying and ultimately redeeming outcome of civilisation, figured as Christian. Pitted against the word 'innocence', then, is the word 'teach' and the monolithic, instrumental view of culture this reveals. For to be taught where salvation lies is to redeem innocence and so to be acquitted not only of Original Sin, but also of its ignorance. Religious instruction takes its place alongside other forms of learning: how to read, how to use implements and tools, how to play a musical instrument, and so on. Indeed, the erection of the cross is preceded by an account of the locals' amazement at the iron tools used by the Portuguese sailors, which they compare to their own more imprecise, roughly hewn implements of stone. Both knowledge and labour are thus moralised; but, more than this, they constitute a submission to the rules of an established order that 'carries the double meaning of having submitted to these rules and being constituted within sociality by virtue of this submission' (Butler, 1997: 118). The celebration of the Mass and the acquisition of manual skills are thus coupled as gestures through which value is mimicked and reproduced, spawning a latently 'civilised' – that is to say, Christian – subject. Caminha's *Letter* reveals, then – and Victor Meirelles' painting embodies – the ways in which the occupation and cultivation of a terrain are hatched into the imperative of instruction as a form of subjection.

Spliced onto an image of melancholy pregnancy, such a construct suggests an analogy with the psychic life of the subject, and the loss of a prior coherence that such education – indeed that all development and instruction – entails, presenting us with a hypothesis of the cost of civilisation, of the paradise that must be renounced (the maternal, the Imaginary) in order for the signifying and ideologically positioned subject to be born.

The two masses celebrated in Caminha's account are condensed into a single pictorial event in Meirelles' painting. A triangle structures the composition, with the amazed natives forming the base and the cross at the apex. The lighting reinforces this heavy-handed symbolism of ascent, with the cross and the clergymen in their white surplices brightly illuminated, the Portuguese lay congregation in soft light in the middle distance, and the indigenous people in the foreground immersed in shadow. The image of un-illumined natives is reinforced by their bodily positions: reclining, standing around, or sitting in the trees, they act out a nineteenth-century stereotype of native indolence. Indeed, the chiaroscuro of Meirelles' painting, while stylistically related to the theatricality of Baroque tableaux, also invokes the civilising and Christianising mission as the vehicle of enlightenment for the dark people.

As a talented student at the Academy of Fine Arts in Rio de Janeiro, Meirelles had, in 1853, been awarded the prize of a trip to Europe, and after a long sojourn in Italy he settled in Paris, where his work was influenced by that of the Romantic painters he copied, such as Géricault, Gros and Ary Scheffer. He painted *The First Mass in Brazil* in 1860 under the aegis of his Brazilian mentor, Araújo Porto Alegre, a poet, painter, dramatist and journalist, and an early exponent of Brazilian Romanticism. Porto Alegre advocated the formation and expression of a 'Brazilianism' – the word he coined was *brasiliana* – a cultural identity specific to the newly independent nation. Yet 'read Caminha five times' was his advice to his acolyte, stressing also the importance of capturing the tropical nature of Brazil: 'Remember our tall trees with their straight trunks, weighed down by diverse plants, interspersed with coconut and palm trees, for these grow in the shadow of the big trees. Sparse, but truly characteristic, genuinely Brazilian' (Porto Alegre to Meirelles, 4 letter dated 4 February, cited by Coli, 1998: 120).

A foundational text and a cultural trope thus join forces in the articulation of 'Brazilianness' paradoxically as both the product of a Portuguese heritage *and* autochthonous. Just as empirical observation in Caminha's letter was absorbed into the rhetorical figure of paradise, so Meirelles' painting harnesses text to pictorial convention. For the iconic status of Meirelles' painting also drew its authority mimetically, through the direct appropriation of a motif from a painting completed in 1854 and exhibited at the Paris Salon a year later. This was Horace Vernet's *First Mass at Kabylia*, a painting that, like Meirelles' own, aimed to contribute directly to a narration of nation. Vernet was famous for his painted 'machines': immense battle-scenes commemorating French military prowess. In *First Mass at Kabylia*, his interest in religious narrative is melded to an orientalist fascination with, and defence of, the French colonisation of Africa.

Vernet's *First Mass at Kabylia* was a triumphalist response to a local mission to establish an independent, theocratic, Islamic state, and thus, for Meirelles, served as a contemporary analogue to the historical subjugation and Christianisation in Caminha's narrative. Constructed as a pictorial eyewitness report, Vernet's painting served for Meirelles as a material correlative to Caminha's *Letter* from three and a half centuries earlier. Together, Vernet and Caminha provided the parameters for Meirelles' ambition to create a work of direct import to the emergence and formation of the Brazilian nation. Vernet's example, reinforced by his position in the French academy, legitimated Meirelles' enterprise, and acceptance of the Brazilian artist was sealed when *The First Mass in Brazil* was shown at the Paris Salon of 1861.

Both Meirelles' painting, and the ideological uses to which the engraving based upon it was put, are appeals to the past pressed at the service of the present. Such uses of the past urge us to ask whether it is ever truly over and done with – the question, of course, has psychoanalytic resonance. But, also, they animate all sorts of other discussions: 'about influence, about blame and judgement, about present actualities and future priorities' (Said, 1993: 1). Just as the later engraving was useful to Salazarist ideology, so Meirelles' evocation of the sixteenth century and his intertextual allusion to the French 'adventure' in Algeria served to promote an image of 'Brazilianness' at a time of anxiety about autonomous, if not fully autochthonous, identity.

Caminha's *Letter* and Meirelles' painting both played their part in the lengthy ideological process of construction of alterity that underpins the self-definition of 'Brazilianness', and the concomitantly troubled familial relation between Portugal and Brazil. Such definition, which today may find its place in the contested field of identity politics, has never been clear-cut in Brazil. 'There is no Brazil. And who's to say Brazilians exist?' (translation de Castro Rocha, 2001) reads the last line of the ironically titled poem *Hino Nacional* – 'National Anthem' – by twentieth-century Brazilian poet Carlos Drummond de Andrade. There is, this phrase suggests, no such thing as a Brazilian essence, and the poem makes it clear that multiple ethnicities constitute Brazilianness.

Not published until 1817, Caminha's *Letter* partook of the 'invention of Brazil' as a nineteenth-century construct. Clearly, the search for nativist myths stood in awkward relation to the idea of Brazil as a country 'discovered' by the Portuguese. In such a context, why was it that a Romantic artist as significant as Meirelles' mentor, Porto Alegre, committed to stamping cultural production with a mark of national – and indeed native – originality, should have insisted that Meirelles 'read Caminha five times'? The answer may lie in the ways in which Caminha's text details the relationship between the Portuguese navigators and the indigenous inhabitants of the land. The celebration of the Mass serves as the apotheosis of this relationship, a symbol of contact figured as harmonious, non-violent, complicit: crucially, the bows and arrows borne by the locals 'were of no use to them' (Caminha, 1990: 158). Similarly, the iconic status of Meirelles' painting in Brazilian culture hinges in part upon the imaging of a paradise of peaceful racial co-existence. At the heart of Brazilian self-invention lies an image of mingled ethnicities, mutually wary but peaceable. This was the Brazilian myth of 'racial democracy' in the making.

But underlying the mythical import of miscegenation and its central role in the narration of nation, there lay the hierarchical ordering of the colonial encounter, and the relationship between masters and slaves: slavery was not abolished in Brazil until 1888. Shortly after independence in 1822, more than a third of Brazil's population consisted of slaves. Substantial numbers of African slaves were still acquired at this time to work on the coffee plantations of the Paraiba Valley. Emilia Viotti da Costa observes that 'owning land and owning slaves were among the highest aspirations of the age' (Viotti da Costa, 1985: 128), for both signalled wealth and conferred social prestige. So, in addition to the soft-skinned French women and fat German girls that, in Drummond de Andrade's *Hino Nacional,* both play their parts in the constitution of Brazilian identity, 'Brazil' as a place and an idea was substantially modified by the enforced presence of Africans as slaves.

If Meirelles' painting is indebted to its textual source for its representation of ethnic co-existence, it is also, like both its textual and pictorial sources, clearly underpinned by the hierarchical racial ordering of Social Darwinism. It is therefore not surprising that its reproduction should have enjoyed popularity in Portugal during Salazar's regime. For the *Estado Novo,* the ethnic mix constituting Brazilian identity served as an exemplum in two opposing ways in the periods 1933–51 and 1951–74, coloured by the divergent responses to the doctrine of Lusotropicalism.

The myth of racial democracy

The Portuguese colonies were legitimated as the bedrock of the *Estado Novo* in the Portuguese Constitution of 1933. That same year, Brazilian sociologist Gilberto Freyre (1900–87) published what was to be his most famous book, *Casa Grande & Senzala* (literally 'The Big House and the Slaves' Quarters', translated as *The Masters and the Slaves,* Freyre, 1970a). This served as the foundations of the theory he called Lusotropicalism. *The Masters and the Slaves* takes as its principal object the decadent, slave-owning aristocracy of north-eastern Brazil in the eighteenth and nineteenth centuries, with particular emphasis on the *fazenda* – the estate or plantation structured around the so-called big house – as a classic example of paternalistic race and gender relations. The book formed part of Freyre's *Introduction to the History of the Patriarchal Society of Brazil*, which included two more volumes published in 1936 and 1959 respectively (Freyre 1968, and 1970b). A projected fourth volume was never written. Freyre further elaborated the notion of Lusotropicalism in a celebrated lecture delivered in Goa in 1951, and in several other texts culminating in *O Luso e o Trópico* (*The Portuguese and the Tropics*, Freyre, 1961) published in 1961, a crucial year, and a turning point in the decline of Salazar's regime.

The year in which Rego made the collage painting *When We Had a House in the Country*, 1961, was a key one for the *Estado Novo*. In addition to the attempted military coup that was instigated by the hijacking of the ocean-liner *Santa Maria*; the occupation by the Indian Union of Goa, Damão and Diu; and the start of the armed conflict in Angola, this was also the year in which the 'Native Statute' in the so-called Portuguese 'provinces' of Guiné, Angola and Mozambique was repealed. The legislative distinction between the Portuguese and the locals was officially and euphemistically replaced by a representation of the co-existence of diverse 'Portuguese subjects' in an ostensibly 'harmonious multiracial society on the outer limits of the Portuguese territory' (quoted in Castelo, 1998: 62).[3] Apparently liberal, but in fact also regionalist and in many ways conservative, Freyre's theories were ideally suited to the interests of Salazarism in the late 1950s and 1960s. For Freyre's endeavour to locate an affinity between the 'Portuguese' and the 'tropical', and his proposal of a third, hybrid culture, a 'luso-tropical' synthesis of the two, provided a perfect ideological foil to the new political climate. Rego's painting *The First Mass in Brazil* alludes, in its detailed inclusion of the painting by Meirelles, to the Lusotropical climate of its reception and reinterpretation in the twentieth century.

The works for which Freyre became famous constitute a monumental construction of Brazilian history as the nation's childhood, viewed in developmental terms in the context of the relationship between the Portuguese patriarchal planter family and its slaves. Problematising the relationship between race and culture, Freyre's writing attests to a concerted effort to short-circuit the predominantly racist mould of contemporary ideas of Brazilian miscegenation by turning it into a redeeming feature. However, the redemption represented by miscegenation was in effect that of ethnic 'whitening'. The triumphalism of Freyre's reversion to a racialised discourse emerges in his celebration of the contribution made by the 'Negro' to Brazilian culture, but also – frequently more than implicitly – in a ratification of slavery itself as the condition under which this became possible. Freyre points to African slaves as the historical *raison d'être* for miscegenation, which he sees as the core of Brazilian identity, reiterating his confidence in ethnic amalgamation as a means of overriding racial conflict. Thus is spawned an egalitarian myth, positing the success of racial integration in the Portuguese empire.

It is tempting today to spurn Freyre's writings as deeply reactionary, but, as Cláudia Castelo reminds us – at a time when institutionalised racism was rife, and when, in Brazil, miscegenation was generally regarded as one of the principle causes of 'degeneration' – Freyre's work was also innovative. It occupied, in other words, shifting ideological positions. By being the first study to examine race, gender and colonialism, and to stress the foundational role of African slaves in the formation of Brazilian culture, *The Masters and the Slaves* constitutes an important break from a nativist tradition. Yet in its approbation of miscegenation as a source of revivification and libidinal energy, Freyre's writing falls prey to a different kind of stereotype. 'It was the Negro', he notes – whose presence in the plantation household would have been in the role of servant or slave – 'who gave to household life in Brazil its cheerful note' (Freyre, 1970a: 472). But more than cheer, the Brazilian women slaves were also seen as sources of libidinal energy and experimentation. He notes how 'every Brazilian' – and his prototype of Brazilian identity is male – 'even the light-skinned fair-haired one' carries with him 'the mongrel mark', and with it, the memory of 'the mulatto girl who relieved us . . . of a pruriency [*sic*] that was so enjoyable. Who initiated us into physical love and, to the creaking of a canvas cot, gave us our first complete sensation of being a man' (Freyre, 1970a: 278).

If Freyre stresses that Brazilian society must be understood in terms of race rather than class, it is in this relationship of the white family with the *mulata* or African woman that he reveals the extent to which race and class are mutually entwined, and, with them, gender and sexuality. Behind the much-vaunted Brazilian miscegenation lies not a democratisation of race, but a network of hierarchical and sexual relations directly tied to class and social positioning. Bluntly, for Freyre, the sexual domination of black slave-women by their white masters is foundational to Brazilian identity. He is explicit about the violence visited upon black women by white planters, and if he presents white women as insipid, his romantic, essentialising evocation of racial mixing as the core of 'Brazilianness' implies a rigorous policing of these same women's sexuality, and a classing of miscegenation itself. Freyre is hard-nosed in his grasp that miscegenation also had direct and immediate practical benefits as a means of territorialisation, revealing the extent to which European demographics in the colonies were shaped by attitudes to sex, and indeed suggesting that the 'procreative fervor' with local women in the colonies was not due to 'violent instincts on the part of the individual' alone, but also to 'a calculated policy stimulated by the State for obvious economic and political reasons' (Freyre, 1970a: 10–11).

In the 1930s, the idyllic picture Freyre painted of Brazil as a society of racial and cultural integration came to play the part of a non-official Brazilian state ideology. So-called racial democracy was mythologised as existing beyond social or class conflict, and miscegenation was the 'lubricating oil' (Freyre, 1970a: 182) that made this possible, as well as the vehicle for the constitution of an ideal new prototype, a 'modern man for the tropics, European but with African or Indian blood'. Freyre finds the roots for this paradigmatic being in the Portuguese colonisers themselves. Located, as he sees it, between Europe and Africa, pre-'Discovery' Portugal spawned colonists born of 'the intimate terms of social and sexual intercourse on which they had lived with the colored races that had invaded their peninsula or were close neighbors to it' (Freyre, 1970a: 11) and who thus displayed so remarkable an ability to acclimatise to the tropics, that they triumphed where other Europeans failed. Miscegenation is thus presented as a form of liberalism, but it is ultimately valued as the key to successful colonisation.

In a series of lectures in the 1930s, Freyre summarised what he considered to be the cultural traits common throughout the 'Portuguese' world: Brazil, Portuguese Africa and India, Madeira, the Azores and Cape Verde. In addition to miscibility and adaptability, he finds a 'fraternal' and 'lyrical' form of Christianity and a noteworthy exercise of racial tolerance. Gathered together and published in 1940, these lectures were collectively titled *O mundo que o português criou* – literally, 'the world created by the Portuguese'. In chiming with the name and tenets of the Great Exhibition of the Portuguese World that took place in Lisbon the same year, this rubric itself reveals the extent to which Freyre's theory was adaptable to the ideological ends of the *Estado Novo*. And so it was that Freyre's concept of 'the Portuguese way of being' (*o modo português de estar no mundo*) became part of a discourse of nation in Portugal in the 1950s, simultaneous with the introduction of the study of Lusotropicalism in academic curricula.[4] Such reductionism rests upon the belief that there exist specifically Portuguese ways of relating to alterity, as well as to the cultural spaces opened up by colonialism, ways which are invariably qualified by positive adjectives such as 'tolerant', 'flexible' or 'fraternal'. Freyre's emphatic belief in the important influence of 'Portuguese Christianity' on the formation of Brazil, his conviction that in 'the tropics', the Portuguese were unique among colonisers for being more 'Christocentric' than 'ethnocentric', found resonance in the Christian rhetoric of the Portuguese *Estado Novo*.

If in the 1930s – a period marked by the affirmation of empire and a predominant conception of 'race' seen through the prism of social Darwinism – Freyre's stress on miscegenation was a source of discomfort to the *Estado Novo*; by the 1950s, it had granted an official, academically legitimated imprimatur to the way in which the Portuguese state wished to represent itself as tolerant. Freyre's idealisation of the Portuguese coloniser as intrinsically more 'humane' was pressed at the service of a regime that, from the latter part of the 1940s, found itself increasingly isolated and under international pressure to renounce its colonies. By the mid-1950s, Lusotropicalism had clearly been appropriated by the *Estado Novo* to justify its overdue stay in Africa. This coincided with the acceptance of Portugal into the United Nations in December 1955. Under the terms of Article 73 of the United Nations Charter of 1945, the old colonial powers found themselves obliged to encourage and sponsor self-government and the development of political institutions 'according to the particular circumstances of each territory and its peoples and their varying degrees of advancement' (Charter of the United Nations, 1945). However, this last clause made it possible for Portugal to deny the very existence of its colonies by stressing the nominal amendments in the constitution of 1951, now designating the territorial possessions 'overseas provinces' of a single, integrated country. In short, Freyre's invocation of Portugal's traditional and mythical non-racism was ideally suited to support national foreign policy, and Lusotropicalism provided the academic backdrop for diplomatic justifications of the sustained presence of the Portuguese in Africa.

In this context and operating at the level of myth, the circulation of the engraving after Meirelles' *First Mass in Brazil* in Portugal during the *Estado Novo* exercised distinct ideological functions. It revealed the co-existence of indigenous people and the Portuguese, while everywhere acknowledging the hierarchies that structured such proximities. It reinforced an image of Christianity not only in its historically inscribed missionary role, but also as tightly woven into the fabric of nationalism itself. The engraving would also have potently imaged a sense of historicist nationalism by locating a founding moment in the history of Portugal's Atlantic expansionism. Both the Christian zeal of the regime and the mystique of empire as the backbone of the *Estado Novo* were reinforced. At a time when the integrity of national identity was endangered by the inevitable demise of colonialism, and when Portuguese foreign policy thus deemed it important to promote a programme of apparent integration, such an image would have allayed anxiety about loss of definition and place.

Memory Holloway suggests other, less officially monitored ways in which the circulation of the engraving would have worked, gesturing to contemporary immigration and to familial links to Brazil. But she stresses its darker meaning, the way in which its performance pulls against the grain of its overt claims, acting as a reminder of loss: 'loss of the colony, loss of wealth, loss of control' (Holloway, 2000/01: 699). Seen this way, the print would have served fetishistically to disavow and symbolically to compensate for such a loss by covering up its scars with a scene of mastery.

Eat the one you love

If the print after Meirelles' *First Mass in Brazil* was a covert reminder of loss, Paula Rego's *First Mass in Brazil*, with its invocation of the powerful ideological forces that shaped the artist's childhood, also calls up another loss in the sustained melancholy of the figure of a pregnant woman alone on a bed, her cheek pressed to a sailor's jumper. The painting has strong autobiographical resonance, for before she reached twenty, Rego was pregnant with her first child, Caroline, and for a period was uncertain as to whether Victor Willing, her future husband and the child's father, would join her in Portugal.

It is the loss of the child's father that establishes a narrative link between the reclining woman and the homosocial bonding of the members of the Portuguese landing party in the image behind her. As there were no women on the discovery expedition described in Caminha's narrative, Rego's figure serves as a reminder of staying-at-home as a condition of femaleness in the so-called Age of Discovery. Her glazed expression evokes not a resistance to the institutions – including maternity – that pin her to the home, but rather, a transformation of the quarrel-with-the-other ('why did you leave me?') into the berating of the self that is the stuff of melancholy, a process of mourning gone awry.

A similar anguish of loss lies at the heart of the series *Dog Women* made a year later. Rego's first body of work in pastel, the *Dog Women* emerged out of a procedure that is typical of Rego's method: the convergence of the artist's will-to-narrative – an endless hunger for what she calls 'stories' – and formal experimentation and improvisation in the studio. Here is Fiona Bradley's account of the genesis of the series:

> A friend sent Rego a story about a woman living alone in a house surrounded by sand-dunes, with only a houseful of animals for company. One winter's evening, driven mad by the isolation and the wind whistling through the dunes, which sounds like her child's voice, the woman gets down on all fours and devours her pets. This story of loneliness, disappointment and frustration returned to Rego during a drawing session when, casting about for something to do, she asked [her model] Lila to settle into a snarling squat. She drew the pose quickly, modified it later having tried out the pose physically herself to see what it felt and looked like, and recognised the resulting woman as a dog woman, heir to the woman in the story . . . who carries her history and her familiars within her. (Bradley, 2002: 69)

An act of violent incorporation, then, simultaneously expresses and staves off solitude and madness, for to swallow those one loves is one way of ensuring they will never leave. This, surely, is also the meaning of Rego's earlier drawing *The Dybbuk* (Figure 13): the cannibalisation of that which one does not want to lose. 'The melancholy cannibalistic imagination', Julia Kristeva observes, 'manifests the anguish of losing the other through the survival of self, surely a deserted self but not separated from what still and ever nourishes it and becomes transformed into the self – which also resuscitates – through such a devouring' (Kristeva, 1989: 12).[5]

What this also tells us, however, is that the loss of one's objects is a necessary condition for our sustained possession of them. Carrying 'her history and her familiars within her' as internal objects, the Dog Woman might be described as a materialisation of the ego itself, which, as convincingly formulated by Freud, emerges through a series of identifications with, and incorporations of, the remnants of external objects.[6] Objects are loved and taken in, as fragments or in various guises: 'a visual image, a voice, a set of values, or some other key feature' (Silverman, 1983: 134). Such an incorporation of the object represents both its survival and its annihilation as its remnants are transformed into the subject. Leo Bersani, for one, brilliantly highlights the relationship between identity and death as foundational for certain literary works: 'Biological death accomplishes, or literalizes, the annihilation of others that Proust tirelessly proposes as the aim of our interest in others' (Bersani, 1990: 7), he shockingly tells us. This is resonant of the Freud of *Civilization and its Discontents.* It also suggests that if the possession of others is only possible when they are 'dead', when we have somehow killed them off, then such 'posthumous possession of others is always an unprecedented *self-* possession' (Bersani, 1990: 7). But if the *Dog Women* invoke the loves that we have already digested and that make us who we are, they also more explicitly concern love as an ongoing affliction and a dependence that compromises the subject's autonomy.[7] These, then, are women in the suspended state of wanting and waiting.

Reminiscent of late Goya, the first *Dog Woman* (Figure 23), wild

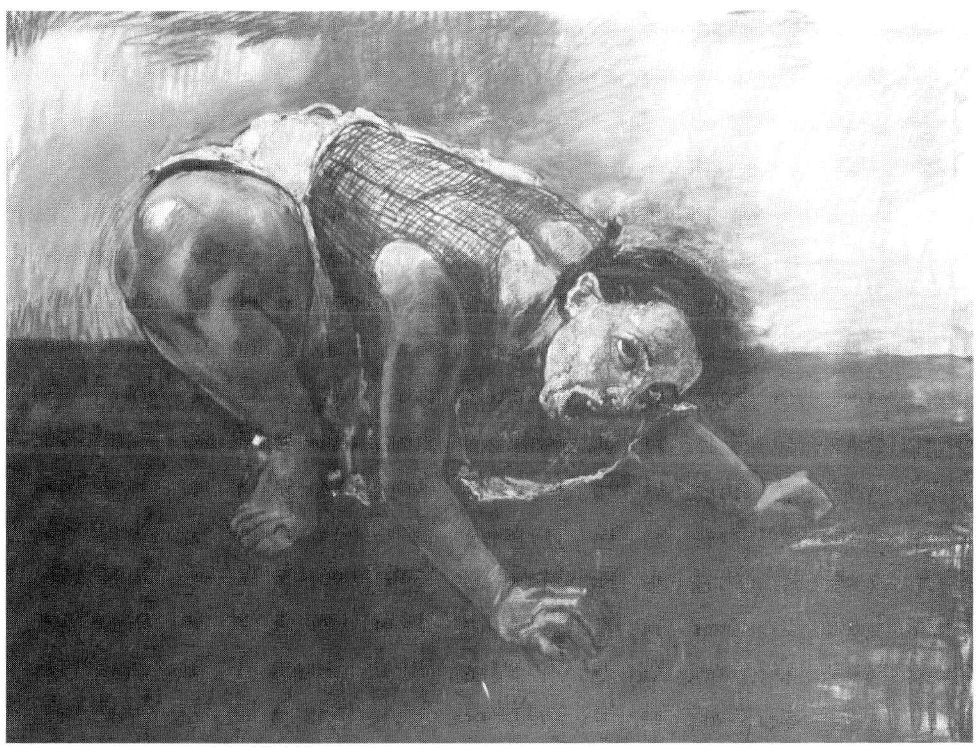

Paula Rego, *Dog Woman,* 1994   Figure 23

and hurt, huge but supple, crouches in a barren, landscape evoked by a simple horizon line, eyes rolling back, mouth gaping in a silent scream. Her body and the turbulent sky behind her are described in gestural hatchings from which the massive forms of her sculptural right knee and thigh awkwardly jut. The articulation of this leg with the shoulder and arm closest to it clearly has no anatomical accuracy: it seems more like a body dismembered and then re-assembled. In effect, this is what has taken place, for Rego worked this knee not from her model Lila, but by posing and viewing herself in the mirror. This contiguity of limbs opening about a central fissure brings a raw and violent sexuality to the work, suggesting, as the *Policeman's Daughter*'s arm had done, something of the fetishising articulations of Hans Bellmer's trussed *Poupées*. As in the *Poupées*, where legs violently torn asunder are then brought together again, literally re-invaginated in the service of the gendered viewer's sadistic pleasure, this tearing and joining of limbs in Rego's first *Dog Woman* puts before our eyes a gusset-like shape that starkly eroticises the image, linking libido to pain.

This embodiment of private agony gives way to quieter, but no less unsettling images, all of which – within the overtly heterosexual matrix of Rego's work – allude to, but never realise, a man, an absent other, the cipher of the Dog Woman's longing. In one work, she rebelliously lifts her leg to piss on 'the master's' bed, but in all other instances, whether hunkering, waiting for food, faithfully lying on her master's jacket, or sitting on command, the *Dog Woman* is a docile subject, one that gestures to the later, disturbingly submissive figure of *Obedience* (Figure 21). In both the *Dog Women* and in *Obedience*, it is the body that materialises the convergence and mutual formation of desire and the law that curtails it, exposing the coalescence of eroticism and violence occurring within conditions of intimacy.

If, like *Obedience*, the *Dog Women* expose compliance as social law brought into the psyche from the outside, they stand as realisations of the very structure of subject formation, where it is in the process of regulation that the frontier itself – the boundary between outside and inside – is drawn. What emerges is a subject riddled with ambiguity, so that while, in the artist's words, 'to be a dog woman is not necessarily to be downtrodden . . . not downtrodden but powerful' (McEwen, 2006: 216), the *Dog Women* also evoke 'humiliation, love, the complicit submission of women, a certain female masochism in love and in betrayal . . . the tacit silence of women, their endurance and sense of honour' (Rego in Macedo, 1999a: 12). Here, in these images and in the words she uses to frame them, Rego explores the extent to which the psychic is acted upon by the enticements and control of the social, experienced at as a psychic rather than social pressure.

While the lack of resistance in these bodies – their apparent complicity with their own subjection as they patiently await the powerful object of their fierce and blind devotion – seems to situate Rego at the very edge of feminism, crucially, the *Dog Women* are not submissive by external coercion. In figuring these robust young women as dogs, Rego exposes an equivocation between self-determination and dependence, rendering visible the ways in which attachment readily turns into submission. If it is a dogged capacity to remain loyal despite adversity and humiliation that characterises canine love, Rego's *Dog Women* are appositely named: in forging the woman's body as the site of a desire whose lack of fulfilment is forever suspended in the pictorial present, they reveal the patience and suspension of will of a loving subject, of a subject in love.

Here, then, is docility by and for love. In extremis, the narrative invoked by both *Obedience* and the *Dog Women* is anti-emancipatory, telling us how we are in effect chained to those to whom we are most attached; telling us that we do not have the last say in who we are or, as Freud puts it, that 'the ego is not master in its own house' (Freud, 1917a: 143). The bodies of the Dog Women thus point to exploitation not by men, but by the unconscious processes that shape the ego itself, which in very limited circumstances sheds its instinct for self-preservation. For Freud, writing in 'Mourning and Melancholia', such a loss of the shelter of narcissistic self-investment occurs under only two conditions: when the subject is either in love or suicidal (Freud, 1917b: 252).[8] Love, then, is not only a narcissistic wound, but rather, a death sentence to the ego itself. In *Civilization and its Discontents*, Freud observes:

> At the height of being in love the boundary between the ego and object threatens to melt away. Against all the evidence of his senses, a man who is in love declares that 'I and 'you' are one, and is prepared to behave as if it were a fact. (Freud, 1930: 66)[9]

With this blend of euphoria and humility, the subject in love admits and embraces alterity, while losing itself. It is in the spirit of such incorporative erasure that Bernardo Soares, one of the heteronyms of Portuguese poet Fernando Pessoa, writes in his fragmentary

Book of Disquiet: 'To possess is to be possessed, and therefore to lose oneself' (*possuir é ser possuído, e portanto perder-se.* Pessoa, 2001: 235). In figuring robust young women as dogs, Rego exposes an equivocation between self-determination and self-loss: an equivocation that hinges about the very experience of love. If the object of that love remains unnamed and outside of representation, the heterosexual matrix of Rego's pictorial world ensures that 'falling in love – far from signifying the return to some presymbolic affective sentience – in fact comes to be coterminous with falling into cultural laws' (Bronfen, 2001: 215–216). It is just such a falling in love – such an alignment with the Symbolic Order – that is elaborated in Rego's composite work *Possession* (2004; Plate 11).

Possessed: pregnant with meaning

A young woman lying listlessly on a sofa removes her black socks. She wriggles and writhes, leans against the back of the sofa, stretches across it, folds her arms, turns this way and that. Her contortions suggest some level of distress. Finally, in the last of the seven panels, she sits up, addressing us with a bemused yet knowing gaze. In this gesture of cognition, Paula Rego seems to be telling us something about her subject's coming-into-consciousness and its relation to her corporeality.

With its pared down inventory of props and costumes and its single protagonist, *Possession* (2004; Figures 24 and 25) stages a personal drama as the intimate choreography of an isolated body. How are we to read *Possession* and the reflexivity of its final address? How, in this series of connected images, do we, as viewers, occupy the position of the object of that cognizant gaze in the last panel, and to what extent is its subject empowered or compromised by being, in turn, the object of our scrutiny? The answers to these questions reside, as I hope to show, in the ambivalent bond – the bond of transference – underpinning the logic of *Possession*, pointing to an underlying politics of female subject formation in Rego's work that hinges on the economy of the Freudian family romance.

Here, then, is a young woman lying down. There is an intimate sensuality in the contact of her skin and the wine-coloured, velvety garments she wears with the worn ochre leather upon which she lies. The pastel marks caress her contour and haptically configure her physiognomy. Her clinging skirt and top follow the volume of her body, occasionally lifting to reveal glimpses of white skin, a lacy

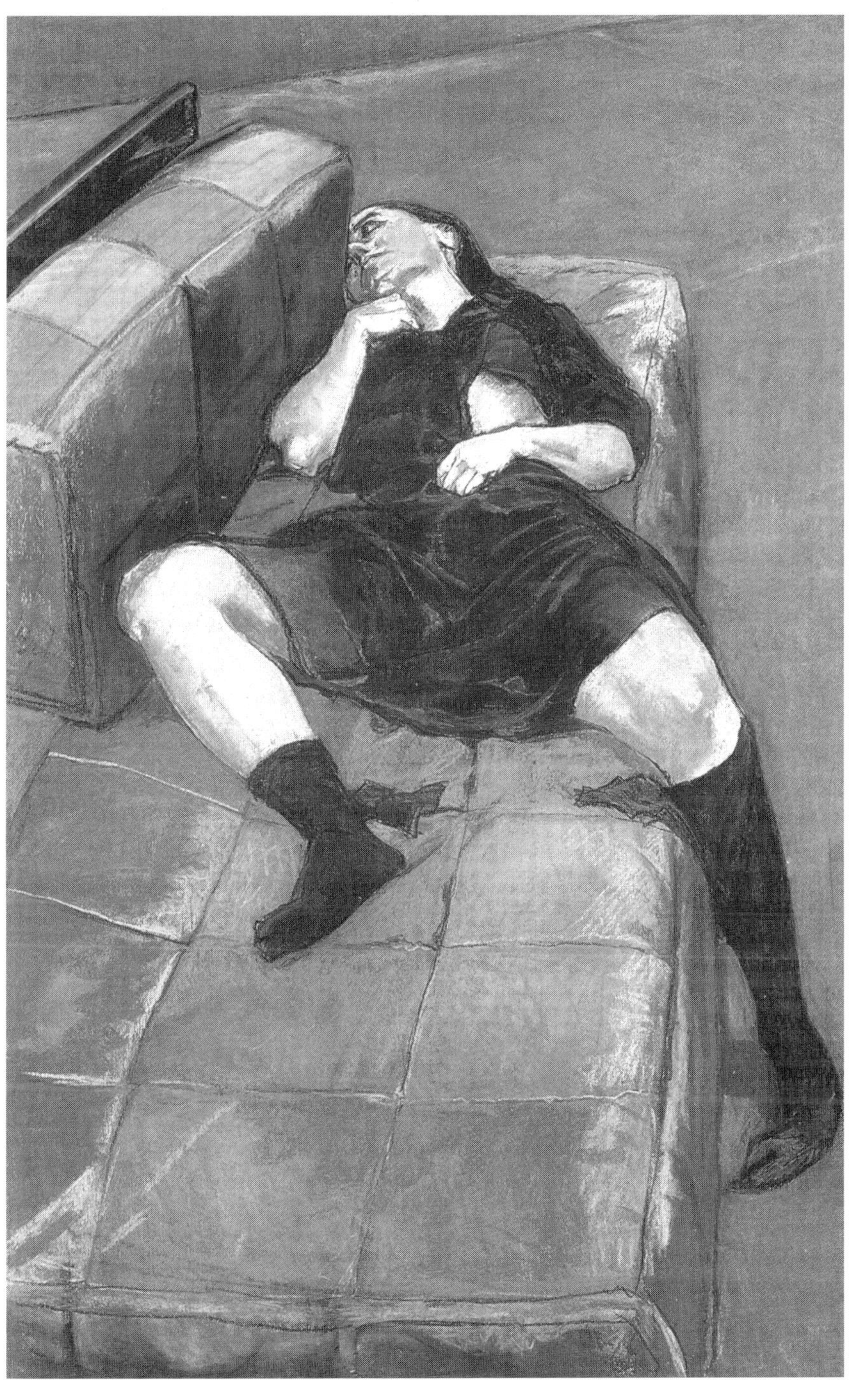

Paula Rego, *Possession I*, 2004

Figure 24

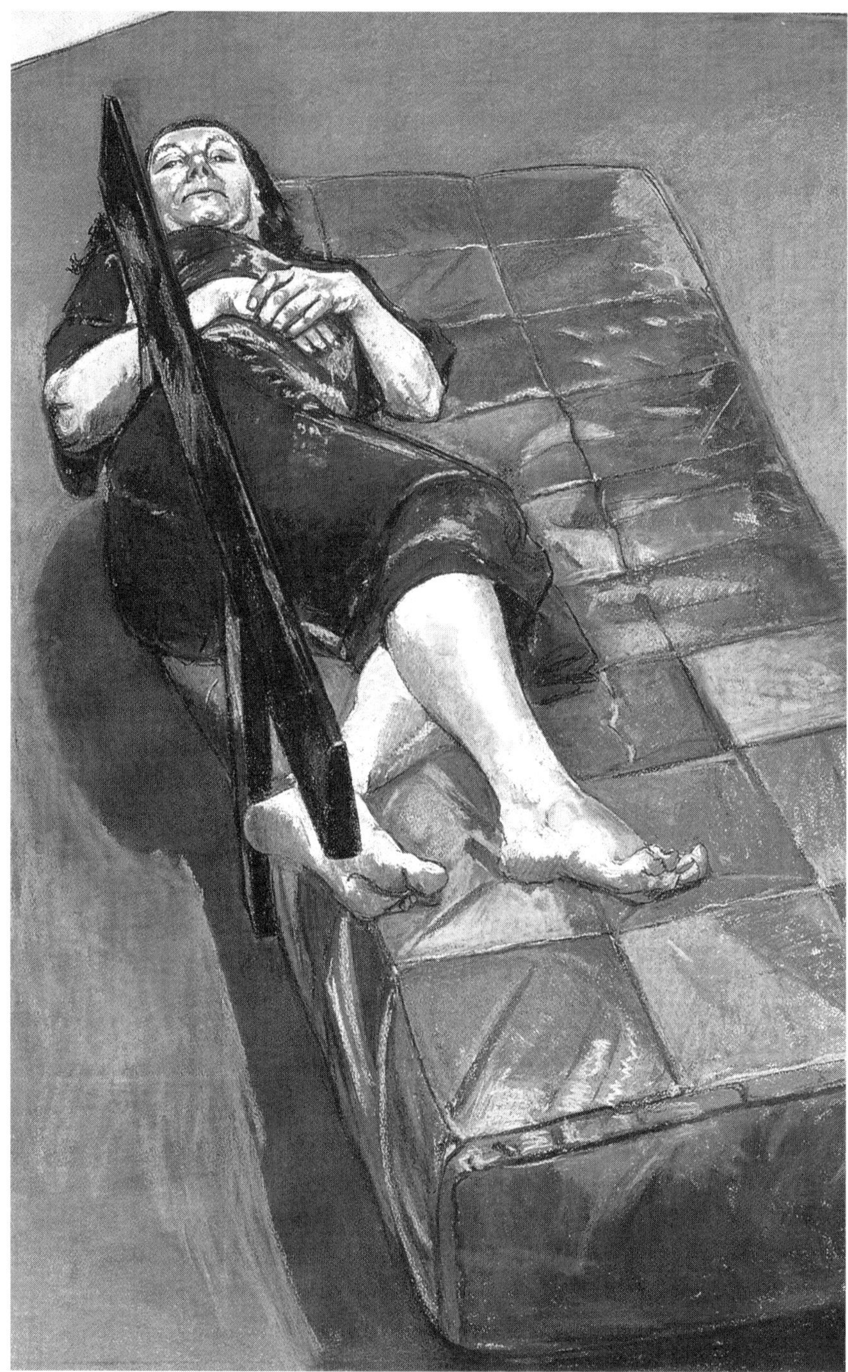

Figure 25   Paula Rego, *Possession V*, 2004

bra. This display offers itself up to the gaze of a viewer implicitly positioned at the foot of the sofa, on our side of the picture plane.[10] In regarding her from this position, it is as if we unveil what is not for our eyes to see, for we imaginatively perform an inversion of the psychoanalyst's position in relation to the couch. And as if to affirm this, Rego tells us the couch was given to her by her psychoanalyst of long standing (Rego: in conversation). This, then, is what goes on behind the analyst's back, while paradoxically remaining, as we shall see, an address to the analyst's authority.

In the body of the protagonist of *Possession*, the binding together of passivity and an inviting eroticism seems to play a traditional role in a gendered economy of vision in which 'woman' is constructed as both spectacle and symptom. The body on the sofa extends itself to an empowered gaze, underlining the subject's earliest impressionability. Such exposure also makes visible the body's violability, duplicating the vulnerability of the patient in relation to the analyst, and, in the scene replayed in psychoanalysis, of the child in relation to the parent. This, then, may be described as a corporeal performance of the transference occurring within the psychoanalytic scene of address as a re-routing of the unconscious back to the site of an originary attachment: a re-staging of the subject's earliest bonds with those people it first loved and feared.

In a postscript to his famous 'Dora' case, Freud defines transferences as 'new editions or facsimiles of the impulses and phantasies which are aroused and made conscious during the progress of analysis [that] have this particularity . . . that they replace some earlier person by the person of the physician' (Freud, 1905c: 116). The object of the patient's address occupies, in other words, the place of an earlier object, and the ensuing speech-act seeks a retrospective redress of buried events in relation to that person. At the heart of transference, then, lies a substitution, the replacement of a primary caretaker. Transference, in other words, is the re-creation, within the analytic space, of a primary relationality and its objective is, through the constraints exerted by the contractual nature of this new scene of address, to yield a new or altered relationship.

Freud observes that the repressed memory that psychoanalysis aims to release – the primal scene of a knowledge that is traumatically disabling – erupts not in the content of verbal enunciations, but in performative repetition that occurs 'under the pressure of a compulsion' (Freud, 1920: 21), in the presence of a professional surrogate. The patient, in other words, unconsciously re-enacts early helplessness and inaugural desires as contemporary event. This mimetic process at the heart of the analytic relationship presupposes a hierarchic relation to the analyst, and, previously, to the parents or primary caretakers as objects of attachment and longing, but also as authorities. As Lacan famously puts it, transference is the subject's relation to another subject who is 'presumed to know' (Lacan, 1979: 232). What is at stake here is not epistemological competence *per se*, but the presumption or fantasy of it. Transference-love – the condition of the patient who thinks she has fallen in love with her analyst – is, as Julia Kristeva observes, for that very reason 'the royal road to the state of love' (Kristeva, 1987a: 8–9), its prototype and epitome. Because, as Freud reminds us, psychoanalytic treatment 'does not *create* transferences, it merely brings them to light like so many other psychical factors' (Freud, 1905c: 117, emphasis in the original); the productive psychoanalytic encounter is a kind of falling in love. Conversely, every falling in love involves both a regression and an idealisation, and hands over its subject to the process of transference: submits the subject's will to the mastery of an other who – by virtue of that very submission – is experienced as authoritative, powerful.

A link between transferential availability and love emerges in the affinity between the figure in *Possession* and an earlier work, made shortly after the *Dog Women*. In *Love* (1995; Figure 26), a young woman lies – her body twisted, head turned awkwardly onto one shoulder – on a counterpane whose lush red velvetiness, rendered in dense pastel markings, occupies almost the full picture plane. Only at the very bottom of the work does a small sliver of shadow create an edge that suggests a tilting into three-dimensional space. The woman is thus splayed against the picture surface like a specimen given to view. As in *Possession*, her clothes are casually disarrayed, allowing us to glimpse the naked flesh of knees and thighs, a triangle of stomach. The woman's gaze, as in *The First Mass in Brazil* and the first six panels of *Possession*, is abstracted and distant: a woman on view, but not looking. Holding her hands together across her chest – over her heart – this body rhetorically stages love as pain of loss.

In the repetition that constitutes transference, the subject identifies its desire and its history not as reconstructed memory, but as present performance in relation to an object occupying simultaneously, as the parents once did, the place of the loved object and the place from which knowledge and power issue. As the site of such over-investment, the object of transference becomes the fantasised

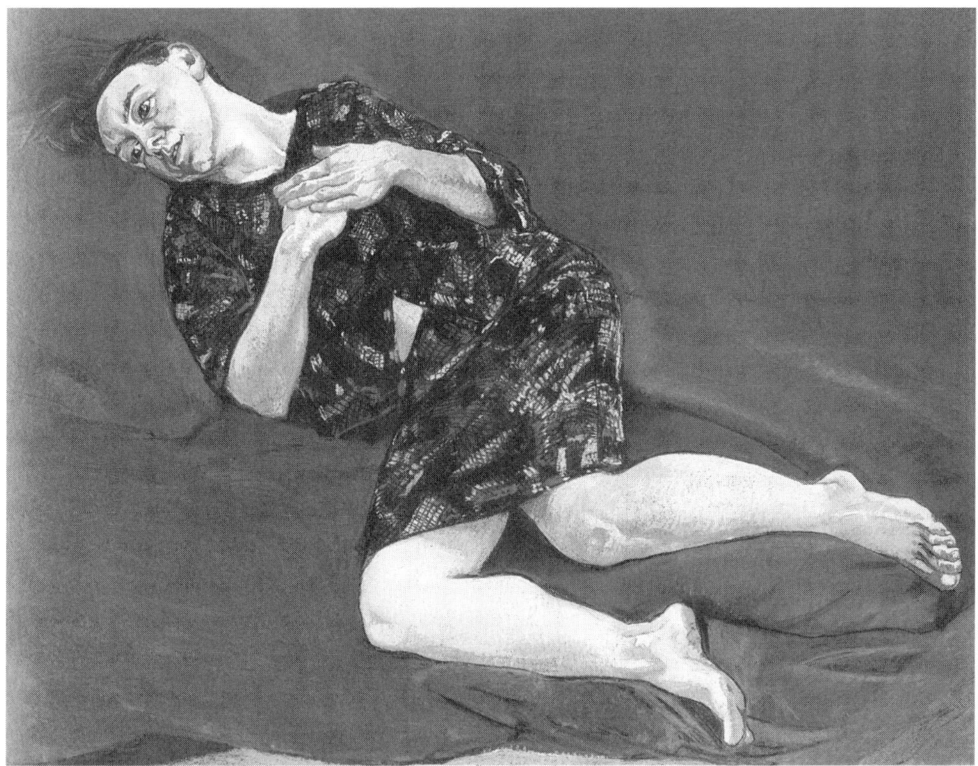

Paula Rego, *Love*, 1995   Figure 26

source of a cure and, as such, also exposes love as ultimately impersonal, structural. It is because the talking cure is so intimately bound up with such 'love' that, for Kristeva, Freud was 'first among the moderns' to conceive of 'turning love into a cure'. He went 'straight to the disorder that love reveals . . . in the speaking being, with its retinue of errors, deceits, and hallucinations, and even physical ailments' (Kristeva, 1987a: 8).

Historically, the psychic malady in which the physical ailments provoked by love take pride of place is hysteria. It is not enough to say that, with hysteria, the psyche speaks through the body. It is, rather, that the body itself speaks belatedly and *instead* of words. Hysteria, then, points to a subjective ailment with regard to the Symbolic Order. A traumatic event (of which an incestuous seduction is the prototype) is repressed – is made to disappear – in order to protect the cherished image of an idealised other, and, with it, the integrity of the picture of the subject's world: this underlies the classic hysterical representation. Arguably, in refusing to disclose the cause of clandestine knowledge, the hysterical fit promises to keep the family intact. The outcome is a psychic gap, the 'nothing' around which the hysterical performance is so much ado. As the somatic eruption of a repressed desire or trauma that is too dangerous to find its way into linguistic representation, the hysterical symptom performs the conversion of mind to body, 'letters of suffering' inscribed 'in the subject's flesh' (Lacan, 1953: 92). 'The unique condition of the hysteric', Moustapha Safouan has observed, is to be 'a possessed body: a body that spits, vomits, bleeds, grows fat, and symptomatizes. Of all that she understands nothing' (Safouan, 1980: 57–58).

This is an address in extremis; an elaborately rhetorical attempt to lure the interlocutor into an engagement so as to affirm the hysteric's very existence. In turn, the interlocutor's passive authority plays the role of a disciplinarian, a policeman that 'can manage to extort admissions, stifle resistances, [and] replace defensive motives with other, more powerful ones' (Kofman, 1985: 44). But, as we have seen, from the point of view of the hysteric, the symptom speaks to someone for whom the physician is a mere substitute. Being fundamentally transferential in nature, then, hysteria repeatedly sets the stage for love. In short, the hysterical performance hyperbolises the condition of transference that underlies all love.[11]

By placing her protagonist on her psychoanalyst's couch, Rego brings the condition of love into the visual field through the invocation of Freudian transference. But she has also acknowledged that the writhing body on the couch in *Possession* was inspired by the photographic tableaux of hysterical patients that Freud's one-time mentor, the neurologist Jean-Martin Charcot, commissioned from Désiré Magloire Bourneville and Paul Régnard for his *Iconographie Photographique de la Salpêtrière* (1876–80) (Rego: in conversation).[12] It was famously Freud's contact with Charcot's use of hypnosis, '[performing] the service of restoring to the patient's memory what had been forgotten' (Freud, 1924c: 195), that alerted him to the possibility that hysteria restaged a repressed sexual trauma. If, historically, hysteria was seen as an affliction of women outside the circuit of heterosexual exchange and patriarchal transmission (virgins or nuns were thought to be particularly susceptible), the atrophied womb wandering in search of moisture, for centuries regarded as the explanation of hysteria, now became a metaphorical figure for a disease of unfulfilled, thwarted or traumatised desire.

As has been well documented, one of the most striking features of Charcot's project to collect and categorise – and indeed to provoke – evidence of the 'great hysterical fit' was its representational nature: the photographs that were intrinsic to his procedure instated the hysteric as visible object. On the one hand, such evidential proof of a disease marked by the mobility and diversity of its symptoms invented the disease as a knowable entity. On the other hand, hysteria itself, as staged by Charcot, came to be regarded as a disease *of* representation, a disease structured by simulation. As handmaiden to positivism, photography was the ideal vehicle for bringing this mimetic disease into a discursive framework.

Although Charcot's *Iconographie* ostensibly documents the effects of hysteria on the body, present-day readings reveal the complex traffic of expectation and desire between the patient's strategy and that of the physician as a process of mutual seduction.[13] Charcot is now portrayed as having taken advantage of his position of class and professional status by physically and psychically manipulating his patients – by relying on their transference love – to perform the symptoms of hysteria as a tautological means of ratifying and legitimating his own expertise. Transference and the love it performs might, in this context, have been the only form of redress for the subject's narcissistic wound, a kind of affirmation to the subject. Better to be seen to be hysterical than not to be seen at all. The image repertoire deployed in this collusion between patient and physician derived from the excesses of religious ecstasy and demonic possession. Performed before a primarily male audience, the grand hysterical fit expropriated the subject of her suffering, allowing it to be incorporated into the body of medical knowledge. The spectacle of hysteria became the reification both of male desire and of a medical master narrative fixated on the image of woman's otherness, figured as possession.

The articulation of the epistemological competence of the practitioner and the epistemological frailty of the patient is fundamental to the theorising of hysteria – and to its feminist critiques – while serving as the prototype of analytic practice. With the corporeal narrativisation of her symptom directed towards an idealised, masterful other – 'a "you" [that] is variable and imaginary at the same time as it is bounded, recalcitrant, and stubbornly there' (Butler, 2005: 51) – the hysterical patient, with her investment in paternal knowledge, becomes the blueprint of the relation between analyst and analysand in the Freudian schema.

It is now a critical commonplace that the most significant and innovative aspect of Freud's reformulation of the representational nature of hysteria as a disease of 'reminiscence' (Freud and Breuer, 1893–95: 7) was his conversion of Charcot's regime of visuality to one of aurality. Put schematically, when the hysteric eventually comes to articulate what previously only her body could express, when speech replaces spectacle, when repetition is converted into memory, the hysteric is 'cured'.[14] The cure, in other words, enables a return to the scene previously shielded by a gap in memory. Thus it is that the divan, which for Charcot was the site of a corporeal spectacle, for Freud became the place from which a voice issues. The analysis of a symptom, then, is an invitation to narrative as a condition of knowledge.

In *Possession*, then, Rego addresses the symptom's story: the compression of bodiliness and narrative. Whether held and possessed by the diagnostic gaze; or possessed, and therefore lost, like Pessoa's subject; or possessed of her symptom, as if by that restless, demonic foreign body, the *dybbuk*, the body in *Possession* is wracked by its inchoate internality. Finally, as we have seen, in the last panel, the woman sits up straight, returning the spectator's gaze with a bemused and knowing gaze of her own (Figure 27). This disjunctive last panel invites us to read the series as a linear sequence. Talking of this last panel, Rego remarked laconically: 'It's as if she's now got it' (Rego: in conversation). It is tempting to see this as a narrativisation of the hysteric's passage from symptom to speech.

The hysteric's move from acting out to cognition is a performance of the subject's trajectory from the Imaginary to the Symbolic: starkly put, it is the conversion of the mother tongue into the language of the father. Some feminist critics argue that this unitary story would not only satisfy the patient's wish to know herself, but also the analyst's fantasy of masterful knowledge. Indeed, the scene of the hysteric's cure, entailing as it does the appropriation of the master discourse, converts 'woman' from enigma to knowable entity.[15] It is for this very reason that these feminists theorise hysteria not as helplessness and inarticulacy, but as a form of resistance against paternal law. Hélène Cixous and Catherine Clément, for instance, examine the hysteric as a figure of excess that challenges the limits of intelligibility, and thus the Symbolic Order itself (Cixous and Clément, 1986: 3–6). For Luce Irigaray it is because the psychoanalyst, being on the side of language rather than body, is a placeholder for masculinity, that 'when it is a matter of *analysis of women, between women*' the

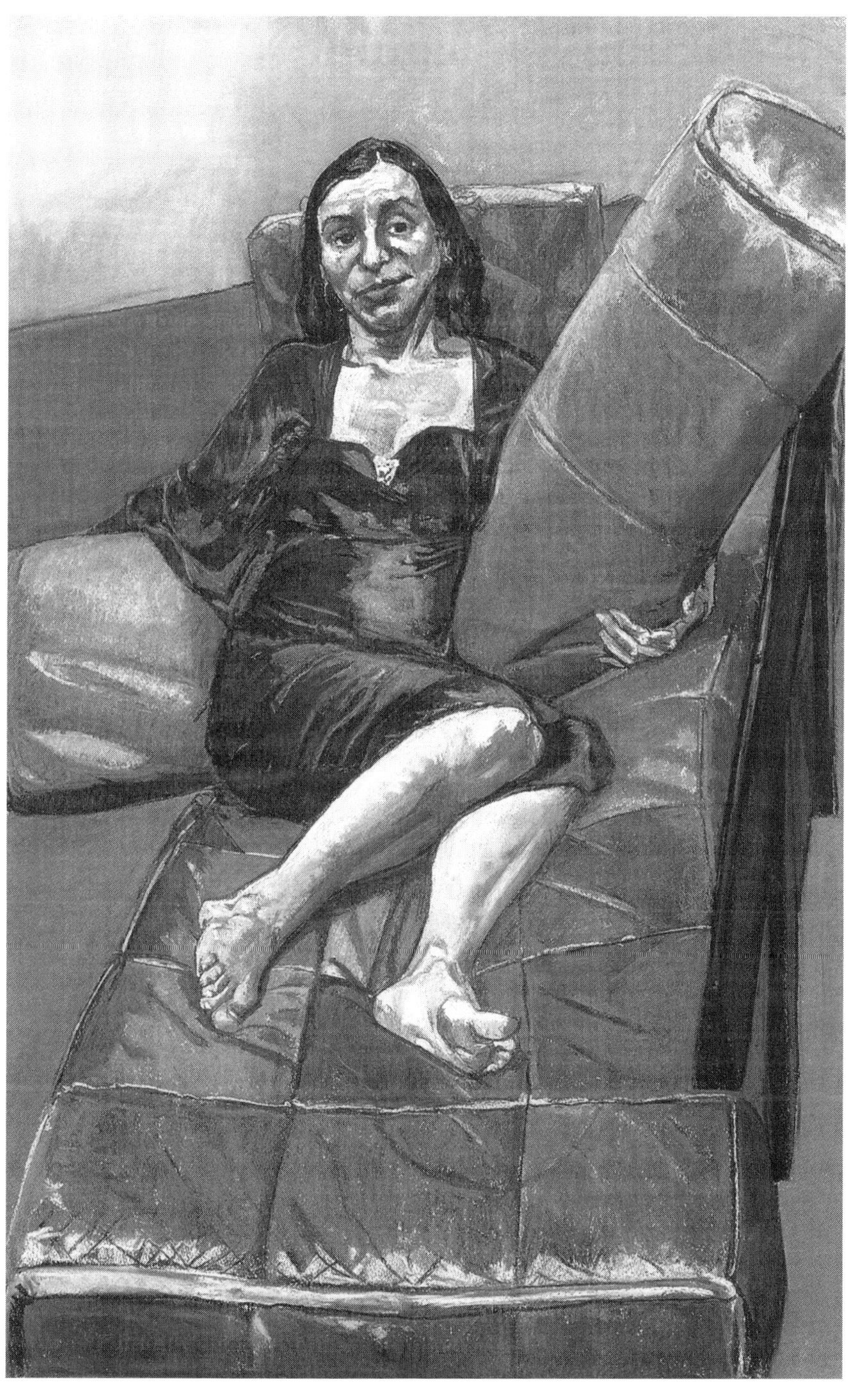

Paula Rego, *Possession VII*, 2004   Figure 27

route of transference 'has to be invented, created' (Irigaray, 1991b: 105). The woman constituting Freud's enigma – hyperbolised in the body of the hysteric – is, Irigaray repeatedly insists, the object of masculine discourse, 'of a debate among men, which would not consult her, would not concern her. Which, ultimately, she is not supposed to know anything about' (Irigaray, 1985: 13). Against such erasure and expropriation, there is, she proclaims, a revolutionary potential in hysteria. For her, it is precisely women's identification with the maternal that makes hysteria so powerful a tool of resistance to patriarchy. In considering mother–daughter relations to be primary (in opposition to Freud's and Lacan's male genealogies), she posits an idealised identity construction that entails a 'female' relation to Otherness, one that is not contained by the phallic logic of the Symbolic.

Yet, clutching the unambiguously phallic cushion, Rego's young woman, no longer possessed of the demonic forces of her own interiority – no longer, as it were, pregnant with bodily meaning – seems to be announcing her own alignment not with the maternal, not with the hysterical as the symptomatic locus of the Imaginary, but with the Symbolic as paternal legacy. Her self-conscious look announces an engagement with a cultural grammar that is the price she has to pay for her refusal to be used as the object of discourse.

Now the hysterical symptom, as we have seen, is an expression of – a ventriloquised performance pointing to – an impossible love. The prototype for this is incestuous love: as the foundation of the psychoanalytic edifice, the process of Oedipalisation is precisely the vehicle through which desire within the family is transformed into desire outside of it. Family members must love each other, but 'they clearly must do so only up to a point' (Lisboa, 2003: 76). If the excess of the hysteric's performance speaks of a barred incestuous desire, the substitution of the mimetic symptom by the symbolic currency of language acknowledges an acceptance of the prohibition of that desire. The route away from hysteria announces the subject's acceptance of the law of desire underpinning not only family life, but also co-existence with others within the social body. The female subject who is prohibited from desiring her father may now desire some other man in his place. In being freed from familial ties and enabled to re-cathect to another object within a heterosexual economy, the female subject fully recognises the impossibility of the father as an object of desire, while never fully demolishing his symbolic authority. Here is a paradox that remains a stumbling block for feminism: as Jane Gallop puts it, 'the daughter submits to the father's rule, which prohibits the father's desire . . . out of the desire to seduce the father by doing his bidding and thus pleasing him' (Gallop, 1982: 70–71).

To articulate *Possession* thus, and to see it from our own viewing position of mastery, is also to expose the scene of psychoanalysis – and the very operations of subject formation that it mimes in transference – as one where someone else's expertise is invoked, that of a master-narrator, legitimated by external discourse. So that in sitting up, in addressing the viewer of the painting with self-consciousness, the young woman in *Possession* puts paid to her relation of inequity with the analyst/viewer, leaving behind her the ignorance that filled her with 'nothing'. But she does so at a cost: to speak the language of self-possession is to incorporate the authority of an external address, to turn to meet the call of the other. If, in other words, hysteria is associated with marginality and alterity, then its cure strikes a compromise between the wayward ego and social law, under the sign of the paternal. If this formulation has been misunderstood by some feminists as an acceptance of the ascendancy of 'men' – Irigaray stays close to such an essentialising view – others recognise, with Kristeva, that this 'paternality' refers more to a structural position than to a biological one, acknowledging that no access to the Imaginary is possible except via the route of the Symbolic (Kristeva, 1984: 50).

Put otherwise, the protagonist of *Possession* is faced with 'love' as a choice of possession *by* another and possession *of* another's discourse. She performs the transition from unconscious symptom to cognition as the subjection of the symptomatic body to paternal law. Rego suggests that in the return to signification – and, indeed, as is attested by many of her works, in the making of art itself – there is no externality to such a law. The subject of *Possession* throws light on a paradoxical simultaneity of submission and mastery, and suggests that, for Rego, a bargain must be struck with the paternal if the female subject is to become the maker of meaning rather than its bearer.

Mother love

If hysteria presents a potential point of resistance to the normative Oedipalisation underpinning patriarchal culture, it nevertheless remains prey, as we have seen, to the tropes of that culture. In my reading of *Possession* through Charcot and Freud, I have alluded to the difficulty that this culture experiences in describing feminine desire without attaching it to maternity. Both the symptomatic body (the body pregnant with meaning), I have argued, and its erasure (as pain is translated into language) are ultimately bound to the Law of the Father, the first because it reproduces Oedipal desire on the site of the female body, the second because it accepts the law of desire upon which 'correct' Oedipalisation is based. As we have seen, Freud's teleological association between female desire and reproduction is cast in Oedipal terms upon the precept of penis envy and the symbolic transformation of 'father's penis' to 'baby', for it is in the context of the transformation of her desire for the father into a desire for his baby that the girl turns into 'a little woman' (Freud, 1925: 256).

For Paula Rego, the girl child and adult woman are often connected in a scrambling of age codes – the ambiguous age of those serious, grown-up girls that inhabit her works. The artist's recollection of a girl she saw at a fair in the Portuguese seaside town of Ericeira is a direct account of the rationale for the conflation of adulthood and childhood in her work. The girl she describes was about twelve years old and assisted her father, who ran a puppet-show stall. She was 'small, very short. She had bleached blonde hair, a perm. She didn't have lipstick,' Rego announces with characteristic precision, 'but she had a tight pullover, a pleated skirt'. Aside from the perm, she could be describing any one of the innumerable girl characters in her own works from the mid-1980s on. 'And she seemed to me to be so efficient', Rego continues.

> She did everything her father wanted her to . . . In effect she was both the madam and a prostitute; she ran the operation but also performed the tasks herself. And that seemed to me to be like the character of all the children I do. It seems to me to be more that way round, rather than that when you are grown up you're a child as well – obviously you are . . . I think that all these children I've done ever since have been to do with that girl, you know. (Livingstone and Stuart-Smith, 1999: 40–1)

While to recognise and reawaken the child surviving within the adult is commonplace, to find the adult already foretold in the child is more startling, more disturbing. Here, it is through the relationship with the father, confirming the pattern of Oedipalisation, that the girl fulfils her destiny by taking the place of the mother.

A reversal between mothers and daughters emerges in Rego's

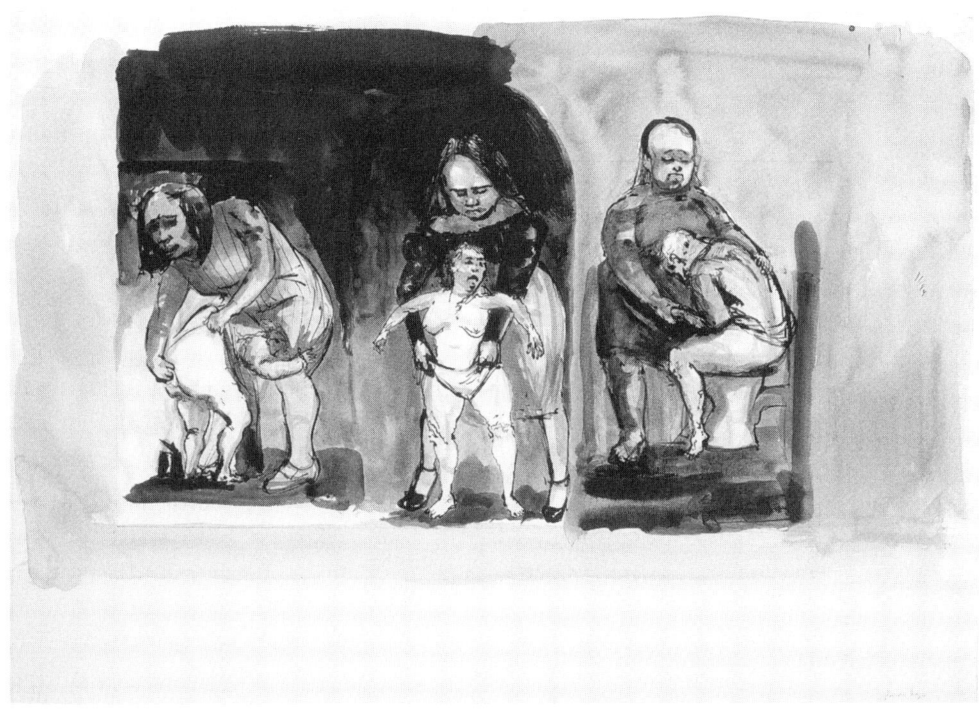

Paula Rego, *Misericordia II*, 2001

Figure 28

work of the early 2000s, perhaps as a meditation on her own shifting position in the genealogical chain. In *Celestina's House* (2000–01; Plate 12), an old woman has become a pathetic and helpless baby. In Rego's most personal and intimate drawings, the series *Misericordia* (2001; Figure 28), with the eponymous novel of Benito Peréz Galdós serving as a pretext more than a source, we are made privy to an ever-shrinking perimeter closing in around the aged subject's infantilised body. In *A Girl with Two Mothers* (2000), the bond of nurturance and discipline is clearly inverted, as indeed is the relative scale: the child is mother to the woman.

The suffocating kiss of *Grandmother* (2000) – mother love trans-mitted contagiously down the generations – announces all that is both desirable and unbearable in these bonds. As we are clearly shown in the drawing *Mothers and Daughters* (1995; Figure 29), the mother is both adversary and burden; incorporated and regurgi-tated, she is, ultimately, the locus of both reunion and rejection of the female subject. The withdrawal of her love would leave the girl devastated and abandoned, yet her overwhelming presence and

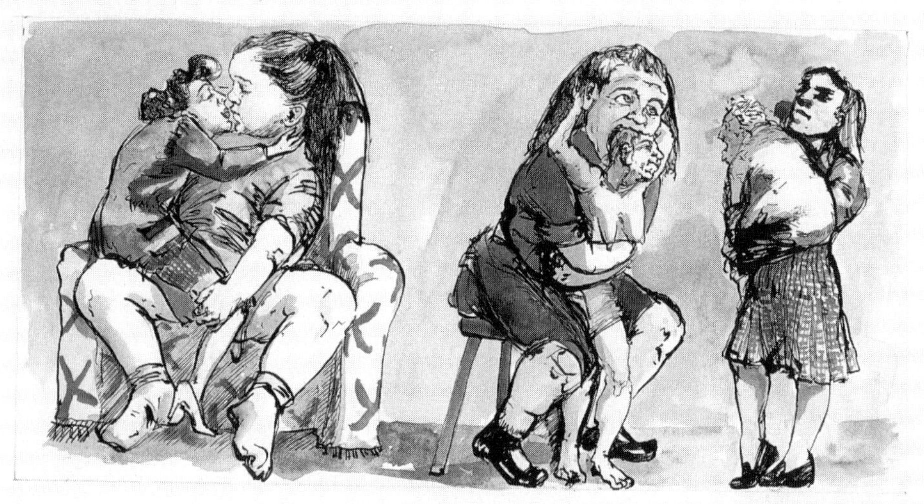

Figure 29   Paula Rego, *Mothers and Daughters II*, 1995

stifling physicality constantly threaten the girl with her own annihilation. The mother is also the embodiment of the future as constraining, a living example of the range of possibilities and limitations available to the female subject. Finally, far from being an altruistic carer, the mother occupies a place of tyrannical authority traditionally associated with paternity, a position that must be contested if it is not to be imitated.

From the 1980s on, we see in Rego's work the protracted performance of such a conflict: the subject, divided and overdetermined, struggles for agency and autonomy within a field that is, of necessity, constrained by external conditions, of which her mother is the first. The mother, as the initial source of nurturance, but also as the child's first object of hostility, remains always tied up with the subjects' identity and destiny. This is particularly so, as Freud recognised, in the female subject – the principal focus of Rego's work – for whom the fierce pre-Oedipal attachment to the mother is a blueprint for other bonds, even for the girl's relationship with her father. 'We knew, of course, that there had been a preliminary stage of attachment to the mother', Freud summarises in 1933,

> but we did not know that it could be so rich in content and so long-lasting, and could leave behind so many opportunities for fixations

and dispositions . . . Almost everything that we find later in her relations to her father was already present in this earlier attachment and
has been transferred subsequently on to her father. In short, we get
an impression that we cannot understand women unless we appre-
ciate this phase of their pre-Oedipus attachment to their mother.
(Freud, 1933: 119)

As we saw in Chapter 1, in a similar theoretical context, Freud
famously, if rhetorically, compares the discovery of the maternal
to the historical discovery, of 'the Minoan-Mycenaean civilisation
behind the civilisation of Greece' (Freud, 1931: 226). In the view
that the subject's later attachments are subtended by the pre-Oedipal, pre-symbolic maternal bond, Freud seems to be hinting at the
possibility of a family romance that precedes and bypasses the logic
of Oedipalisation and that offers, particularly to feminists, an escape
route from the tyranny of paternal law.[16]

Yet, Rego's work suggests, separation and individuation are especially trying tasks for the female subject, leaving her charged with
ambivalence. Split off from an originary body to which she clings in
fantasy, the female subject remains always connected to it, whether
in mimetic identification or in disgusted repudiation. In *Convulsion*
(Figure 30) and drawings made around it such as *Nursing* and *Don't
Leave me* (all of 2000) – works which, in raising the ghost of the hysterical symptom, gesture towards the later *Possession* – Rego reveals
the undisguised horror of the girl as she watches the adult woman
twitching on the floor, or the vengeful determination of the girl
ignoring the tiny, moribund old woman on her lap. This is rage and
horror born of a visceral connection, the subject's hapless struggle
for freedom from the snares of maternal attachment.

While the paternal exercises a subterfuge seduction on Rego's
female protagonists, it is in relation to their mothers that they strive
to gain autonomy. 'I wasn't repressed by Salazar,' the artist has
affirmed, 'I was repressed by my mother' (Rego: in conversation).
Of course if the subject is interpellated, at the most intimate level, in
the home, the two forms of repression are in fact one, for the mother's collusion with authoritarian patriarchy is ideologically achieved
through the positioning of women in the system of the unconscious.

In the *Estado Novo*, as in various other authoritarian regimes,
production and reproduction were categorically divided and gendered. Maternity was simultaneously valued as the symbolic bedrock
of the ideology itself, and for the biological service it rendered
in safeguarding demographies and securing national continuity.

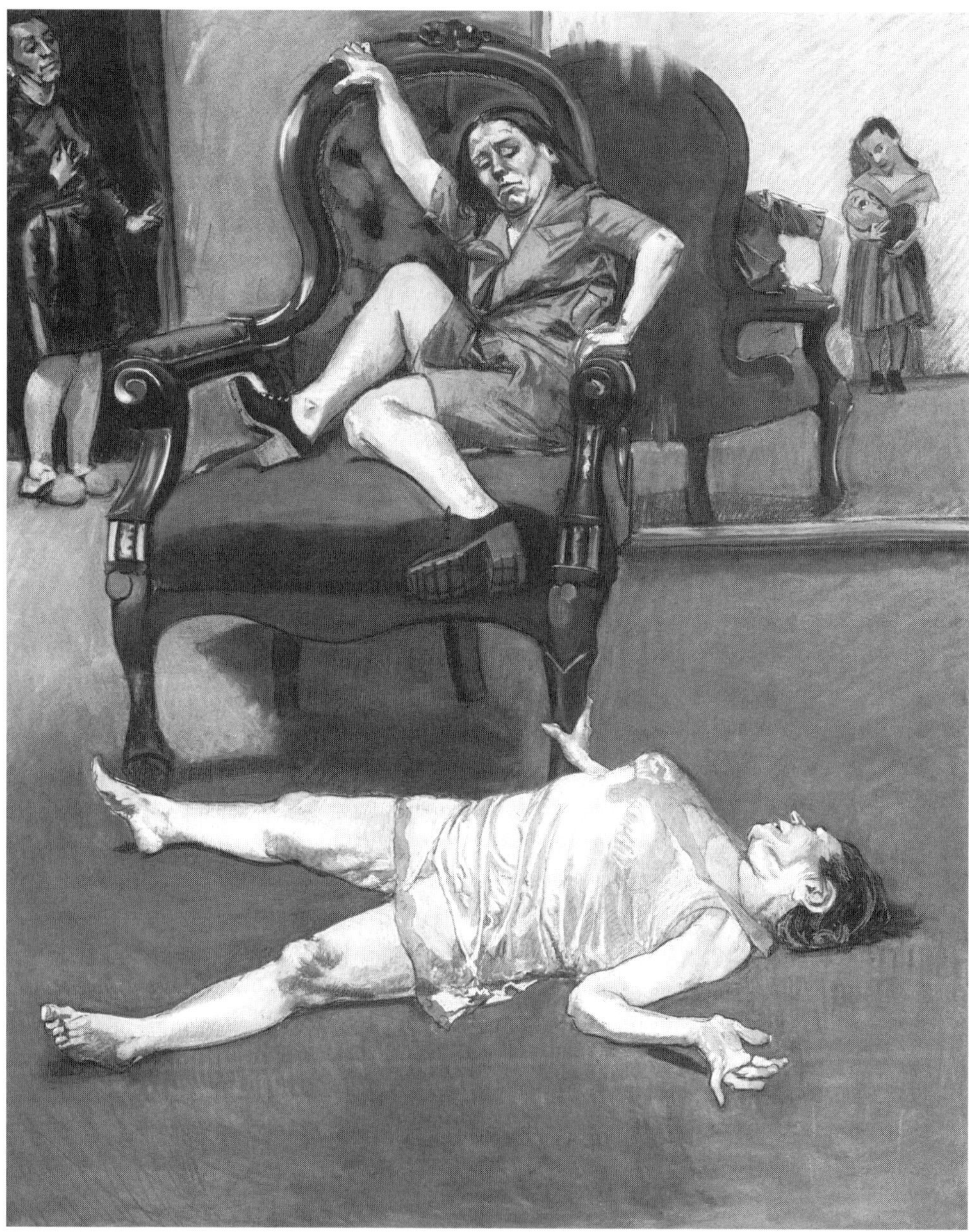

Figure 30   Paula Rego, *Convulsion*, 2000

Wilhelm Reich tells us that on the occasion of Mother's Day in Germany in 1933, the newspaper *Angriff* proclaimed the virtues of the German mother as 'protectress of the family life from which sprout the forces which will lead again our nation forward ... the sole bearer of the idea of the German nation' (Reich, 1972: 57). A year later, in his article 'Machine and Woman', Mussolini claimed that while work furnished men with 'an extremely powerful physical and moral virility', it distracted women from their real role, reproduction, encouraging 'habits that are incompatible with childbearing' (Durham, 1998: 15). The compensation for women's enforced domestication – Salazar's affirmation that 'the great nations should set an example by confining women to their homes' (Garnier, 2002: 30) – was their symbolic status as stay and support of the nation itself through maternity. Through maternity, then, women played a part in the reproduction of ideology itself. Indeed, masochism plays a part here: the pain of childbirth becomes pleasurable through the ideological role it plays.

While on a symbolic register the roles of the sexes in fascist ideology were intertwined in complex ways,[17] on a more practical level, for Salazar – as for Mussolini and Hitler – enlisting the support of the female population was as seminal as stressing the symbolic primacy of maternity. In her excoriating analysis of the relationship between female sexuality and fascism, Maria Antonia Macciocchi points an accusatory finger at the silence and disavowal, among feminists, of women's role as accomplices to fascist regimes, the important part they played in the implementation and reproduction of authoritarian mystique (Macciocchi, 1972: 67–82).

It was in order to canvass the consent of the female population that OMEN – *Obra das Mães para a Educação Nacional* (Mothers' Work for National Education) was founded in Portugal in 1936. Ostensibly non-political, as an organism of the state OMEN nevertheless mobilised the official ideology. As Irene Flunser Pimentel observes in her extensively researched history of women's movements during the *Estado Novo* (Pimentel, 2001, 2007b), OMEN was not created through pressure from below of women wanting to claim political agency, but was, rather, created from above with the aim of 're-educating' women and aligning them with the predominant 'mentalities' of the *Estado Novo*. These were nourished by the close link between church and state, a link that was sealed with the signing of the concordat with the Vatican in 1940. Slotting seamlessly into the institutionally reproduced condition of *Estado*

Novo ideology, Mariolatory elevated maternity, while simultaneously keeping women in their place.

In Rego's work, the mother as representative of the regime, 'a kind of substitute for effective power in the family and the city but no less authoritarian, the underhand double of explicit phallic power' (Kristeva, 1987b: 245) prompts a series of interrelated questions: how to be separate but not alienated; how to love without fusing with the other; how to exercise duty within the field of the social without being subservient. It is possible to argue, with Julia Kristeva, that a symbolic matricide is the precondition of the subject's very being *as* subject. In order to exist outside of the charmed circle of family love, we have to have killed off our first attachment, mourned our primary objects. The loss of the mother is a necessary step, in other words, in our becoming autonomous. Symbolically, matricide 'is our vital necessity, the sine-qua-non of our individuation, provided that it takes place under optimal circumstances and can be eroticized' (Kristeva, 1987a: 27). Provided, in other words, that the subject is able to transform that loss into a new attachment.

While a subjective teleology must always incorporate the mother's metaphoric death as the condition of its emergence, the pregnant body itself – at once a vessel and a dangerous pivot – also gestures to mortality. Indeed, as point of origin and fantasised locus of return, the maternal receptacle typifies what Kristeva calls the abject by posing a threat to the proper boundaries of the self. The abject is thus intimately tied to the violence of mourning for the maternal, taking the ego back to its source 'on the abominable limits from which, in order to be, [it] has broken away', assigning it a source 'in the non-ego, drive, and death' (Kristeva, 1982: 15). In short, as a threshold between non-being and being, the maternal evokes that other threshold that is our destiny.

The lost object

Paula Rego's *The First Mass in Brazil* materialises, in the figure of imminent maternity, just such a conflation between the maternal and death. Indeed, here we see melancholy (the anticipation of, and attachment to, lost objects) as a corollary to maternity: it is, one might postulate, a maternal bequest.

In *The First Mass in Brazil*, death is most overtly introduced by the arum lilies, which, as John McEwen observes in his brief appraisal of the painting, traditionally signify death (McEwen, 2006: 207). Death is also evoked by the figurine of Rego's erstwhile nanny, Luzia, her apron spattered in blood, announcing, perhaps, the plump turkey's fate. These objects seem to be significantly played off against the sacrificial theme of the Easter mass celebrated by the Portuguese landing party in the painting by Meirelles, hanging behind the pregnant girl. A ceramic jug in the shape of a naked woman's torso swallowed by infernal flames and the two lifeless fish on the side of the bed would flesh out such a reading. The insinuation of loss in the generative body of the woman invokes Kristeva's notion of maternal sacrifice as necessary to the working of patriarchy, and supports McEwen's reading of *The First Mass in Brazil* as a painting 'about sacrifice' (McEwen, 2006, 2007), a view seconded by Fiona Bradley, who sees the pregnant girl as a sacrificial victim of her circumstances (Bradley, 2001–02: 61).

Yet if sacrifice occupies the geometric centre of this painting, it does not seem to be at its heart. Sacrifice implies a bargain struck between an individual and an abstract force: a metaphysical trade-off realised either in order to prevent some danger from taking place, or to expiate a misfortune that has already occurred. The sacrificial core of Christianity, symbolically performed in the Eucharist, falls into the second of these categories: Christ dies so as to ransom humanity from the guilt of an earlier sin. But, rather than seeing the woman's body in this painting as sacrificial, her propitiation on the altar of sex as a profane analogy, I would argue that Rego alerts us to the dangerous liminality of pregnancy itself. In her blood-smeared apron, Luzia would then be not a celebrant, but a homely midwife, the inverse of the back-street abortionist. She cannot help but remind us of the female body's link to biology, to nature. As Memory Holloway forcefully argues, such a link binds *The First Mass in Brazil* to the *Dog Women* made a year later, through their shared insistence on the axis of horizontality (Holloway, 2000–01).

Holloway channels her reading of the *Dog Women* through the idea of the formless, theorised by Yve-Alain Bois and Rosalind Krauss, after Georges Bataille. Although there is nothing in the facture and materiality of *The First Mass in Brazil* that aligns it with what Krauss has called 'the operation of horizontality' that characterises the *informe* (Bois and Krauss, 1997), an operation of dissolution that functions as a formal analogue to Kristeva's notion of the abject, Holloway identifies in Rego's painting the cultural association of horizontality with subjugation, carnality, femininity and nature, in opposition to the equally overdetermined vertical axis, which – identified with the masculine – is the field of culture, the axis of painting, and the plane of beauty and of vision itself. Like Rosalind Krauss (1999: 129), Holloway leans on Freud's analysis of the consequences to the human being of the shift in bodily orientation from the earth-bound and its prioritisation of the olfactory, to the distance-bound and its prioritisation of the visual, as the outcome of the transition from crawling on the ground to the erect position. This transition is one in which visceral carnality is sublimated by culture. Each subject's entry into the compromised civilised world that it will henceforth always inhabit, involves an axial change realised, in Lacan's formulation, in the child's earliest self-recognition and self-alienation in the mirror. This introduces verticality into a chain of sublimatory cultural signifiers.

Reading *The First Mass in Brazil* alongside two works made at approximately the same time, Holloway perceptively links the verticality that positions 'man' within culture with the idea of 'the aesthetic'. While *Caritas*, like many of Rego's works, probes the relationship between nurture and maternity, in *The Artist in her Studio* we see an ironic reflection on verticality as the effect of the artist's command of her world and her capacity to transform the bounty of nature into mediated objects of contemplation. The horizontality of Rego's pregnant body, as if reclaimed by the landscape in the picture behind her, apparently assimilates these traditionally gendered tropes that link masculinity to culture and to verticality, and femininity to nature and to horizontality. Yet, for Holloway, *The First Mass in Brazil*

> marks out a territory in which the horizontality of the body and all that it evokes . . . is a forceful match for the heightened verticality offered in that very instant when the Host is raised in the name of King and Country. If we read this picture as an allegory, the moment of subjugation is indeed the very moment when resistance and independence begins. (Holloway, 2001–02: 703)

Importantly, then, Holloway stresses the interpellative moment as decisive, simultaneously in the formation of the subject, and in the trajectory of its resistance to the ideological forces that shape it.

However, I would like to suggest that in the bonding of subjection and resistance Rego's painting proposes a subject whose autonomy is more ambivalent than Holloway's analysis suggests, where melancholy marks the limits of that resistance. Here, then, is a subjectivity that not so much asserts its autonomy, as is caught between a melancholy attachment to lost objects and the hope of renewed and autonomous agency. For, while presenting single motherhood as resistant to the patriarchal and paternalistic underpinnings of Meirelles's painting, Rego's work also performs a depressed acknowledgement of gender (rather than anatomy) as destiny.

This is perhaps where the fish come in. As an early symbol of Christian baptism, and appearing in several allegorical or miraculous incidents in the gospels, fish also came to symbolise Christ himself. Read as an emblem snatched from traditional iconography, the fish in Rego's painting restates the incorporative symbolism of the Eucharist performed in the metapicture. But, as in *The Policeman's Daughter*, an examination of Rego's painting also throws up numerous verbal idioms in both English and Portuguese that might illuminate the peculiar juxtaposition of the pregnant woman with a couple of dead fish.[18] Metonymically linked to the ocean that acts as a historical backdrop to this work, they are perhaps a reminder that, for the solitary woman, there are many more fish in the sea. Or is the artist telling us that in patriarchy a pregnant girl without a husband is a fish out of water? Are we being warned that 'daughters and dead fish are no keeping wares' (*Ao peixe fresco gasta-o cedo e havendo tua filha crescido, dá-lhe marido*)? Parents, marry off your grown daughters quickly, for not only do women, like fish, quickly decay, but also, unmarried women are dangerous, their sexuality unanchored and uncontained: they could cause a stink in the patriarchal family, in the communal body. Has the pregnant protagonist of *First Mass in Brazil* caused such a stink?

Here, then, as in several other works, Rego troubles the 'expecting' body, removing it from the reassuringly familiar scene of legitimate triangulation. Whether in suggestions of adultery and thus of uncertain paternity (*Red Monkey Beats His Wife* and *Wife Cuts Off Red Monkey's Tail*, of 1981), of accidental or unwanted fecundation (*Pregnant Rabbit Telling her Parents*, 1982) or of single motherhood (the series *The Crime of Father Amaro* and *Untitled*, of 1997–98), Rego disrupts the reassurance to paternity of legitimate continuity.

Similarly, in the image of a miraculous pregnancy announced in *The Family* (1988; Figure 5), where a little girl stands, backlit, displaying her protruding belly to those who, engaged in a scene of domestic sadism, ignore her – she hints at 'virgin birth' as a prototype for continuity without paternity. What, this painting asks, does a family without a father look like? In the foreground, a wily maid and a knowing girl pin down a terrorised man: the one firmly grasps his wrist; the other presses herself between his parted legs, beginning to remove his jacket. Impending murder or incest threaten to shatter the familiar structures of kinship and, with them, any vestigial image of cosy domesticity. Yet as a reading of this painting alongside the later *Possession* may reveal, such miraculous pregnancy can only be a hysterical symptom and as such, an ambivalent address *to* the father, reinstating his symbolic authority.

Virgin birth, as an image of continuity without paternity, is a suggestion that had, more elliptically but more richly, been present in *Joseph's Dream* (Figure 17), where, as in *The Artist in her Studio* and *Martha, Mary, Magdalene*, continuity is assured not by progeny, but by the making of art. 'Art' as significant and signifying artifice presents itself in *The First Mass in Brazil* in the metapainting, an image historically appropriated, as we have seen, to cover up the site of a cultural wound: Portugal's loss of its African colonies. Seen against this image, with its sublimatory, fetishistic associations, the pregnancy announces – indeed anticipates – a similar dispossession. The expulsion from the paradise of existence *in utero* forces subjectivity to take up its residence in exile. Against the exotic Eden of a newly 'discovered' territory, Rego presents us not with a spiritual world organised through sacrifice and the compliant humility of the Madonna; not, in other words, with the ransoming of Eve's carnality. Rather, she unveils a postlapsarian, unredeemed world in which the female body bears the burden of its desire, binding the young woman to a future contemplated as loss. This loss, as both past and as destiny, shapes the female subject's trajectory: from the founding loss of her mother, then her father, through the loss of the lover, to the eventual and inevitable loss of her child as it is released from its fusional bonds into an autonomy that must figure her own metaphorical death as its condition.

We must now turn to the absent father/husband/lover in *The First Mass in Brazil*, and the hypothetical conditions underpinning the portrayed pregnancy. An initial reading of the juxtaposition of pregnancy and 'Brazilianness' may suggest not only the more obvious 'colonisation' of the body, but a historical allusion to rape, to the slave women or so-called 'concubines' that were left pregnant by their masters, whose mestizo progeny were both a testament to violence and a form of demographic capital, serving to increase the masters' stock. Gilberto Freyre tells us of the vices into which planters' sons fell, in a culture that valued, as Fascism was later to do, an explicit exhibition of masterful virility. 'No Big House in the days of slavery wanted any effeminate sons or male virgins' (Freyre, 1970a: 395), he proclaims.

> [T]he freedom that was soon accorded the white boys to loaf around ... to deflower young Negro girls, to take slave women, and to abuse animals – represented vices in the upbringing of the child that were, perhaps, inseparable from the slave-holding regime under which the formation of Brazilian society took place. (Freyre, 1970a: 399)

The naturalisation of the planters' progeny as male, and the effortless dehumanisation implicit in the elision and treatment of 'young Negro girls', 'slave women' and 'animals' speaks of the extent to which racialised sexual violence was a trope for colonial rule itself, propagating and perpetuating it. Underlying the celebrated Brazilian 'mixed race' identity is not, as the myth of racial democracy will have it, an easy conviviality between the ethnic groups in the tropics but, rather, repeated acts of violence born of, and in turn reinforcing, racial, class and sexual inequity. In short, the production and maintenance of a violent masculinity was pressed at the service of a politics of exclusion, holding the social structure of colonial domination firmly in place, for it goes without saying that the children born of these forced unions could not compete for property with the legitimate heirs of the paternal estate. Although the ethnic identity of the girl is probably Caucasian, a reading of *The First Mass in Brazil* as an invocation of the ghost of gendered violence would be supported by other allusions to rape and sexual coercion in Rego's work as a whole.

The question of sexual violence is also a crucial one in the dynamic between politics and psychoanalysis, although, as Jacqueline Rose has brilliantly shown, the very opposition between them may be specious (Rose, 1989). Masochistic images in Rego's work (addressed above in Chapter 3) clearly unsettle the distinction between a violence whose agency is social, and one whose origin lies in the subject's death drive. Rego's allusions to rape play along this dangerous edge. For instance, discussing the Pieta-like configuration in the triptych *After 'Marriage à la Mode' by Hogarth* (1999), the artist comments that young wife bearing the drunken husband across her lap 'is doing what she feels she must do: be obedient to her husband', invoking the *Estado Novo* ideology of hierarchic familiarism. But then she adds in a chillingly matter-of-fact way: 'It's a little bit of a rape, I guess' (Gleadell, 2000: 54).

Celestina's House (2000–01 Plate 12) is a painting that uses as its initial springboard Fernando de Rojas's 'novel in dialogue', probably published in 1499. While the family carouses in postprandial jollity, seduction turns into a threatening scene of rape or coercion in the background. The scene is reminiscent of the sense of menace in Degas' possibly misnamed *Le Viol* (1868–69). Similar hints of intimidation or brutality are conjured by the undressed woman in the background of *The Interrogator's Garden* (Plate 2); the scene of sexual domination in the 'seduction' taking place in the left hand panel of *After 'Marriage à la Mode' by Hogarth*; the more ambiguously dishevelled and half-undressed *Wedding Guest* and its preparatory sketches (1999–2000); the woman lying fully dressed but splay-legged alongside an overturned chair in *Bruised* (2000). All these works point to rape as the ultimate scene of female vulnerability.

These scenes of rape might also be regarded, as Mieke Bal has forcefully argued in discussing the iconography of the Rape of Lucretia (Bal, 2001: 71), as 'really' about political tyranny. Yet, as Bal also recognises, while allegory performs the fundamentally polysemous nature of the sign, the depiction of rape as allegory can never ignore the literal and the real in such a scene. While the representation of the raped woman may be linked to the politics at stake, it cannot be separated from a unique, particular and traumatically lived experience. In *Celestina's House*, in relentlessly logical response to the threat of such a bodily invasion – in answer to the vulnerability of the nubile female body, but also in response to her desire – Rego seats a heavy-set, practical, elderly woman before us, feet pressed politely together, sewing closed the vagina of a little girl, who quietly submits to what seems to be a standard procedure of grooming or hygiene. Such images insert a seam of ambivalence into the work, raising the ghost of masochism and asking how desire and violence are situated in relation to one another.

On the one hand, to place rape at the centre of our reading of *The First Mass in Brazil* would be to literalise its narrative and pinpoint the consequences of the painting's historical allusion, eliciting a recognition of the brutal disruptions of kinship bonds suffered by the violently disenfranchised and dispossessed. On the other hand, to pull away from the specificity of such a view brings love into the equation and accommodates a reading of the domestic politics of colonialism and the effects of the colonial enterprise on the women either abandoned by unavailable, powerful men, or left at home. Taken together, what we have, then, is the violent possession of the female body pitted against its abandonment as the physical expressions of the twinned forces of colonial and patriarchal power.

Under scrutiny here are the conditions that underwrote both sexuality and domesticity in the colonial context. For, as Ann Laura Stoler has suggested, 'the very categories of "coloniser" and "colonised" were secured through forms of sexual control that defined the domestic arrangements of Europeans and the cultural investments by which they identified themselves' (Stoler, 1997: 345). In light of this, pregnancy stands not only as an analogue to a geographical terrain invaded and possessed, not only as the incubator of imperial, patriotic manhood, but also – in its liminality, in its challenge to coherent, unified identity – as a material sign of the contestation of the very boundary dividing 'us' from 'them', citizen from colonial subject.

A prelude to this reflection on the fecund but dangerous consequences of an encounter with the cultural other – the encounter literalised in the painting after Meirelles' print on the wall – may be found in Rego's painting *Pregnant Rabbit Telling her Parents* (1982). The work is part of an extensive, loosely connected series of paintings in acrylic on paper made in the early 1980s, in which anthropomorphic animals give body to homely themes – shame, jealousy, betrayal, cruelty. As in Goya's dark *Caprichos*, masquerading creatures enlist the viewer's engagement by holding a mirror up to the human subject. Here, a defiant teenage rabbit makes an announcement to her parents: a shadowy, authoritative dog, and a passive, simpering cat. The consternation aroused within the family circle by an illegitimate pregnancy is economically sketched in the rhetorical and clichéd gestures: the father, blotted out by shadow and smoking a phallic cigar, the mother anxious, but withdrawn and conciliatory, the daughter shrugging to indicate her honesty. In her inspired reading of this painting, Maria Manuel Lisboa points not only to the transgression represented by a pregnancy not sanctified by matrimony, but more emphatically to the 'generational repetition of transgressive reproduction' across the species, raising the spectre of miscegenation (the union of dog and cat producing a morally aberrant rabbit) (Lisboa, 2003: 67–68).

But now there is more. While Rego leaves the narrative open ended, she clearly uses *The First Mass in Brazil* in order to explore the losses that underpin both love and maternity. If fecundation is infiltration by, and possession of, an alien other, its outcome, pregnancy, is a form of transubstantiation, a fullness that both announces and redresses a loss. It is the pregnancy, Rego's painting may suggest, that secures for its subject a psychic hold on the lost object, the man gone to sea, the absent father: his incorporation and metabolisation. He has gone, but his baby remains. The transformation of desire for the man into desire for his baby follows, as we have seen, a classic Oedipal pattern. The father's existence as an object of desire is sustained in a physical transformation that assures his symbolic continuity through succession, but it is a transformation that, for the female subject, simply postpones the loss, holds it temporarily at bay.

Holding together these complex and contradictory meanings, Rego's image of a pregnant woman lying on a sailor's jumper before a picture of cultural possession and sacralisation is also, arguably, an emblem of the workings of the ego itself. 'The pregnant woman', Diana Fuss observes, is in many ways 'the perfect figure for a psychoanalytic model based upon incorporation' (Fuss, 1995: 24). Fuss cites Otto Fenichel, for whom pregnancy represents the 'full realization of identificatory strivings to incorporate an external object bodily into the ego and to enable that object to carry on an independent existence there' (Fuss, 1995: 24). Such identificatory strivings, in turn, are experienced by the offspring in their bid to incorporate parental power, yet to be independent of it. The totem meal – the sons murdering and cannibalising their father – as the foundation of civilisation in Freud's *Totem and Taboo* is recapitulated in individual history. The parents – first the mother, then the father – must be both demolished and swallowed, internalised, in order for subjective autonomy to be launched. A subjectivity thus configured must always bear within itself the melancholy traces of the losses upon which it was founded, and in particular the price of the loss of the original symbiosis with the mother. This is what is entailed in the staking out of the boundaries that separate inside from out, ego from world. Yet without the acknowledgement of such a loss, there is no egress from the enchanted circle of the family.

Although Freud's model of 'normal' subjectivity is developmental, a progress narrative that recounts the stages of a selfhood gained incrementally, he also shows repeatedly that we are torn between a desire for autonomy that impels us forward, and a desire for a fusional identification that pulls us back towards the maternal. Indeed, as it might be argued that it only because 'the path backward is obstructed that we move forward at all . . . Desire craves its original form of satisfaction, and only accepts later symbolic substitutes reluctantly' (Kilgour, 1998: 246). In this sense, love is always conservative, impelling us to abandon our hard-won autonomy. The ego strains to fuse with the love object as once it was fused to the mother, so that '[a]gainst all the evidence of his senses, a man who is in love declares that "I" and "you" are one, and is prepared to behave as if it were a fact' (Freud, 1930: 66).

While the ego struggles to affirm its autonomy, love aims to break through this isolation and return the subject to its first state of union with the maternal, a fusion that is, I have argued, also a kind of death. It is therefore no coincidence that, as a meditation on various sorts of love – the love that keeps us in the family and the love that strives to lead us outside of it – Rego's *The First Mass in Brazil* should pit the melancholy body of a pregnant woman against a performance of the Eucharist, that ritual of symbolic revivification through incorporation. In this confrontation, we see not only a meditation on the inextricability of the life and the death drives, but also a reflection on possession and loss, and on the incorporation of Otherness that is a precondition of the subject's emergence.

Notes

1 The word initially used, *descoberta* (discovery), has more recently given way to the less ideologically charged *achamento* (finding).

2 The *Letter* was completed the day before the Portuguese party set sail again. Hans Ulrich Gumbrecht suggests that Pero Vaz de Caminha began composing the text halfway through his sojourn in the newly found land, and that we may thus assume that the first half was written retrospectively, while the second 'ended up adopting the rhythms of a diary' (Gumbrecht, 2000/01: 425).

3 Ministério do Ultramar, *Legislação de 6 de Setembro de 1961*, Lourenço Marques: Imprensa Nacional de Moçambique, 1961, p. 5.

4 In 1955–56, Adriano Moreira introduced the study of Lusotropicalism in a second-year course; other curricula in the social sciences and agronomy followed suit, generating numerous published research projects. Moreira was a sociologist, lawyer and politician, who was to hold the portfolio of the Overseas Territories (*Ultramar*) from 13 April 1961 to 4 December 1962.

5 Melanie Klein (to whom Kristeva pays homage, see Kristeva, 2001) theorises a relationship between (cannibalistic) incorporation, melancholia and mania. The depressive position is, for Klein, the subject's response to a withdrawal of its earliest loved object, and results in later depressive states only if the subject has failed to introject its lost object and so establish it within the ego. Contrariwise, the manic position results from the fantasy of being able to control both the internalised

parents and the real ones, 'for the child's gratification of being fed is not only felt to be a cannibalistic incorporation of external objects (the "feast" in mania, as Freud calls it) but also sets going cannibalistic phantasies relating to the internalized loved objects and connects with the control over these objects' (Klein, 1935: 287).

6 Speaking of the ego's first object choice, Freud observes how it – the ego – 'wants to incorporate this object into itself, and, in accordance with the oral or cannibalistic phase of libidinal development in which it is, it wants to do so by devouring it' (Freud, 1917b: 249).

7 For Lacan and for Kaja Silverman reading him, on the rare occasions when love occurs as an 'active gift' rather than as an event that befalls a passive subject, it brings out the subject's autonomy through the recognition of the other as a truly 'other' subject. The 'active gift of love', inadequately theorised by Lacan, is for Silverman the cornerstone of an ethics that permits the conferral of ideality upon socially disprized bodies. The process she proposes is an identification with the object that is excorporative rather than incorporative, allowing us to remain at a distance from – and thereby to respect – the 'otherness of the newly illuminated bodies' (Silverman, 1996: 2).

8 Melanie Klein makes a different connection between love and suicide, seeing in suicide the murder, by the ego, of an introjected bad object, while at the same time 'it also always aims at saving its loved objects, internal or external'. Thus, in suicide, 'the ego is able to become united with its loved objects' (Klein, 1935: 276).

9 Freud had made a similar point earlier, when saying that, in love, 'the object has, so to speak, consumed the ego. Traits of humility, of the limitation of narcissism, and of self-injury occur in every case of being in love … The whole situation can be completely summarized in a formula: *The object has been put in the place of the ego ideal*' (Freud, 1921: 113).

10 For an inspiring account of how the picture plane becomes active in the engendering of representation and embodiment of the viewer, see Harrison, 2005.

11 Kaja Silverman's formulation of 'the active gift of love' (Silverman, 1996) is intended to counter such a view of love, as is Irigaray's use of the preposition 'to' in the formulation 'I love to you' (Irigaray, 1996).

12 Bourneville wrote the texts under the supervision of Charcot, and Régnard took the photographs. In the 1880s, Albert Londe was the director of photography at the Salpêtrière, and in 1888 the first volume of the *Nouvelle Iconographie de la Salpêtrière* appeared, by Gilles de la Tourette, Paul Richer and Londe, still under Charcot's auspices.

13 In his seminal analysis of Charcot's project, Georges Didi-Huberman proposes that hysteria, as a disease constructed by medical discourse, was nourished by a mutual complicity between patient and physician.

Being a 'good' hysteric, he points out, would have also served a practical purpose and operated as a form of seduction, gaining material advantages for the patient (Didi-Huberman, 2003: 170).

14 Joan Copjec inverts this teleology, pointing out that in Freud's later writings in particular, memory comes to be 'less and less [the] direct aim or assured victory' of psychoanalysis, but, rather, its by-product: 'one remembers because one is cured, not the other way round'. With memory thus figured, transference becomes 'the place where the desires which structured fantasies could be analyzed and not ... the place from which to restore a forgotten event' (Copjec, 1984: 66).

15 In his famous address to an imaginary audience on the riddle of feminine sexuality, Freud bluntly quips: 'To those of you who are women ... you are yourselves the problem' (Freud, 'Femininity', in Freud, 1933: 113.) The 'riddle' of femininity is, for Freud, the question of how women might be knowable to men. For a brilliant feminist reading of Freud's 'lecture' in relation to his other work – a reading that does not, as Irigaray does, simplistically reduce Freud to 'the enemy' – see Kofman, 1985. Kofman shows how 'Femininity' had strategic value for Freud, serving to legitimate his powerful knowledge in the face of several female psychoanalysts whose findings on the relation between neuroses and the Oedipus complex undermined his own theories (Kofman, 1985: 16–19).

16 Nancy Chodorow's work on the pre-Oedipal bond between daughters and mothers has offered feminists the possibility of a new paradigm outside of the patriarchal drama (Chodorow, 1999). Nevertheless, continuing to label it 'pre-Oedipal' emphasises the primacy of the Oedipus complex as a referent.

17 Fascism, like many totalitarian discursive regimes, enforced a compulsory heterosexuality and a strict distribution of gender roles. Yet, as Barbara Spackman has shown, in Italy, while the adjective 'virile' was applied to women as a term of insult, the Fascist cult of virility universalised and was also adopted by women (Spackman, 1996: 43).

18 Common Portuguese examples might include *fazer render o seu peixe* (literally, to make the most of one's fish; to be parsimonious or thrifty), *vender o seu peixe* (literally, to sell one's own fish; to blow one's own horn), and *tudo que vem à rede é peixe* (literally, everything that the net picks up is fish; there is nothing that cannot be put to some use).

Conclusion: Painting history

The finding of an object is in fact a refinding of it. (Sigmund Freud, *Three Essays on the Theory of Sexuality*)

But no fact that is a cause is for that very reason historical. It became historical posthumously, as it were . . . (Walter Benjamin, 'Theses on the Philosophy of History')

The history that Paula Rego's works repeatedly rehearse is, as I have shown, that of the Portuguese *Estado Novo*. This regime was finally toppled in the Carnation Revolution of April 1974. If that dictatorship has furnished Rego's work with an abundant image repertoire, it has also provided her with fertile abstractions, tapping the mutual penetration of the personal and the political, the family and the state, subjectivity and sociality. Repression, humiliation, obedience and subversion are all intimately rehearsed at home. But why, we want to ask, this investment in anteriority, this obsessive re-configuring of the past? To what extent is the reiteration of pastness only apparently a 'working through' (Freud, 1914c: 145–146), while remaining profoundly cathected to antecedence as origin? What, one wonders, would Rego's work look like stripped of this repetition?

Underpinning this book is the notion that such reiteration of historical referents serves a structural role in Rego's work. The regime to which she implicitly or explicitly returns time and time again – its reliance on repressive measures, its dependence on territorial possession, its alignment with the values of a conservative Catholicism, its perpetuation of the structures of the patriarchal family – seems to offer Rego a mirror: a surface upon which both the self-recognition and the self-alienation of identity might be essayed. The past in

Rego's work is therefore not a prehistory in a causal or chronological sense. Rather, it is constantly revivified in present utterance. As both trace and construct, it is figured as the condition – the ideological possibility – for the emergence of her subjects. Through their invocation of different constituent aspects of the *Estado Novo*, and with their representations of the home as an intimate locus of ideological elaboration, I have argued, the three paintings that have served as case studies here underline the extent to which subjectivity cannot be ideologically innocent.

If it is through the mutual interpenetration of the ideological and the psychic that Rego's works engage with history, it is also on the site of such interpellation that the female subject's placement is secured, first in its family of origin, and then in subsequent relationships. Crucially, then, invoking that particular historical context seems to offer Rego a frame through which to address the central concerns that drive her work, an investigation into the ways in which women may be implicated in history, and an exploration of the ways in which human subjects simultaneously strive towards inter-subjective bonds (most ardently, the bond of love), and suffer subjection through such attachment. Rego's work, then, stages the subject's ambivalent responses to subjectification and to the values in which it is inevitably immersed; not least, those values that organise subjectivity along lines of sexual difference. Such values are exercised on an intimate level through the process of Oedipalisation, to which I have repeatedly returned in the course of this study.

Oedipalisation – the trajectory of the Oedipus complex from inception to dissolution (or irresolution) – situates the subject in a structure of relations and in a form of narrativity that Freud calls 'the family romance'. This is a way of saying that, for the adult, to love is always, in effect, to love again. For, as an incomplete project, the family romance suggests that there is no final breach with the past, no absolute egress, in our choice of objects and our negotiation with them, from the representations of childhood and from the determination of our earliest attachments. These attachments, Freud suggests in his essay 'Family Romances' and makes explicit later, operate under the sign of paternal law. It is to such a law that I turned in my examination of *The Policeman's Daughter*, where the father invoked by the title, but absent from the representation, announces the centrality, for Rego, of relations of kinship in general, and of a relation to the paternal in particular.

Here, I argued in favour of a reading of Rego's subjects in the light of those terms first defined by Freud and then refracted through the prism of structural linguistics by Lacan, stipulating that for his inability to be the definitive author of his child, the father is given compensation by the law that is exercised in his name. Legitimacy resides, in other words, in a bond celebrated, by paternal dispensation, on the symbolic plane. The role of the paternal (for Lacan, as placeholder) is fundamental to the structuring of the Symbolic Order as the domain of signification and exchange within culture. Paternal law thus entails the set of injunctions and limitations governing desire, framed as the prohibition against incest: desire must be deferred and find its place outside of the family of origin. It is, therefore, coterminous with the law of exogamy, the effect of which is to establish a grid of structural relationships not only within the family, but also among members of a group, within a context of normative heterosexuality. This is the structure that Oedipalisation puts into place. Oedipalisation, I have therefore urged, is a primary vehicle for socialisation in patriarchy.

If a normative heterosexuality marks the Freudian family romance, for Lacan, Oedipus and its consequence in 'castration' operates on a symbolic plane as a marker of the subject's entry into both difference and consensual meaning. Following Lacan, I consider the Oedipus complex not so much as a narrative of real relationships within the family, but as the architecture positioning the subject in relation to its objects. I have found convincing support in those feminist theories that see in the Oedipus complex not the triumph of actual paternity over maternity, but a structure of triangulation through which a signifying subject emerges, transforming the family triangle into a symbolic constellation where a relation to the mother's image and the father's name places the subject in culture. Understood in the broadest sense, 'Oedipus', as I stress in Chapter 2, is a mechanism through which the subject joins a broader collectivity, is conscripted into the social contract, and participates in a cultural and symbolic order that pre-exists and anticipates it. For the subject, there is nowhere else to go.

Clearly, such a picture of subject formation suggests that there is no easy exit from the geometry that produces a conservative subject. Clearly, too – as feminism has shown – this is not necessarily or universally the case, and the history of feminism might be tracked as a trajectory of resistance to such a model. For instance, in regarding the umbilical cut rather than symbolic castration as the first act of division, Luce Irigaray proposes, in an idealising vein, a language in the feminine, one that purportedly eschews the logic of the Phallus. Moreover, the notion of a de-Oedipalised family, as I have suggested, resides at the core of some of those intellectual projects wishing to loosen the stranglehold of the model that acts as the keystone to Freud's theories. As a normative heterosexuality is the outcome of the Oedipalised family romance, such views attempt to locate a position for other kinds of desire. But, I would argue, the Oedipus myth seems to be not one of many possible hermeneutic tools, but the story that most profoundly sounds the emergence of subjects in families, even if those groupings are governed by new and differently gendered kinship and family arrangements. And regarding Oedipus as structural, as Lacan and his followers have done, crucially detaches the mythical/Freudian narrative from the fixed gendering of its placeholders. This, nevertheless, tends to remain largely theoretical, re-introducing a question mark over Freud's famous harnessing of destiny to anatomy. For, as Juliet Mitchell has pointed out,

> if [Freudian] psychoanalysis is phallocentric, it is because the human social order that it perceives refracted through the individual human subject is patrocentric. To date, the father stands in the position of the third term that *must* break the asocial dyadic unit of the mother and child. We can see that this third term will always need to be represented by something or someone. Lacan returns to the problem, arguing that the relation of mother and child cannot be viewed outside the structure established by the position of the father. (Mitchell and Rose, 1982: 23)

The father (or the placeholder of the paternal), in other words, generally and archetypally occupies the structural position that symbolises the constitutive break between child and mother. It is this structure, I have argued, that organises Rego's work: a triangulated formation inhabited, for the most part, though not always, by traditionally gendered placeholders.

The relative positions of mothers and fathers have, in different ways, informed the three central chapters of this book. Taking, as Rego does, the female subject (the subject that, through the very process described, is constituted in 'femininity') as my point of departure, my narrative has inverted the developmental chronology whereby the paternal violently disrupts the child's bond with the maternal. I have begun, in other words, with the father, and ended with the mother. This chronological reversal has enabled me to rehearse a brief history of the *Estado Novo* as a more or less chrono-logical narrative. While in Chapter 4, I have explored the sense of loss that constitutes the maternal bequest to the female subject as a consequence of such an intrusion; in Chapter 2, I have examined that subject's compliance with, and struggle against, paternal law. However, these two chapters hinge around an investigation into gender enactment in Chapter 3, where a transvestite performance realises the relativity of maternal and paternal roles, and underlines the mobility of those gender positions that might otherwise seem quite fixed in Rego's work. Underlying all three chapters – and underpinning the three paintings at the heart of each of these chapters – is a notion of identification, of *being* as 'being like', of the mimesis and incorporation entailed in the constitution of identity.

I have argued that Rego's reprises of the past – both of an image repertoire embedded in the *Estado Novo*, and of the earliest identifi-cations of infants – are means of exploring the ways in which libidi-nal attachments are framed by relations of, and to, authority and power. But it is also tempting to hypothesise, with regard to Rego's continued evocations of the Portugal of her childhood, the urge to reiterate the past in order to redeem it, as if to renegotiate the scope of its determinations; to repeat what is over until it is done with.

Clearly, the reiteration is itself a measure of the failure of such a project. This has a dimension that is addressed by psychoanalysis as a process of repeating repressed material as contemporary event: transference, as Freud recognised, was a way of invoking the past 'with unwished-for exactitude' (Freud, 1920: 18), while failing to remember it. The talking cure entails, as we have seen, converting into conscious memory the unwitting acting-out that characterises the process of transference as a veiled address to earliest authority. This takes place as the analysand 'works through' the resistances that hinder recollection. 'It has been the physician's endeavour', Freud tells us, 'to keep this transference neurosis within the narrowest limits: to force as much as possible into the channel of memory and to allow as little as possible to emerge as repetition' (Freud, 1920: 19). It is, I am suggesting, in the failure to work through, in the reit-erations of its field of reference, that Rego's work keeps transference alive. Indeed, here transference emerges as a pressure to memori-alise the traumatic effects not only of historical events, but also of intimate ones; indeed, compressing and compacting the historical and the intimate. Considered more broadly, the process of transference enables a retrospective construction of the very category of 'the historical'.

If Freud's therapeutic methods aim gradually to familiarise the subject with things that are strange and menacing in his or her own trajectory, there is, Rego's work tells us, something valuable in allowing that strangeness to remain so; something to be gained by not allowing repressed material to be fully absorbed and integrated. There is, I am therefore suggesting, a political dimension to Rego's desire to hold on to her ghosts, her refusal to permit tyranny to be transformed into a placid memorial. For the paradox of the idealised – and never entirely realisable – wish to 'remember, repeat and work through' is that, in bringing the past into conscious focus, remembering also ushers in its opposite. Remembering, in other words, may become a way of forgetting. For, once it has been processed, an event threatens to slip, as if for a second time, into oblivion. Contrariwise, the unacceptable – repeatedly invoked and acted out, constantly de-familiarised and somatised – remains a rebuke. In refusing to relegate the past to the past, Rego's work keeps it alive as a matter of acute contemporary concern, announcing that its legacy survives in the present as a haunting and as a caution.

This brings me to a methodological point, for it sharpens the importance of the encounter between psychoanalytic theory and artistic practice. Here, I wish to invoke Jacqueline Rose's productive definition of the staging of that encounter as reiterating uncertainties that are already in place. That encounter, then,

> draws its strength from . . . repetition, working like a memory trace of something we have been through before. It gives back to repetition its proper meaning and status: not lack of originality or something merely derived (the commonest reproach to the work of art), nor the more recent practice of appropriating artistic and photographic images in order to undermine their previous status; but repetition as insistence, that is, as the constant pressure of something hidden but not forgotten – something that can only come into focus now by blurring the field of representation where our normal forms of self-recognition take place. (Rose, 1986: 228)

Paradoxically, then, something comes into focus by a smudging, an obfuscation. That 'blurred field' of self-recognition may also be the site where gender identity is staged, with its interpellations and appropriations, its incorporations and disavowals. It is, of course, precisely because of such mobile identifications that I have chosen to focus on the three principal works around which this book has been constructed. Rego's work shows us what Freud's had already implied – that identifications sometimes comply with, and at other times run across and against the grain of, gender expectations, whose lines of division are, in Rose's words, 'fragile in exact proportion to the rigid insistence with which our culture lays them down' (Rose, 1986: 227). Oedipalisation is the intimate structure whereby those laws are rigidly declared; yet Freud also recognises, if only in what he considers to be the subject's inherent bisexuality, the extent to which this process remains an ideal, never fully realisable.

For Rose, then, psychoanalysis can be recruited for a particular account of the image, in a field of vision always invested with the idea of sexuality, not only as content but as form: an account, in other words, of practices of looking as inextricably bound to gendering. The submission of the image to a sexual reference becomes the site where aesthetics and politics converge. This is where feminism announces itself as the politics that 'holds the image accountable for the reproduction of norms' (Rose, 1986: 231). For if the 'aesthetic' as a category is traditionally linked to a mastery of vision and its origin located in a masculine body, feminism has served as the political consciousness that underlines the ways in which that 'aesthetically acclaimed form serves to maintain a particular and oppressive mode of sexual recognition' (Rose, 1986: 232). Yet finally, Rose recognises that it is by looking obliquely *within* the parameters of that given field of representation – just as Lacan looked obliquely at Holbein's *Ambassadors* – that 'we can surely relinquish the monolithic view of that history, if doing so allows us a form of resistance which can be articulated *on this side of . . .* the world against which it protests' (Rose, 1986: 233, emphasis in the original). Rose, like Kristeva, apprehends that there is no possible resistance outside the field of the symbolic.

Surely, it is an oblique look at history – a look which, in being oblique, shows that history as already containing its 'moments of unease' (Rose, 1986: 233) – that Rego offers, in her obsessive invocation of a time now gone, but not lain to rest. This, I propose, is how we should consider her claim to a place within canonicity,[1] represented, in the first instance, by the collection of the National Gallery in London, where she held a residency in 1990; her invocation of older styles of figurative painting that some, following Buchloh, might see as restorative of a reactionary academicism.[2]

The hailing of the past, not only as historical event, but also as 'style', marks a turn away from Rego's earlier embrace of the matrix-ial and the inscriptive, the formless and the abject in Rego's works of the 1960s: modes of pictorial production that, it may be argued, eschew the phallocentric and phallocratic Symbolic Order, and that might therefore more readily be identified with a feminist project. A turn towards mimetic figuration – towards a form of figuration that seems to ventriloquise those very historical referents it also criticises – places Rego at a far remove from any practice that endeavours to imagine new signifiers for the feminine, signifiers that are situated outside of the phallic regime. Such a practice is generally associated with *écriture féminine* in the verbal arts, and either with deconstruc-tion, non-representational inscription, or the abject in the visual arts.[3]

Indeed, if feminism is regarded in terms of the historical cargo borne by the materials and forms of art themselves, Rego has to be seen as excluded from this camp. But, as Griselda Pollock has rightly pointed out, feminist practice cannot be reduced 'to a question of "painting" [versus] scripto-visual forms' (Pollock, 2001: 105). We cannot, she affirms 'be debating women's right to use oil or acrylic paint on canvas' (Pollock, 2001: 86). If, however, feminism is more broadly viewed as a crisis in knowledge, or as an endeavour that allows the 'woman's body' to inhabit the 'body of the painter' (Pollock, 2001: 73), or as the vexation of the difference that under-pins subject formation, then, by troubling the codes that underpin that underpins representation of female bodies and women's lives, Rego's work remains attached to a project that must be seen as fol-lowing a feminist impulse. Indeed, if, as Denise Riley has shown, the category of 'woman' cannot be homogeneously encapsulated and is not only too generic but is also historically determined (Riley, 1988: 106), then it is through the honed exploration of the specific (neither 'Woman' nor 'woman', but 'women') as it is played out in history that Rego engages with feminism.

This is not – though some have claimed it so – a triumphalist cele-bration of 'women's' power; not, as Riley drolly puts it 'a celebratory identification with a rush of Women onto the historical stage' (Riley, 1988: 8). Neither is it an unalloyed trespassing of social norms, or an autonomous femininity (a femininity not defined by its otherness, not branded by 'difference') voiced, as Cixous or Irigaray proposes, in a revolutionary new language. But in the volatility of identifica-tions it performs, and in its aggressive de-aestheticisation and con-comitant de-fetishisation of women's bodies, Rego's work remains awkwardly difficult to assimilate into the canonicity to which it also submits.

If in her evocation of the porous division between vitality and aggression, between love and submission, between psychic and social law, Rego presents the viewer with ways of thinking the body as a threshold, the transactions across the body are also invocations of, and interventions in, history. But, more than this, in Rego's work, it is the body or, more appositely, bodies that not only perform *in* history, they also perform histories. In the most intimate sense, Rego revives – and simultaneously disorders – the outmoded genre of history painting by aligning it with contradictory, unstable female subjectivities. Embracing the subject's necessary insertion in the Symbolic Order where meaning is produced and reproduced, her works give material form to a struggle with the emergence in history of the very concept of 'feminine' meaning. The ambivalence and tension that her works reveal in relation to the family triangle – and the romance that holds it in place – is a token of that struggle.

Notes

1 The relationship between feminism and the canon, as it is played out in Rego's work, has remained outside the ambit of my field of enquiry in this thesis. For the interplay between canoncity and feminism, see Pollock, 1999.
2 Alexandre Pomar sees in 'the process of continued renovation . . . of the outmoded language of painting' in Rego's work, not a 'return to order' with its 'politically or artistically reactionary connotation', not 'as some say . . . the survival of that outmoded language of painting', but a sign of its vitality (Pomar, 1999c: 22).
3 Many names may be invoked here, in all three fields and their various overlaps and correlations, among them: Helen Chadwick, Rose Garrard, Laura Godfrey-Isaacs, Ann Hamilton, Mona Hatoum, Susan Hiller, Mary Kelly, Barbara Kruger, Rosa Lee, Ana Mendieta, Annette Messager, Laura Mulvey, Therese Oulton, Martha Rosler, Carolee Schneemann, Cindy Sherman, Lorna Simpson, Jo Spence and Nancy Spero.

Bibliography

Abel, Elizabeth. 1990. 'Race, Class, and Psychoanalysis? Opening Questions', in Marianne Hirsch and Evelyn Fox Keller (eds) *Conflicts in Feminism*, London and New York: Routledge, 184–204.

Acciaiuoli, Margarida. 1991. 'Os Anos 40 em Portugal: O País, o Regime e as Artes, "Restrauração e Celebração"' PhD thesis, Lisbon: Universidade Nova.

Adams, Parveen. 1989. 'Of Female Bondage', in Teresa Brennan (ed.) *Between Feminism and Psychoanalysis*, London and New York: Routledge, 247–265.

Alexandre, Valentim. 1998. 'The Colonial Empire', in António Costa Pinto (ed.) *Modern Portugal*, Palo Alto, CA: The Society for the Promotion of Science and Scholarship, 41–59.

Alpers, Svetlana. 1983. *The Art of Describing: Dutch Art in the Seventeenth Century*, London: Penguin.

—— 2005. *The Vexations of Art: Velázquez and Others*, New Haven, CT and London: Yale University Press.

Althusser, Louis. 1971a. 'Ideology and Ideological State Apparatuses (Notes towards an Investigation)', in *Lenin and Philosophy and Other Essays*, trans. Ben Brewster, New York: Monthly Review Press, 127–186.

—— 1971b. 'Freud and Lacan', in *Lenin and Philosophy and Other Essays*, trans. Ben Brewster, New York: Monthly Review Press, 181–202.

Amnesty International. 1984. *Torture in the Eighties*, an Amnesty International Report, London: Amnesty International Publications.

Arriaga, Lopes de. 1976. *Mocidade Portuguesa: Breve História de Uma Organização Salazarista*, Lisbon: Terra Livre.

Associação de Ex-Presos Políticos Antifascistas. 1976. *Elementos para a história da PIDE*, Lisbon: AEPPA.

Avillez, Maria João. 1991. 'A arte de pintar histórias', *O Público*, 25 August, 7–16.

Bakhtin, Mikhail. 1984 (1964). *Rabelais and His World*, trans. Hélène Iswolsky, Bloomington: Indiana University Press.

Bal, Mieke. 1991. *Reading 'Rembrandt': Beyond the Word-Image Opposition*, Cambridge: Cambridge University Press.

—— 1996. 'Reading Art?', in Griselda Pollock (ed.) *Generations and Geographies in the Visual Arts: Feminist Readings*, London: Routledge, 25–41.

—— 2001a. *Louise Bourgeois' Spider: The Architecture of Art-Writing*, London and Chicago, IL: Chicago University Press.

—— 2001b. *Looking In: The Art of Viewing*, with an introduction by Norman Bryson, Amsterdam: G+B Arts International.

—— 2006. 'Dreaming Art', in Griselda Pollock (ed.) *Psychoanalysis and the Image*, Oxford: Blackwell Publishing, 30–59.

—— and Bryson, Norman. 1991. 'Semiotics and Art History', *Art Bulletin*, 73/2, June, 174–208.

Barker, Francis. 1995 (1984). *The Tremulous Private Body: Essays on Subjection*, Michigan, IL: Michigan University Press.

Barrett, Michèle and McIntosh, Mary. 1982. *The Anti-Social Family*, London: Verso.

Barthes, Roland. 1974 (1970). *S/Z*, trans. Richard Miller, New York: Hill & Wang.

—— 1975 (1973). *The Pleasure of the Text*, trans. Richard Miller. New York: Farrar, Straus and Giroux.

—— 2000 (1972). *Mythologies*, trans. Annette Lavers, London: Vintage.

Bastide, Roger. 1972. 'Lusotropicology, Race, and Nationalism, and Class Protest and Development in Brazil and Portuguese Africa', in Roger H. Chilcote (ed.) *Protest and Resistance in Angola and Brazil: Comparative Studies*, Los Angeles and London: University of California Press, 225–242.

Battersby, Christine. 1995. 'Just Jamming: Irigaray, Painting and Psychoanalysis', in Katy Deepwell (ed.) *New Feminist Art Criticism*, Manchester and New York: Manchester University Press, 128–137.

Baudelaire, Charles. 1964. *The Painter of Modern Life and Other Essays*, trans. and ed. Jonathan Mayne, London: Phaidon Books.

—— 1972. 'The Salon of 1846', in *Baudelaire: Selected Writings on Art and Artists*, trans. P.E. Charvet, Harmondsworth: Penguin Books, 47–107.

Baxandall, Michael. 1985. *Patterns of Intention: On the Historical Explanation of Pictures*, New Haven, CT and London: Yale University Press.

—— 2003. *Words for Pictures: Seven Papers on Renaissance Art and Criticism*, New Haven, CT and London: Yale University Press.

Beauvoir, Simone de. 1972 (1949). *The Second Sex*, trans. H.M. Parshley, London: Penguin Books.

Beizer, Janet. 1994. *Ventriloquized Bodies: Narratives of Hysteria in Nineteenth-Century France*, Ithaca, NY and London: Cornell University Press.

Benjamin, Jessica. 1986. 'A Desire of One's Own: Psychoanalytic Feminism and Intersubjective Space', in Teresa de Lauretis (ed.) *Feminist Studies/ Critical Studies*, Bloomington: University of Indiana Press, 78–101.

—— 1990. *The Bonds of Love: Psychoanalysis, Feminism and the Problem of Domination*, London: Virago.

Berger, John. 1972. *Ways of Seeing*, London: Penguin Books.

Bersani, Leo. 1986. *The Freudian Body: Psychoanalysis and Art*, New York: Columbia University Press.

—— 1990. *The Culture of Redemption*, Cambridge, MA and London: Harvard University Press.

Bessa-Luís, Augustina and Rego, Paula. 2001. *As Meninas*, Lisbon: Três Sinais.

Bethencourt, Francisco. 2003. 'Desconstrução da memória imperial: literatura, arte e historiografia', in Margarida Calafate Ribeiro and Ana Paula Ferreira (eds) *Fantasmas e Fantasias Imperiais no Imaginário Português*, Oporto: Campo de Letras, 69–89.

Betterton, Rosemary. 1996. *Intimate Distance: Women, Artists, and The Body*, London and New York: Routledge.

Bhabha, Homi. 1987. 'Of Mimicry and Man', first published in *October: Anthology*, Boston, MA: MIT Press; reprinted in Bhabha, 1994, *The Location of Culture*, London and New York: Routledge, 85–92.

—— 1990. 'Introduction: Narrating the Nation', in Homi Bhabha (ed.) *Nation and Narration*, London and New York: Routledge, 1–7.

Blyth, Jenny. 2003. 'A Sting in the Tale', *Art Review* (October), 47–48.

Bois, Yve-Alain. 1990. *Painting as Model*, Boston, MA: MIT Press.

—— and Krauss, Rosalind. 1997. *Formless: A User's Guide*, New York: Zone Books.

Bollas, Christopher. 1987. *The Shadow of the Object: The Unthought Known*, London: Free Association Books.

—— 1992. 'Why Oedipus', in *Being a Character*, London: Routledge, 218–246.

Bosi, Alfredo. 1992. *Dialética da Colonização*, São Paulo: Companhia das Letras.

Bowie, Malcolm. 1993. *Psychoanalysis and the Future of Theory*, Oxford: Blackwell Publishers.

Boxer, Charles. 1963. *Race Relations in the Portuguese Colonial Empire, 1415– 1825*, Oxford: Clarendon Press.

—— 1975. *Mary and Misogyny: Women in Iberian Expansion Overseas, 1415– 1815*, London: Duckworth.

Bradley, Fiona. 1997. 'Introduction: Automatic Narratives', in *Paula Rego*, exhibition catalogue, Liverpool: Tate Gallery, 9–32.

—— (ed.) 2000. *Victor Willing* (with contributions from Lynne Cooke, John McEwen, John Mills, Paula Rego and Nicholas Serota), London: August Media Ltd.

—— 2001–02. 'Paula Rego, Recent Works', in *Paula Rego: Celestina's House*, exhibition catalogue, Kendal: Abbot Hall Art Gallery, and New Haven, CT: Yale Center for British Art, 5–7.

—— 2002. *Paula Rego*, London: Tate Publishing.

Braga da Cruz, Manuel. 1988. *O Partido e o Estado no Salazarismo*, Lisbon: Editorial Presença.

—— 1998. *O Estado Novo e a Igreja Católica*, Lisbon: Bizâncio.

Braidotti, Rosi. 1989. 'The Politics of Ontological Difference', in Teresa Brennan (ed.) *Between Feminism and Psychoanalysis*, London and New York: Routledge, 40–59.

Brecht, Bertolt. 1972. *Compact Poets: Bertolt Brecht*, selected and introduced by Denys Thomson, trans. H.R. Hays, London: Chatto & Windus.

Bronfen, Elisabeth. 1998. *The Knotted Subject: Hysteria and its Discontents*, Princeton, NJ: Princeton University Press.

—— 2001. 'Redressing Grievances: Cross-Dressing Pleasure with the Law', in Elisabeth Bronfen and Misha Kava (eds) *Feminist Consequences: Theory for the New Century*, New York: Columbia University Press, 213–253.

Brontë, Charlotte. 1996 (1847). *Jane Eyre*, ed. Michael Mason, London: Penguin Classics.

Brooks, Peter, 1984. *Reading for the Plot: Design and Intention in Narrative*, Oxford: Clarendon Press.

—— 1993. *Body Work: Objects of Desire in Modern Narrative*, Cambridge, MA and London: Harvard University Press.

Brown, Wendy. 1995. *States of Injury: Freedom and Power in Late Modernity*, Princeton, NJ: Princeton University Press.

Brunner, José. 1995. *Freud and the Politics of Psychoanalysis*, New Brunswick, NJ: Transaction Publishers.

Brunswick, Ruth Mack. 1928. 'A supplement to Freud's "History of an Infantile Neurosis"', *International Journal of Psychoanalysis*, 9, 439–476.

Buarque de Holanda, Sérgio. 1985 (1959). *Visão do Paraíso: Os Motivos Edênicos no Descobrimento e na Colonização do Brasil*, São Paulo: Nacional.

Buchloh, Benjamin. 1984. 'Figures of Authority, Ciphers of Regression: Notes on the Return of Representation in European Painting', *October*, 16 (Spring), 39–68. Reprinted in Brian Wallis (ed.) 1984, *Art After Modernism: Rethinking Representation*, New York: The New Museum of Contemporary Art, and Boston: David R. Godine Publisher, 107–134.

Buck, Louisa. 2003b. 'Playtime: Interview with Paula Rego', *The Times*, 18 October, 36–45.

Buhle, Mari Jo. 1998. *Feminism and its Discontents: A Century of Struggle with Psychoanalysis*, Cambridge, MA and London: Harvard University Press.

Butler, Judith. 1990. *Gender Trouble: Feminism and the Subversion of Identity*, London and New York: Routledge.

—— 1993a. *Bodies That Matter: On the Discursive Limits of 'Sex'*, London and New York: Routledge.

—— 1993b. 'The Body Politics of Julia Kristeva', in Kelly Oliver (ed.) *Ethics, Politics and Difference in Julia Kristeva's Writing*, New York and London: Routledge, 164–178.

—— 1997. *The Psychic Life of Power: Theories in Subjection*, Stanford, CA: Stanford University Press.

—— 2000. *Antigone's Claim: Kinship Between Life and Death*, London and New York: Columbia University Press.

—— 2005. *Giving an Account of Oneself*, New York: Fordham University Press.

Caminha, Pero Vaz de. 1990. 'A Carta de Pero Vaz de Caminha', in Cortesão, Jaime, *Obras Completas, Vol. VII*, Lisbon: Imprensa Nacional Casa da Moeda, 153–173.

Campbell-Johnson, Rachel. 2002. 'Divinity Comes Down to Earth', *The Times*, 4 September, 16–17.

—— 2004. 'Tales from a True Life Class', *The Times*, 27 October, 16.

Caplan, Jane. 1979. 'Introduction to Female Sexuality in Fascist Ideology', *Feminist Review*, 1, 59–66.

Capucho, Teresa. 2001. 'Paula Rego: O desenho como ponto de referência, o deseno como factor de mudança', MA dissertation, Lisbon: Universidade de Lisboa.

Cardoso Pires, José. 1982. *Ballad of Dog's Beach*, trans. Mary Fitton, London: J.M. Dent and Sons.

Castelo, Claudia. 1998. *O Modo Português de Estar no Mundo: O Luso-Tropicalismo e a Ideologia Colonial Portuguesa (1933–1961)*, Oporto: Edições Afrontamento.

Castro Rocha, João Cezar de. 2001. 'Brazil as Exposition', online text, paper delivered at the conference *Grand Expositions*, Yale University, 2001, www.lehman.cuny.edu/ciberletras/vo8/rocha.html (accesed on 5 March 2005).

Cavalcanti de Albuquerque, Roberto. 2000. *Gilberto Freyre e a Invenção do Brasil*, Rio de Janeiro: José Olympio Editora.

Cavarero, Adriana. 1997. *Relating Narratives: Storytelling and Selfhood*, trans. Paul A. Kottman, London and New York: Routledge.

Chassegueut-Smirgel, Janine. 1985. *The Ego Ideal: A Psychoanalytic Essay on the Malady of the Ideal*, trans. Paul Barrows, London and New York: Penguin Books.

Chodorow, Nancy. 1994. *Femininities, Masculinities, Sexualities*, London: Free Association Books.

—— 1999 (1978). *The Reproduction of Mothering*, Berkeley, Los Angeles and London: University of California Press.

Christie, Ian and Dodd, Philip. 1996. *Spellbound: Art and Film*, exhibition catalogue, texts by Gordon Burn, Christopher Frayling, Martin Kemp, Marcia Pointon and Peter Wollen, London: Hayward Gallery.

Cixous, Hélène and Clément, Catherine. 1986. *The Newly Born Woman*, trans. Betsy Wing, Manchester: Manchester University Press.

Coldwell, Paul. 2003. 'Paula Rego's Graphic Technique', in Tom Rosenthal, *Paula Rego: The Complete Graphic Work*, London: Thames and Hudson, 249–252.

—— 2005. 'Paula Rego, Printmaker', in *Paula Rego: Printmaker*, exhibition catalogue, London and travelling: Marlborough Graphics, 11–28.

Coli, Jorge. 1998. 'A Primeira Missa e Invenção da Descoberta', in Adauto Novaes (ed.) *A Descoberta do Homem e do Mundo*, São Paulo: Companhia das Letras, 107–121.

Constituição Política da República Portuguesa e Colonial. 1935, Lisbon: Imprensa Nacional.

Copjec, Joan. 1984. 'Transference: Letters and the Unknown Woman', *October*, 28 (Spring), 61–90.

Cork, Richard. 1997. 'Postcards from Wonderland', *The Times*, 11 February, 40.

Cornell, Drucilla. 1995. 'What is Ethical Feminism?', in Seyla Benhabib, Judith Butler, Drucilla Cornell and Nancy Fraser (eds) *Feminist Contentions: A Philosophical Exchange*, London and New York: Routledge: 75–105.

Costa Pinto, António. 1995. *Salazar's Dictatorship and European Fascism: Problems of Interpretation*, New York: Social Science Monographs, distributed by Columbia University Press.

—— 2001. *O Fim do Império Português: A Cena Internacional, a Guerra Colonial e a Descolonização, 1961–1975*, Lisbon: Livros Horizonte.

—— and Monteiro, Nuno G. 1998. 'Cultural Myths and Portuguese National Identity', in António Costa Pinto (ed.) *Modern Portugal*, Palo Alto, CA: The Society for the Promotion of Science and Scholarship, 206–217.

Coward, Rosalind. 1983. *Patriarchal Precedents: Sexuality and Social Relations*, London, Boston, Melbourne and Henley: Routledge and Kegan Paul.

Damisch, Hubert. 1975. 'Semiotics and Iconography', in Thomas A. Sebeok (ed.) *The Tell-Tale Sign: A Survey of Semiotics*, Lisse: Ridder Press, 27–36. Reprinted in Donald Preziosi (ed.) 1998, *The Art of Art History*, Oxford: Oxford University Press, 234–256.

Darwin, Charles. 1896. *Journal of Researches into the Natural History and Geology of the Countries Visited During the Voyage of the HMS Round the World, Under the Command of Capt. Fitz Roy, RN*, New York: D. Appleton.

Deepwell, Katy. 1987. 'In Defence of the Indefensible: Feminism, Painting and Postmodernism', *Feminist Art News*, 2/4, September, 13–15.

Didi-Huberman, Georges. 2003. *The Invention of Hysteria: Charcot and the Photographic Iconography of the Salpêtrière*, trans. Aliza Hartz, Cambridge MA: MIT Press.

Doane, Janice, and Hodges, Devon. 1992. *From Klein to Kristeva: Psychoanalytic Feminism and the Search for the 'Good Enough' Mother*, Ann Arbor: University of Michigan Press.

Doane, Mary Anne. 1997. 'Film and Masquerade: Theorizing the Female Spectator', in Katie Conboy, Nadia Medina and Sarah Stanbury (eds), *Writing on the Body: Female Embodiment and Feminist Theory*, New York: Columbia University Press, 176–194. First published in *Screen*, 23 (1982), 78–87.

Dubow, Jessica. 2000. 'Colonial Space, Colonial Identity: Perception and the South African Landscape', PhD thesis, Royal Holloway, University of London.

Duncan, Carol. 1973. 'Virility and Domination in Early Twentieth-Century Vanguard Painging', *Artforum*, December, 30–39.

—— 1975. 'When Greatness is a Box of Wheaties', *Artforum*, October, 60–64.

Durham, Martin. 1998. *Women and Fascism*, London and New York: Routledge.

Eça de Queirós, José Maria. 1962. *The Sin of Father Amaro*, trans. Nan Flangan, Manchester: Carcanet Press.

Faria, Óscar. 2001. 'Narrar o Maravilhoso', *O Público*, 10 November, 22.

—— 2004a. 'Paula Rego: devo ser surrealista, com certeza', *O Público*, 14 October, 2–3.

—— 2004b. 'Paula Rego: Da beleza convulsiva ao devir animal', *O Público*, 23 October, 16–17.

Feldstein, Richard and Roof, Judith (eds) 1989. *Feminism and Psychoanalysis*, Ithaca, NY and London: Cornell University Press.

Felman, Shoshana. 1987. *Jacques Lacan and the Adventure of Insight*, Cambridge, MA and London: Harvard University Press.

—— 1993. *What Does a Woman Want? Reading and Sexual Difference*, Baltimore, MD and London: Johns Hopkins University Press.

Ferreira, Virginia. 1998. 'Engendering Portugal: Social Change, State Politics, and Women's Social Mobilization', in António Costa Pinto (ed.) *Modern Portugal*, Palo Alto, CA: The Society for the Promotion of Science and Scholarship, 162–188.

Ferro, António. 1933. *Salazar: O Homem e a Sua Obra*, Lisbon: Empresa Nacional de Publicidade.

Flügel, J.C. 1930. *The Psychology of Clothes*, London: Hogarth Press.

Fortnum, Rebecca. 1991. 'Paula Rego: Tales from the National Gallery', *Women's Art Magazine*, 40, May–June, 12–13.

Foucault, Michel. 1977 (1975). *Discipline and Punish*, trans. Alan Sheridan, London: Penguin Books.

—— 1978 (1976). *The History of Sexuality, Vol. 1: An Introduction*, trans. Robert Hurley, London: Penguin Books.

—— 1984. 'Space, Knowledge, and Power', interview by Paul Rabinow, trans. Josué V. Harari, in Paul Rabinow (ed.) *The Foucault Reader: An Introduction to Foucault's Thought*, London: Penguin Books, 239–256.

França, José-Augusto. 1974. *A Arte em Portugal no Século XX (1911–1961)*, Lisbon: Livraria Bertrand.

Freud, Sigmund. 1892–99. 'Extracts from the Fliess Papers', in *The Standard Edition of the Complete Psychological Works* (henceforth *SE*), 2001 (1974), trans. under the general editorship of James Strachey, in collaboration with Anna Freud, assisted by Alix Strachey and Alan Tyson, London: Vintage, vol. 1, 173–280.

—— 1900a. *The Interpretation of Dreams* (first part), *SE*, vol. 4.

—— 1900b. *The Interpretation of Dreams* (second part) and *On Dreams*, *SE*, vol. 5.

—— 1905a. *Jokes and their Relation to the Unconscious*, *SE*, vol. 8.

—— 1905b. *Three Essays on Sexuality*, *SE*, vol. 7, 125–243.

—— 1905c. 'Fragment of an Analysis of a Case of Hysteria', 1905, *SE*, vol. 7, 3–122.

—— 1908. 'On the Sexual Theories of Children', *SE*, vol. 9, 209–226.

—— 1909. 'Family Romances', *SE*, vol. 9, 235–241.

—— 1910a. *Leonardo da Vinci and a Memory of his Childhood*, *SE*, vol. 11, 59–137.

—— 1910b. 'A Special Type of Choice of Object Made by Men (Contributions to the Psychology of Love, I)', *SE*, vol. 11, 164–175.

—— 1912a. 'The Dynamics of Transference', *SE*, vol. 12, 99–108.

—— 1912b. 'On the Universal Tendency to Debasement in the Sphere of Love: Contribution to the Psychology of Love, II', *SE*, vol. 11, 177–190.

—— 1913. *Totem and Taboo. SE*, vol. 13, 1–161.

—— 1914a. 'The Moses of Michelangelo', *SE*, vol. 13, 211–237.

—— 1914b. 'On Narcissism: An Introduction', *SE*, vol. 14, 67–102.

—— 1914c. 'Remembering, Repeating and Working-Through (Further Recommendations on the Technique of Psycho-Analysis, II', *SE*, vol. 12, 145–156.

—— 1915. 'Observations on Transference-Love (Further Recommendations on the Technique of Psycho-Analysis, II)', *SE*, vol. 12, 159–171.

—— 1917a. 'A Difficulty in the Path of Psychoanalysis', *SE*, vol. 17, 137–144.

—— 1917b. 'Mourning and Melancholia', *SE*, vol. 14, 237–258.

—— 1919a. '"A Child is Being Beaten": A Contribution to the Study of the Origin of Sexual Perversions', *SE*, vol. 17, 175–204.

—— 1919b. 'The Uncanny', *SE*, vol. 17, 217–256.

—— 1920. *Beyond the Pleasure Principle. SE*, vol. 18, 7–64.

—— 1921. *Group Psychology and the Analysis of the Ego, SE*, vol. 18, 67–143.

—— 1923. *The Ego and the Id, SE*, vol. 19, 3–66.

—— 1924a. 'The Economic Problem of Masochism', *SE*, vol. 19, 159–170.

—— 1924b. 'The Dissolution of the Oedipus Complex', *SE*, vol. 19, 173–179.

—— 1924c. 'A Short Account of Psycho-analysis', *SE*, vol. 19, 191–209.

—— 1925. 'Some Psychical Consequences of the Anatomical Distinction Between the Sexes', *SE*, vol. 19, 248–258.

—— 1926. *The Question of Lay-Analysis*, *SE*, vol. 20, 183–258.

—— 1927a. *The Future of an Illusion*, *SE*, vol. 21, 3–56.

—— 1927b. 'Humour', *SE*, vol. 21, 161–166.

—— 1927c. 'Fetishism', *SE*, vol. 21, 149–157.

—— 1930. *Civilization and its Discontents*, *SE*, vol. 21, 59–145.

—— 1931. 'Female Sexuality', *SE*, vol. 21, 223–243.

—— 1933. *New Introductory Lectures on Psycho-Analysis*. *SE*, vol. 22, 3–182.

—— 1940. *An Outline of Psychoanalysis*, *SE*, vol. 23, 141–207.

—— and Breuer, Josef. 1893–95. *Studies on Hysteria*. *SE*, vol. 2.

Freyre, Gilberto. 1961. *The Portuguese and the Tropics: Suggestions Inspired by the Portuguese Methods of Integrating Autocthonous Peoples and Cultures Differing from the European in a New, or Luso-Tropical Complex of Civilisation*, trans. Helen M. D'O and Matthew and F. de Mello Moser, Lisbon: Executive Committee for the Commemoration of the Fifth Centenary of the Death of Prince Henry the Navigator.

—— 1968. *The Mansions and the Shanties: The Making of Modern Brazil*, trans. Harriet de Onís, New York: Alfred A. Knopf.

—— 1970a (1948). *The Masters and the Slaves: A Study in the Development of Brazilian Civilization*, trans. Samuel Putnam, New York: Alfred A. Knopf.

—— 1970b (1959). *Order and Progress: Brazil from Monarchy to Republic*, trans. Rod. W. Horton, New York: Alfred A. Knopf.

Friedlander, Saul (1978). *History and Psychoanalysis: An Inquiry into the Possibilities and Limits of Psychohistory*, trans. Susan Suleiman, New York and London: Holmes and Meier Publishers.

Fuller, Peter. 1980. *Art and Psychoanalysis*, London: Writers and Readers.

Fuss, Diana. 1995. *Identification Papers*, London and New York: Routledge.

Gallop, Jane. 1982. *Feminism and Psychoanalysis: The Daughter's Seduction*, London: Macmillan.

—— 1992. *Around 1981: Academic Feminist Literary Theory*, New York and London: Routledge.

Gamman, Lorraine and Makinene, Merja. 1994. *Female Fetishism: A New Look*, London: Lawrence & Wishart.

Garber, Marjorie. 1992. *Vested Interests: Cross-Dressing and Cultural Anxiety*, London: Penguin.

Garnier, Christine. 2002 (1954). *Férias com Salazar*, Lisbon: Parceria.

Gee, Maggie. 1999. 'Painter of Shocking and Painful Truths', *Daily Telegraph*, 15 February, 19.

Gilbert, Sandra M. 1980. 'Costumes of the Mind: Transvestism as Metaphor in Modern Literature', *Critical Inquiry*, 7/2 (Winter), 391–417.

Gleadell, Colin. 2000. 'A Twist in the Tale', *Daily Telegraph* (Magazine), 3 June, 50–54.

Gombrich, E.H. 1966. 'Freud's Aesthetics', *Encounter,* 26/1, January, 30–40.

Gooding, Mel. 1988. 'Paula Rego', *Art Monthly,* 121, November, 16–17.

Gorjão, Vanda. 2002. *Mulheres em Tempos Sombrios: Oposição Feminina ao Estado Novo,* Lisbon: Imprensa de Ciências Socias.

Graham-Dixon, Andrew. 1998. 'Heroine Addiction', *The Independent,* 1 November, 16.

Grandville: Dessins Originaux. 1986–87. Exhibition catalogue, texts by S. Guillaume and C.F. Getty, Nancy: Musée des Beaux-Arts.

Green, André. 1986. 'The Dead Mother', trans. Katherine Aubertin, in *On Private Madness,* London: The Hogarth Press and the Institute of Psychoanalysis, 142–172.

Greer, Germaine. 1988. 'Paula Rego', *Modern Painters,* 1/3 (Autumn), 29–34.

—— 2004. 'Untamed by Age', *The Guardian,* 20 November, 18–19.

Grosz, Elizabeth. 1994. *Volatile Bodies: Towards a Corporeal Feminism,* Bloomington: Indiana University Press.

—— 1995. *Space, Time, and Perversion,* New York and London: Routledge.

Gumbrecht, Hans Ulrich. 2000–01. 'Who was Pero Vaz de Caminha?' *Portuguese Literary and Cultural Studies,* 4–5 (Spring/Fall), 423–434.

Harrison, Charles. 2005. *Painting the Difference: Sex and Spectator in Modern Art.* Chicago, IL: University of Chicago Press.

Hattenstone, Simon. 2009. 'You punish people with drawings', *The Guardian* (Weekend Section), 22 August, 22–28.

Heller, Dana. 1995. *Family Plots: The De-Oedipalization of Popular Culture.* Philadelphia: University of Pennsylvania Press.

Hicks, Alistair. 1985. 'Mischief in Paradise', *The Spectator,* 7 September, 31–32.

—— 1991. 'Women Take Over the Garden', *Sunday Times,* 21 July, 8.

Hill, Andrea. 1982. 'Paula Rego', *Artscribe,* 37, October, 33–37.

Hirsch, Marianne. 1989. *The Mother/Daughter Plot: Narrative, Psychoanalysis, Feminism,* Bloomington: Indiana University Press.

Holloway, Memory. 1999. 'Rear View Mirror: Looking Back, Moving Forward', in *Open Secret: Drawings and Etchings by Paula Rego,* exhibition catalogue, Paris: Calouste Gulbenkian Foundation, and Dartmouth, MA: University Art Gallery, 7–24.

—— 2000–01. 'Praying in the Sand: Paula Rego and the Visual Representations of the First Mass in Brazil', *Portuguese Literary & Cultural Studies,* 4–5 (Spring/Fall), 697–705.

Hubbard, Sue. 1989. 'Paula Rego and Psychoanalysis', *Alba* (Spring), 30–31.

Irigaray, Luce. 1985. *Speculum of the Other Woman,* trans. Gillian C. Gill, Ithaca, NY: Cornell University Press.

—— 1991a. 'Women-mothers, the silent substratum of the social order', trans. David Macey, in Margaret Whitford (ed.) *The Irigaray Reader*, Oxford: Blackwell Publishers, 34–52.

—— 1991b. 'The Limits of Transference', trans. David Macey with Margaret Whitford, in Margaret Whitford (ed.) *The Irigaray Reader*, Oxford: Blackwell Publishers, 105–117.

—— 1993. *Sexes and Genealogies*, trans. Gillian C. Gill, New York and Chichester: Columbia University Press.

—— 1996. *I Love to You: Sketch for a Felicity Within History*, trans. Alison Martin, New York and London: Routledge.

Isaak, Jo-Anna. 1996. *Feminism and Contemporary Art: The Revolutionary Power of Women's Laughter*, London and New York: Routledge.

Jacobus, Mary. 1986. 'Dora and the pregnant Madonna', in Mary Jacobus, *Reading Woman: Essays in Feminist Criticism*. New York: Columbia University Press, 137–193.

—— 1995a. 'In Parenthesis: Immaculate Conceptions and Feminine Desire', In *First Things: The Maternal Imaginary in Literature, Art, and Psychoanalysis*, London and New York: Routledge, 23–42.

—— 1995b. 'Narcissa's Gaze: Berthe Morisot and the Filial Mother', in Mary Jacobus, *First Things: The Maternal Imaginary in Literature, Art, and Psychoanalysis*, London and New York: Routledge, 269–295.

Jaggi, Maya. 2004. 'Secret Histories', *Guardian* (Review), 17 July, 16–19.

Januszczak, Waldemar. 2001. 'The Ecstacy and the Agony', *Sunday Times* (Culture), 5 August, 6–7.

Jardine, Alice. 1982. 'Gynesis', *Diacritics*, 12 (Summer), 54–65.

Kafka, Franz. 1996. 'In the Penal Colony', in *Metamorphosis and Other Stories*, trans. Stanley Appelbaum, New York: Dover Publications, 53–75.

Kahn, Coppélia. 1985. 'The Hand that Rocks the Cradle: Recent Gender Theories and Their Implications', in Shirley Nelson Garner, Claire Kahane, and Madelon Sprengnether (eds) *The (M)other Tongue: Essays in Feminist Psychoanalytic Interpretation*, Ithaca, NY and London: Cornell University Press, 72–87.

Kayman, Martin. 1987. *Revolution and Counter-Revolution in Portugal*, London and Wolfboro: Merlin Press.

Kellaway, Kate. 2004. 'No Flies on Rego', in *The Observer* (Features), 7 November, 11.

Kent, Sarah. 1989. 'Rego's Girls', *Art in America*, June, 158–162 and 205.

Kilgour, Maggie. 1998. 'The Function of Cannibalism in the Present Time', in Francis Barker, Peter Hulme and Margaret Iversen (eds) *Cannibalism and the Colonial World*, Cambridge: Cambridge University Press, 238–259.

King, Edward. 2001. 'Paula Rego Interviewed by Edward King, February 2001', in *Paula Rego: Celestina's House*, exhibition catalogue, Kendal: Abbot Hall Art Gallery, and New Haven, CT: Yale Center for British Art, 8–13.

Klein, Melanie. 1927. 'Criminal Tendencies in Normal Children', in *Love, Guilt and Reparation and Other Works (1921–1945)*, 1998, London: Vintage Books, 170–185.

—— 1928. 'Early Stages of the Oedipus Complex', in *Love, Guilt and Reparation and Other Works (1921–1945)*, 1998, London: Vintage Books, 186–198.

—— 1933. 'The Early Development of Conscience in the Child', in *Love, Guilt and Reparation and Other Works (1921–1945)*, 1998, London: Vintage Books, 148–257.

—— 1934. 'On Criminality', in *Love, Guilt and Reparation and Other Works (1921–1945)*, 1998, London: Vintage Books, 258–261.

—— 1935. 'A Contribution to the Psychogenesis of Manic-Depressive States', in *Love, Guilt and Reparation and Other Works (1921–1945)*, 1998, London: Vintage Books, 262–289.

—— 1937. 'Love, Guilt and Reparation', in *Love, Guilt and Reparation and Other Works (1921–1945)*, 1998, London: Vintage Books, 306–343.

—— 1945. 'The Oedipus Complex in the Light of Early Anxieties', in *Love, Guilt and Reparation and Other Works (1921–1945)*. 1998, London: Vintage Books, 370–419.

Kofman, Sarah. 1985. *The Enigma of Woman*, trans. Catherine Porter, Ithaca, NY and London: Cornell University Press.

—— 1988. *The Childhood of Art: An Interpretation of Freud's Aesthetics*, trans. Winifred Woodhull, New York: Columbia University Press.

Koonz, Claudia. 1988. *Mothers in the Fatherland: Women, the Family and Nazi Politics*, London: Methuen.

Krauss, Rosalind. 1999. *Bachelors*. Cambridge, MA and London: MIT Press.

Kristeva, Julia. 1980. *Desire in Language: A Semiotic Approach to Literature and Art*, trans. Thomas Gora, Alice Jardine and Leon S. Roudiez, New York: Columbia University Press.

—— 1982. *Powers of Horror: An Essay on Abjection*, trans. Leon S. Roudiez, New York: Columbia University Press.

—— 1984 (first published in French in 1974). *Revolution in Poetic Language*, trans. Margaret Waller, New York: Columbia University Press.

—— 1986. 'Women's Time', trans. Alice Jardine and Harry Blake, in Toril Moi (ed.) *The Kristeva Reader*, Oxford: Blackwell, 187–213. First published in *Signs*, 7/1 (Autumn), 1979, 13–35.

—— 1987a. *Tales of Love*, trans. Leon S. Roudiez, New York: Columbia University Press.

—— 1987b. 'Stabat Mater', in *Tales of Love*, trans. Leon S. Roudiez, New York: Columbia University Press, 234–263.

—— 1989. *Black Sun: Depression and Melancholia*, trans. Leon S. Roudiez, New York: Columbia University Press.

—— 2001. *Melanie Klein*, trans. Ross Guberman, New York: Columbia University Press.

—— 2003. 'On Génie Feminine and Art', lecture in the programme *Talks and Discussions* (webcast), Tate Modern, London, 23 November, www.channel.tate.org.uk/channel/search?searchQuery=kristeva (accessed 30 November 2003).

Kuin, Simon. 1993. 'A Mocidade Portuguesa nos anos 30: anteprojectos e Instauração de uma Organização Paramilitar da Juventude', *Análise Social*, 27/122, 555–588.

Kuspit, Donald. 1993. *Signs of Psyche in Modern and Postmodern Art*, Cambridge: Cambridge University Press.

Lacan, Jacques. 1953. 'The function and field of speech and language in psychoanalysis', in *Écrits: A Selection*, trans. Alan Sheridan, 1977, New York and London: W.W. Norton & Company, 30–113.

—— 1957. 'Agency of the Letter in the Unconscious', in *Écrits: A Selection*, trans. Alan Sheridan, 1977, New York and London: W.W. Norton & Company, 146–178.

—— 1979 (1973). *Four Fundamental Concepts of Psychoanalysis*, trans. Alan Sheridan, London: Penguin Books.

LaCapra, Dominick. 1989. 'History and Psychoanalysis', in *Soundings in Critical Theory*, Ithaca, NY and London: Cornell University Press, 30–66.

Lacerda, Alberto de. 1965. 'Fragmento de um poema intitulado Paula Rego', in *Paula Rego*, exhibition catalogue, Lisbon: Sociedade Nacional de Belas Artes.

Langbein, John H. 1976. *Torture and the Law of Proof: Europe and England in the Ancien Régime*, London and Chicago: Chicago University Press.

Lapa, Pedro. 2004. 'Fabulações das muitas figures na pintura de Paula Rego', in *Cinco Pintores da Modernidade Portuguesa (1911–1965)*, exhibition catalogue, Barcelona: Fundació Caixa Catalunya, 53–60.

Laplanche, Jean and Pontalis, Jean-Bertrand. 1973. *The Language of Psychoanalysis*, trans. Donald Nicholson-Smith, London: Karnac Books.

—— 1999. *Essays on Otherness*, various translators, ed. John Fletcher, London and New York: Routledge.

Laqueur, Thomas. 1990. *Making Sex: Body and Gender from the Greeks to Freud*, Cambridge, MA and London: Harvard University Press.

Lee, Rosa. 1987. 'Resisting Amnesia: Feminism, Painting and Postmodernism', *Feminist Review*, 26, July, 5–28.

Léonard, Yves. 1998a. 'O Império Colonial Salazarista', in Francisco Bethencourt and Kitri Chandhuri (eds) *História da Expansão Portugues*, vol. 5, Lisbon: Círculo de Leitores, Série Temas & Debates, 10–30.

—— 1998b. 'O Ultramar Português', in Francisco Bethencourt and Kitri Chandhuri (eds) *História da Expansão Portugues*, vol. 5, Lisbon: Círculo de Leitores, Série Temas & Debates, 31–50.

Lisboa, Maria Manuel. 1995. 'Uma Caixa de Fósforos, ou Como O Mundo Acaba: A Risada Vingativa de Eça de Queiroz', *Revista Arca*, 3, 35–54.

—— 2003. *Paula Rego's Map of Memory: National and Sexual Politics*, Burlington, VT: Ashgate.

Livingstone, Marco. 2004. 'All that Is Left Behind', in *Paula Rego*, exhibition catalogue, Oporto: Serralves Museum, 48–55.

—— 2007. 'Tales to Tell', in *Paula Rego*, exhibition catalogue, Madrid: Museo Nacional Centro de Arte Reina Sofia, 37–57.

—— 2008. 'First Principles', in *Paula Rego: Human Cargo*, exhibition catalogue, New York, Marlborough and London: Marlborough Fine Art.

—— 2009. 'A Philosophy of Life: Themes in the Art of Paula Rego', museum catalogue, Cascais: Casa das Histórias Paula Rego', 12–27.

—— and Stuart-Smith, Stephen. 1999. *Paula Rego: The Children's Crusade*, London: Enitharmon Press.

Lorcin, Patricia M.E. 1995. *Imperial Identities: Stereotyping, Prejudice and Race in Colonial Algeria*, London and New York: I.B. Tauris.

Lourenço, Eduardo. 1999. *A Nau de Ícaro seguido de Imagem e Miragem da Lusofonia*, Lisbon: Gradiva.

Lubbock, Tom. 1998. 'Lost the Plot, Lost her Way', *The Independent*, 23 June, 11.

Lucena, Manuel. 1976. *A Evolução do Sistema Corporativo Português, Vol. I: O Salazarismo*, Lisbon: Perspectivas e Realidades.

Macciocchi, Maria-Antonietta. 1979. 'Female Sexuality in Fascist Ideology', trans. Michèle Barrett, Judy Keiner, Karen Margolis and Jennifer Stone, *Feminist Review*, 1, 67–82.

Macedo, Ana Gabriela. 1999a. 'Paula Rego: a propósito de santas, aranhas e avestruzes . . . ou, a arte dfe contra histórias', *Jornal de Letras, Artes & Ideias*, 19 May, 12–13.

—— 1999b. 'Pintura como denúncia: entrevista com Paula Rego', *Jornal de Letras, Artes & Ideias*, 19 May, 12–13.

—— 2001a. 'Through the Looking-Glass: Paula Rego's Visual Rhetoric, an "Aesthetics of Danger"', *Textual Practice*, 15/1, 67–85.

—— 2001b. 'A Casa da Celestina', *Jornal de Letras, Artes & Ideias*, 11 July, 27.

—— 2001c. 'Material Girls: Feminism and Body Matters', *Cadernos de Literatura Comparada*, 3/4, 145–167.

—— 2003. 'Histórias de mulheres', *Jornal de Letras, Artes & Ideias*, 12 November, 32–33.

Mackenzie, Suzie. 1991. 'Female Forms', *The Guardian*, 31 July, 15.

—— 'Don't Flinch, Don't Hide', *The Guardian* (Weekend), 30 November, 26–28.

Manuel, Alexandre; Carapinha, Rogério; and Neves, Dias 1974. *Pide: A História da Repressão*. Fundão: Jornal do Fundão Editora.

Marques Gastão, Ana. 1999. 'Paixão, culpa, anjos e morte', *Diário de Notícias* (Artes e Multimédia), 2 May, 44–45.

—— 2001. 'As meninas exemplares', *Diário de Notícias* (Suplemento DNA), 2 May, 58–59.

—— 2002. 'Jane Eyre, A Bruxa', *Diário de Notícias* (Artes e Multimédia), 19 July, 40–41.

—— 2003a. 'Aborto – talvez antes da anunciação – Entrevista com Paula Rego', *Diário de Notícias*, 23 January, 40.

—— 2003b. 'Imagem e texto gravados a fogo que não acaba', *Diário de Notícias*, 16 September, 40–41.

Martins, Hermínio. 1968. 'Portugal', in Stuart Woolf (ed.) *European Fascism*, London: Weidenfeld & Nicolson, 302–336.

Masson, Jeffrey. 1984. *The Assault on Truth, Freud's Suppression of the Seduction Theory*, New York: Farrar, Straus and Giroux.

Matlock, Jann. 1993. 'Masquerading Women, Pathologized Men: Cross Dressing, Fetishism, and the Theory of Perversion, 1882–1935', in Emily Apter and William Pietz (eds) *Fetishism and Cultural Discourse*, Ithaca, NY: Cornell University Press, 31–61.

Mauperrin, Maria José. 1982. 'As crianças gostam desta violência', *Expresso*, 3 April, 28–29.

McClintock, Anne. 1995. *Imperial Leather: Race, Gender and Sexuality in the Colonial Contest*. New York and London: Routledge.

McEwen, John. 1981. 'Telling Tales', *The Spectator*, 30 May, 28.

—— 1982a. 'Drawbacks', *The Spectator*, 24 July, 26–27.

—— 1982b. 'Triangles', *The Spectator*, 11 September, 27.

—— 1983. 'Restorative', *The Spectator*, 8 October, 32–33.

—— 1988. 'Telling Tales Out of School', *Sunday Times* (Colour Magazine), 16 October, 62–65.

—— 2006 (1992). *Paula Rego*, London: Phaidon Press.

—— 2008. *Paula Rego: Behind the Scenes*, London: Phaidon Press.

Melo, Alexandre. 1988. 'Entrevista: O mundo mágico de Paula Rego', *Expresso* (Cartaz), 7 May, 69–71.

—— 2003. 'O Menino Mágico', *Expresso* (Revista Actual), 1 March, 34.

Melo, Filipa. 1994. 'Para descobrir o encantamento', *Jornal de Letras, Artes & Ideias*, 23 November, 12–13.

Merleau-Ponty, Maurice. 2002 (1945). *The Phenomenology of Perception*, trans. Colin Smith (1961) revised by Forrest Williams (1981), London and New York: Routledge Classics.

Miller, Sandra. 1991. 'Paula Rego's Nursery Rhymes', *Print Quarterly*, 8/1, 53–60.

—— 2006. 'Fashioning Subversion: Clothes and their Meaning in Paula Rego's Paintings', *Apollo: The International Magazine of Arts and Antiques*, January, 20–27.

Mitchell, Juliet. 1971. *Women's Estate*, London: Penguin.

—— 1974. *Psychoanalysis and Feminism*, London: Pelican Books.

—— 2000. *Mad Men and Medusas: Reclaiming Hysteria and the Effects of Sibling Relations on the Human Condition*, London: Penguin Books.

—— 2003. *Siblings*. Oxford: Blackwell Publishing.

—— and Jacqueline Rose (eds) 1982. *Feminine Sexuality: Jacques Lacan and the École Freudienne*, London and Basingstoke: Macmillan.

Mitchell, W.J.T. 1994. *Picture Theory: Essays on Verbal and Visual Representation.* Chicago, IL and London: The University of Chicago Press.

Mocidade Portuguesa Feminina. 1951. *Legislação sobre a Mocidade Portuguesa Feminina*, Lisbon: MPF.

Moi, Toril. 2000. 'Is Anatomy Destiny? Freud and Biological Determinism', in Peter Brooks and Alex Woloch (eds) *Whose Freud: The Place of Psychoanalysis in Contemporary Culture*, New Haven, CT and London: Yale University Press, 71–92.

Mónica, Maria Filomena. 1978. *Educação e Sociedade no Portugal de Salazar*, Lisbon: Editorial Presença / Gabinete e Investigações Sociais.

Morphet, Richard (ed.) 2000. *Encounters: New Art from the Old*, exhibition catalogue, London: National Gallery.

Morris, David B. 1991. *The Culture of Pain*, Berkeley, Los Angeles and London: University of California Press.

Morrison, Blake. 1996. *Pendle Witches*, with illustrations by Paula Rego, London: Enitharmon Press.

—— 2008. 'Page Turners', *The Guardian*, 19 April, 12.

Mota Ribeiro, Anabela. 2003. 'Paula Rego', *Diário de Notícias* (DNA), 1 February, 3–12.

Mulvey, Laura. 1989. 'Visual Pleasure and Narrative Cinema', in *Visual and Other Pleasures*, London: Macmillan, 14–26. First published in *Screen*, 16/3, 1975, 6–18.

Naro, Nancy Priscilla. 2000. *A Slave's Place, a Master's World: Fashioning Dependency in Rural Brazil*, London and New York: Continuum.

Nead, Lynda. 1992. *The Female Nude: Art, Obscenity and Sexuality*, London and New York: Routledge.

Needell, Jeffrey D. 1995. 'Identity, Race, Gender, and Modernity in the Origins of Gilberto Freyre's Oeuvre', *The American Historical Review*, 100/1, 51–77.

Nietzsche, Friedrich 1974 (1961). *Thus Spoke Zarathustra*, trans. R.J. Hollingdale, Harmondsworth: Penguin Books.

—— 1996. *On the Genealogy of Morals*, trans. Douglas Smith, Oxford: Oxford University Press.

Nixon, Mignon. 1998. 'Louise Bourgeois and the Logic of the Part-Object, 1942–1982', PhD thesis, New York: The City University of New York.

—— 2005. *Fantastic Reality: Louise Bourgeois and a Story of Modern Art.* Cambridge, MA: MIT Press.

Nochlin, Linda. 1989. *The Politics of Vision: Essays on Nineteenth-Century Art and Society*, London: Thames and Hudson.

—— 1991 (1971). 'Why Have there Been no Great Women Artists?', in *Women, Art, and Power and Other Essays*, London: Thames and Hudson, 145–178.

Nolasco, Ana. 2004. 'A Ironia e o Grotesco na Obra de Paula Rego', MA dissertation, Lisbon: Universidade de Lisboa.

Paula Rego: Paintings 1984–5. 1985. Exhibition catalogue, with an introduction by Lynne Cooke, London: Edward Totah Gallery.

Paula Rego. 1988. Exhibition catalogue, with texts by John McEwen, Bernardo Pinto de Almeida, Ruth Rosengarten and Victor Willing, Lisbon: Fundação Calouste Gulbenkian, and London: Serpentine Gallery.

Paula Rego: Tales from the National Gallery. 1991. Exhibition catalogue, with texts by Colin Wiggins and Germaine Greer, London: National Gallery.

Paula Rego: A Retrospective. 1997. Exhibition catalogue, with texts by Fiona Bradley, Judith Collins, Ruth Rosengarten and Victor Willing, Liverpool: Tate Gallery, and Lisbon: Centro Cultural de Belém.

Paula Rego: O Crime do Padre Amaro. 1999. Exhibition catalogue, with an introduction by Jorge Molder and a short text by Paula Rego, Lisbon: Calouste Gulbenkian Foundation.

Paula Rego: Untitled. 1999. Exhibition catalogue, with an introduction by Jorge Molder, Lisbon: Calouste Gulbenkian Foundation.

Paula Rego. 1999. Exhibition catalogue, with an introduction by Desmond Shawe-Taylor and a short text by Paula Rego, London: Dulwich Picture Gallery.

Paula Rego: Jane Eyre and Other Stories. 2003. London: Marlborough Fine Arts.

Paula Rego. 2004. Exhibition catalogue, with texts by João Fernandes, Marco Livingstone and Ruth Rosengarten, Oporto: Serralves Museum.

Paula Rego. 2007. Exhibition catalogue, with texts by Marco Livingstone and Robert Hughes, and commentaries by Paula Rego, Madrid: Museo Nacional Centro de Arte Reina Sofia.

Paulo, Heloisa. 1994. *Estado Novo e Propaganda em Portugal e no Brasil. O SPN/SNI e o DIP*, Coimbra: Minerva.

Pessoa, Fernando. 2001. *The Book of Disquiet*, ed. and trans. Richard Zenith, London: Allen Lane and the Penguin Press.

Peters, Edward. 1985. *Torture*, New York: Basil Blackwell.

Phillips, Adam, 1993. *On Kissing, Tickling and Being Bored*, London: Faber and Faber.

—— 1994. 'Cross Dressing', in *On Flirtation*, London: Faber and Faber, 122–130.

—— 1995. *Terrors and Experts*, London: Faber and Faber.

—— 1998. *The Beast in the Nursery*, London: Faber and Faber.

Pimentel, Irene Flunser. 2001. *História das Organizações Femininas do Estado Novo*, Lisbon: Temas e Debates.

—— 2007a. *A História da PIDE*, Mem Martins: Círculo de Leitores.

—— 2007b. *Mocidade Portuguesa Feminina*, Lisbon: A Esfera dos Livros.

Pinharanda, João. 1988. 'Paula Rego e as meninas exemplares', *Jornal de Letras, Artes & Ideias*, 10 May, 27.

—— 1992. 'Pintar a ilusão', *O Público* (Suplemento Fim de Semana), 8 May, 4–5.

—— 1994. 'Um cão precisa de uma casa', *O Público*, 16 December, 14–15.

—— 1997. 'A pintura no feminino', *O Público*, 16 May, 2–3.

—— and Melo, Alexandre. 1987. 'Paula Rego: "Tudo que pinto vem de Portugal"', *Jornal de Letras, Artes & Ideias*, 15 June, 14–15.

Pinto de Almeida, Bernardo. 2005. *Paula Rego*, Lisbon: Editorial Caminho.

Pires de Lima, Maria. 2001. 'Ecce Femina: Das Paixões. Das Mulheres', preface to José Maria Eça de Queirós, *O Crime do Padre Amaro*, Oporto: Campo das Letras Editores, 7–42.

Pointon, Marcia. 1990. *Naked Authority: The Body in Western Painting, 1830–1908*, Cambridge: Cambridge University Press.

Pollock, Griselda. 1988. *Vision and Difference*, London: Routledge.

—— 1996a. 'Inscriptions in the Feminine', in Catherine de Zegher (ed.) *Inside the Visible*, Kortrijk: Kanaal Art Foundation, 67–87.

—— 1996b. 'The Politics of Theory: Generations and Geographies in Feminist Theory and the Histories of Art Histories', in Griselda Pollock (ed.) *Generations and Geographies in the Visual Arts: Feminist Readings*, London: Routledge, 3–21.

—— 1999. *Differencing the Canon: Feminist Desire and the Writing of Art's Histories*, London and New York: Routledge.

—— 2001. 'Painting, Feminism, History', in *Looking Back to the Future: Essays in Art, Life and Death*, with an introduction and commentary by Penny Florence, Amsterdam, G+B Arts International, 73–111.

—— 2003. 'Does Art Think? How Can We Think the Feminine Aesthetically?' in Dana Arnold and Margaret Iversen (eds) *Art and Thought*, Oxford: Blackwell Publishing, 129–155.

—— 2006a. 'Beyond Oedipus: Feminist Thought, Psychoanalysis, and Mythical Figurations of the Feminine', in Vanda Zajko and Miriam Leonard (eds) *Laughing with Medusa: Classical Myth and Feminist Thought*, Oxford: Oxford University Press, 67–117.

—— 2006b. 'The Image in Psychoanalysis and the Archaeological Metaphor', in Griselda Pollock (ed.) *Psychoanalysis and the Image*, Oxford: Blackwell Publishing, 1–29.

Pomar, Alexandre. 1996. 'Se a palavra fosse visual: pintura de histórias', *Tabacaria* (Revista de Poesia e Artes Plásticas), 2 (Winter), 19–23.

—— 1997. 'Antigo e Moderno', *Expresso* (Revista), 31 May 32–33.

—— 1999a. 'O Eixo Ibérico', *Expresso*, 2 February, 60–66.

—— 1999b. 'Amor e Crime', *Expresso* (Cartaz), 22 May, 23.

—— 1999c. 'Mostrar o Inominável', *Expresso* (Cartaz), 22 May, 22.

—— 1999d. 'O Outro Escândalo', *Expresso* (Cartaz), 22 May, 22.

—— and Diogo, Fernando. 1997. 'Copiar liberta a imaginação', *Expresso* (Revista), 31 May, 22–30.

Pommier, Gerard. 2004. *Erotic Anger: A User's Manual*, trans. Catherine Liu, Minneapolis: University of Minnesota Press.

Porfírio, José Luís. 2004. 'A Leste do Paraíso', *Expresso* (Cartaz), 30 October, 44–45.

Preziosi, Donald (ed.) 1998. *The Art of Art History*, Oxford: Oxford University Press.

Priore, Mary Del. 1993. *Ao Sul do Corpo: Condição feminina, maternidades e mentalidades no Brasil Colónia*, Rio de Janeiro: José Olympio Editora.

—— 2000/01. '*The Mansions and the Shanties:* "The Flesh and the Stone" in Nineteenth-Century Brazil', *Portuguese Literary and Cultural Studies*, 4–5 (Fall/Spring), 65–71.

Proença Rosa, *et al.* 1982. *Victor Meirelles de Lima, 1832–1903*, Rio de Janeiro: Edições Pinakotheke.

Reich, Wilhelm. 1967. *Reich Speaks of Freud. Conversations with Kurt Eissler*, ed. Mary Higgins and C.M. Raphael. New York: Farrar, Straus and Giroux.

—— 1972. *The Mass Psychology of Fascism*, ed. Mary Booth Higgins and Chester M. Raphael, trans. Vincent R. Carfagno, Guernsey: Souvenir Press, E&A Ltd.

Ribeiro, Darcy. 2000. *The Brazilian People: The Formation and Meaning of Brazil*, trans. Gregory Rabassa, Gainesville: University Press of Florida.

Ribeiro, Maria da Conceição. 1996. *A Polícia Política no Estado Novo (1926–1945)*, Lisbon: Editorial Estampa.

Riley, Denise. 1983. *War in the Nursery: Theories of the Child and Mother*, London: Virago.

—— 1988. *'Am I That Name?' Feminism and the Category of 'Women' in History*, Minneapolis: University of Minnesota Press.

Riviere, Joan. 1986. 'Womanliness as Masquerade', in Victor Burgih, James Donald and Cora Kaplan (eds), *Formations of Fantasy*, London and New York: Methuen, 35–44. First published in 1929 in *The International Journal of Psychoanalysis*, 10, 303–313.

Robert Mapplethorpe, 1970–1983. 1983. Exhibition catalogue, with texts by Alan Hollinghurst, Stuart Morgan and Sandy Nairne, London: ICA.

Robinson, Hilary. 1995. 'Border Crossings: Womanliness, Body, Representation', in Katy Deepwell (ed.) *New Feminist Art Criticism*, Manchester and New York: Manchester University Press, 138–146.

—— 2006. *Reading Art, Reading Irigaray: The Politics of Art by Women*, London and New York: I.B. Tauris.

Rodrigues, Dalila. 2009. 'Paula Rego and the Old Masters', museum catalogue, Cascais: Casa das Histórias Paula Rego', 48–67.

Romero Magalhães, Joaquim. 1998. 'O Reconhecimento do Brasil', in Francisco Bethencourt and Kitri Chandhuri (eds), *História da Expansão*

Portuguesa, Vol. 1: A Formação do Império, Lisbon: Círculo de Leitores, Série Temas & Debates, 192–217.

Rosas, Fernando. 1986. *O Estado Novo nos anos trinta: 1928–1938*, Lisbon: Editorial Estampa.

—— 1994. *O Estado Novo (1926–1974)*, in *História de Portugal* vol. 7, ed. José Mattoso, Lisbon: Círculo de Leitores.

Rose, Jacqueline. 1986. *Sexuality in the Field of Vision*, London: Verso.

—— 1988. 'Sexuality and Vision: Some Questions', in Hal Foster (ed.) *Vision and Visuality*, Seattle, WA: Bay Press, 115–127.

—— 1989. 'Where Does the Misery Come From? Psychoanalysis, Feminism and the Event', in Jacqueline Rose. 1993. *Why War? Psychoanalysis, Politics, and the Return to Melanie Klein*, Oxford: Blackwell Publishers, 89–109. First published in Richard Feldstein and Judith Roof (eds), *Feminism and Psychoanalysis*, Ithaca, NY and London: Cornell University Press.

—— 1993. *Why War? Psychoanalysis, Politics, and the Return to Melanie Klein*, Oxford: Blackwell Publishers.

Rosenthal, Tom. 2003. *Paula Rego: The Complete Graphic Work*, London: Thames and Hudson.

Rosengarten, Ruth. 1997. 'Home Truths: The Work of Paula Rego', in *Paula Rego*, exhibition catalogue, Liverpool: Tate Gallery, 43–118.

—— 1999. 'Nurturing the Adult Within: Drawings and Etchings by Paula Rego', in *Open Secret: Drawings and Etchings by Paula Rego*, exhibition catalogue, Paris: Calouste Gulbenkian Foundation, and Dartmouth, MA: University Art Gallery, 25–29.

—— 2006. 'This flesh I purchased with my pains: Paula Rego's Life of the Virgin', in *Paula Rego: Virgin Mary's Life Cycle*, Lisbon: Museu da Presidência da República, 48–95.

—— 2009. 'The Artist in her Studio', in *Paula Rego*, museum catalogue, Cascais: Casa das Histórias Paula Rego', 26–46.

Russo, Mary. 1986. 'Female Grotesques: Carnival and Theory', in Teresa de Lauretis (ed.) *Feminist Studies / Critical Studies*, Bloomington: Indiana University Press, 213–229.

Sadlier, Darlene J. 1989. *The Question of How: Women Writers and New Portuguese Literature*, New York and London: Greenwood Press.

—— 2008. *Brazil Imagined: 1500 to the Present*. Austin: University of Texas Press.

Safouan, Moustapha. 1980. 'In Praise of Hysteria', trans. Stuart Schneiderman, in Stuart Schneiderman (ed.) *Returning to Freud: Clinical Psychoanalysis in the School of Lacan*, New Haven, CT and London: Yale University Press, 55–60.

Said, Edward. 1993. *Culture and Imperialism*, London: Chatto & Windus.

Salazar, António Oliveira. 1934. *Discursos e Notas Políticas, vol. 1 (1928–34)*. Coimbra: Coimbra Editora.

—— 1942. *Defesa Económnica, Defesa Moral, Defesa Política*, Lisbon: SPN.

—— 1945. *Discursos e Notas Políticas, vol. 2 (1935–37)*, Coimbra: Coimbra Editora.

—— 1951. *Discursos e Notas Políticas, vol. 4 (1943–50)*, Coimbra: Coimbra Editora.

—— 1959. *Discursos e Notas Políticas, vol. 5 (1951–1958)*, Coimbra: Coimbra Editora.

—— 1967. *Entrevistas, 1960–1966*, Coimbra: Coimbra Editora.

Scarry, Elaine. 1985. *The Body in Pain: The Making and Unmaking of the World*, Oxford and New York: Oxford University Press.

Schor, Naomi. 1987. *Reading in Detail: Aesthetics and the Feminine*. New York and London: Methuen.

——, Weed, Elizabeth and Rooney, Ellen (eds) 2003. *Differences*, 14/5 (Fall).

Searle, Adrian. 1997. 'Children with Animals – Charming', *The Guardian*, 10 February, 10.

Sebestyen, Amanda. 1988. 'Female Potency', *New Statesman & Society*, 28 October, 40.

Schapiro, Meyer. 1956. 'Leonardo and Freud: An Art-Historical Study', *Journal of the History of Ideas*, 17/2, April, 147–178.

Sheringham, Michael. 1991. *French Autobiography: Devices and Desires, Rousseau to Perec*, Oxford and New York: Oxford University Press.

Silverman, Kaja. 1983. *The Subject of Semiotics*, New York: Oxford University Press.

—— 1986. 'Fragments of a Fashionable Discourse', in Tina Modleski (ed.) *Studies in Entertainment: Critical Approaches to Mass Culture*, Bloomington: Indiana University Press, 139–152.

—— 1996. *The Threshold of the Visible World*, London and New York: Routledge.

Sinclair, Alison. 1993. *The Deceived Husband: A Kleinian Approach to the Literature of Infidelity*, Oxford: Clarendon Press.

Skidmore, Thomas E. 1974. *Black into White: Race and Nationality in Brazilian Thought*, Oxford and New York: Oxford University Press.

Soares de Oliveira, Luisa. 1992. 'Quando os artistas olham para a arte antiga', *O Público (Suplemento Fim de Semana)*, 8 May, 6.

Sophocles. 1999. *Four Dramas of Maturity*, ed. Michael Ewans, trans. Michael Ewans, Graham Ley and Gregory McCart, London: Everyman.

Spackman, Barbara. 1996. *Fascist Virilities: Rhetoric, Ideology and Social Fantasy in Italy*, Minneapolis and London: University of Minnesota Press.

Spector, Jack J. 1969. 'The Method of Morelli and its Relation to Freudian Psychoanalysis', *Diogenes*, 66 (Summer), 63–83.

SPN/MPF. 1964. *25 Anos de Actividades da Mocidade Portuguesa Feminina. 1938–1963*, Lisbon: SPN/MPF.

Sprengnether, Madelon. 1990. *The Spectral Mother: Freud, Feminism and Psychoanalysis*, Ithaca, NY and London: Cornell University Press.

Stallybrass, Peter and White, Allon. 1986. *The Politics and Poetics of Transgression*, Ithaca, NY: Cornell University Press.

Stoler, Ann Laura. 1997. 'Making Empire Respectable: The Politics of Race and Sexual Morality in Twentieth-Century Colonial Cultures', in Anne McClintock, Aamir Mufti and Ella Shohat (eds) *Dangerous Liaisons: Gender, Nation, and Postcolonial Perspective*, Minneapolis and London: University of Minnesota Press, 344–373.

Strathern, Marilyn. 2005. *Kinship, Law and the Unexpected: Relatives are always a Surprise*. Cambridge and New York: Cambridge University Press.

Suleiman, Susan Rubin. 1985. 'Writing and Motherhood', in Shirley Nelson Garner, Claire Kahane and Madelon Sprengnether (eds) *The (M)other Tongue: Essays in Feminist Psychoanalytic Interpretation*, Ithaca, NY and London: Cornell University Press, 352–377.

Suleri, Sara. 1992. *The Rhetoric of British India*, Chicago, IL and London: Chicago University Press.

Szirtes, George. 1991. 'Paula Rego: The Actors in the Playhouse', *Modern Painters* (Winter), 83–86.

Taussig, Michael. 1993. *Mimesis and Alterity: A Particular History of the Senses*, New York and London: Routledge.

Taylor, John Russell. 1982. 'Transitory Joke of a Cartoonist's Dilemma', *The Times*, 7 September, 9.

—— 1992. 'Fearless Poacher is Captured by her Prey', *The Times*, 3 January, 8.

Teale, Polly. 2003. 'Brontë's Eyres', *New Statesman*, 10 November, 42–43.

Teixeira de Pascoaes (pseudonym of Joaquim Pereira Teixeira de Vasconcelos). 1991. *Arte de ser Português* (1920), with an introduction by Miguel Esteves Cardoso, Lisbon: Assírio e Alvim.

Theweleit, Klaus. 1987. *Male Fantasies vol. 1: Women, Floods, Bodies, History*, trans. Stephen Conway in collaboration with Erica Carter and Stephen Conway, Cambridge: Polity Press.

—— 1989. *Male Fantasies vol. 2: Psychoanalyzing the White Terror*, trans. Chris Turner and Erica Carter in collaboration with Stephen Conway, Cambridge: Polity Press.

Turner, Victor. 1977. 'Frame, Flow and Reflection: Ritual and Drama as Public Liminality', in Michel Benamou and Charles Caramello (eds) *Performance in Postmodern Culture*, Milwaukee: Center for Twentieth-Century Studies, University of Wisconsin; and Madison, WI: Coda Press, 33–55.

Tusa, John. 2001. 'Interview with Paula Rego', *The Independent on Sunday*, 3 June, 10–11.

United Nations. 1945. *Charter of the United Nations*, San Francisco, 26 June, www.un.org/en/documents/charter (accessed on 20 March 2010).

Vale de Almeida, Miguel. 2000. *Um Mar da Cor da Terra: Raça, Cultura e Política de Identidade*, Oeiras: Celta Editora.

Vasco, Nuno. 1977. *Vigiados e Perseguidos – Documentos Secretos da PIDE/DGS*, Lisbon: Livraria Bertrand.

Viotti da Costa, Emilia. 1985. *The Brazilian Empire: Myths and Histories*, Chicago: University of Chicago Press.

Wall, Karin. 1995. 'Apontamentos sobre a família na política social portuguesa', *Análise Social*, 131, 431–458.

Ware, Vron. 1992. *Beyond the Pale: White Women, Racism and History*, London: Verso.

Warner, Marina. 1976. *Alone of All her Sex: The Myth and Cult of the Virgin Mary*, London: Picador.

—— 1990. 'Shame of Secrets', *New Statesman & Society*, 26 January, 40–42.

—— 1994. 'Introduction' in *Nursery Rhymes* (with reproductions of etchings by Paula Rego), London: Thames and Hudson.

—— 2003. 'An Artist's Dreamland: Jane Eyre Through Paula Rego's Eyes', in *Paula Rego: Jane Eyre*, London: Enitharmon Editions, 7–15.

Weber, Samuel, 2000 (1988). *The Legend of Freud*, Stanford, CA: Stanford University Press.

Willing, Victor. 1971. 'The Imagiconography of Paula Rego', *Colóquio Artes*, April, 43–49.

—— 1983. 'Forward', *Paula Rego*, exhibition catalogue, London: Edward Totah Gallery; Bristol: Arnolfini; Milan: Studio Marconi (n.p.).

Wills, Clair. 1989. 'Upsetting the Public: Carnival, Hysteria and Women's Texts', in Ken Hirschkop and David Shepherd (eds) *Bakhtin and Cultural Theory*, Manchester and New York: Manchester University Press, 85–108.

Wollheim, Richard. 1973. 'Freud and the Understanding of Art', in *On Art and the Mind: Essays and Lectures*, London: Allen Lane, 249–266. First published in *British Journal of Aesthetics*, 10, 1970, 211–224.

Wood, Gaby. 2005. 'The Woman who put Eroticisim in the Nursery', *The Observer* (Features), 4 September, 13.

Woolf, Virginia. 2005. *A Room of One's Own*, in *Selected Works of Virginia Woolf*, Ware: Wordsworth, 561–633.

Wright, Elizabeth (ed.) 1992. *Feminism and Psychoanalysis: A Critical Dictionary*, Oxford: Blackwell Publishers.

Wright, Karen. 2004. 'The Pain of Paula Rego', *The Independent*, 22 October, 2–4.

Wullschlager, Jackie. 2004. 'Originality from a Wellspring of Tradition', *Financial Times*, 24 November, 15.

Yaeger Kaplan, Alice. 1985. *Reproductions of Banality: Fascism, Literature and French Intellectual Life*, Minneapolis: University of Minneapolis Press.

Young, Robert. 2001. *Postcolonialism: An Historical Introduction*, Oxford: Blackwell Publishers.

Zemon Davis, Natalie. 1975. *Society and Culture in Early Modern France: Eight Essays*, London: Duckworth.

Index